ISBN 978-1-331-73154-2
PIBN 10227370

This book is a reproduction of an important historical work. Forgotten Books uses
state-of-the-art technology to digitally reconstruct the work, preserving the original format
whilst repairing imperfections present in the aged copy. In rare cases, an imperfection in
the original, such as a blemish or missing page, may be replicated in our edition. We do,
however, repair the vast majority of imperfections successfully; any imperfections that
remain are intentionally left to preserve the state of such historical works.

1 MONTH OF
FREE
READING

at

www.ForgottenBooks.com

By purchasing this book you are eligible for one month membership to ForgottenBooks.com, giving you unlimited access to our entire collection of over 700,000 titles via our web site and mobile apps.

To claim your free month visit:
www.forgottenbooks.com/free227370

DIARIES

OF

A LADY OF QUALITY.

LONDON

PRINTED BY SPOTTISWOODE AND CO.

NEW-STREET SQUARE.

DIARIES

OF

A LADY OF QUALITY

FROM 1797 TO 1844.

EDITED, WITH NOTES,

BY

A. HAYWARD, Esq., Q.C.

LONDON:

LONGMAN, GREEN, LONGMAN, ROBERTS, & GREEN.

1864.

PREFATORY NOTICE.

THE manuscript volumes (ten in number) from which this book has been compiled, differ materially from any of the same extent which have fallen under my observation. Although called diaries, they are none of them what is commonly understood or described by that name. They do not profess to be a record of the writer's daily life: they contain no details of a private or purely personal nature: no flights of egotism, no self-communings, nothing that can be called scandal. At the end of half a century the lives of princes and statesmen belong to history, and the only unfavourable impressions noted down by her relate exclusively to *them*. Her very gossip is redeemed by the speakers and the subjects; and her sole object throughout appears to have been to submit her

understanding to an improving exercise, and to store
up for future reference the conversations and compositions which attracted her attention in the course
of her daily intercourse with the most cultivated
people and her assiduous study of curious books and
manuscripts.

How many of us have regretted that we did not make
a note at the time of what we heard fall from persons who
had been prominent actors on the political or literary
stage, or who had even been behind the scenes when
a memorable performance was arranged or in progress!
How unlucky, have we thought, that we did not copy
the striking passage in the now forgotten book, or the
curious letter which we might easily have borrowed for
the purpose; or that we did not cut out and keep the
clever newspaper article or quaint paragraph which so
much struck everybody! Then why, on finding that
this has been judiciously done by another, should we
not profit by his or her sagacity, industry, and taste?
Such were the questions that suggested themselves
to me when I had gone over these diaries with
the view of deciding whether a book, calculated to
reflect credit on the collector, could be compiled from
them.

Gray went a little too far when (as quoted by Horace Walpole) he laid down that 'if any man were to form a book of what he had seen and heard himself, it must, in whatever hands, prove a useful and entertaining one.' But when a woman of thought and feeling, of cultivation and discernment, has enjoyed such opportunities of seeing and hearing as this lady of quality, a book so formed by her could hardly fall short of the degree of value and attraction anticipated by Gray.

Miss Frances Williams Wynn, the lady in question, was the daughter of Sir Watkin Williams Wynn (the fourth baronet) and Charlotte, daughter of George Grenville (First Lord of the Treasury, 1763-1765). The uncles to whom she frequently alludes, were the first Marquis of Buckingham, Lord Grenville, and the Right Honourable Thomas Grenville: the brothers, the Right Honourable Charles Williams Wynn, and Sir Henry Williams Wynn (long English minister at Copenhagen). One of her sisters was married to the late Lord Delamere, and the other to Colonel Shipley, M.P., son of the celebrated Dean of St. Asaph, and grandson of Johnson's friend, the Bishop. Lord Braybrooke and Lord Nugent were her near relatives. She died in 1857, in her 77th or 78th year; when her papers came into the possession of her niece, the Honourable Mrs. Rowley,* under whose sanction these selections from them are published.

Simple and easy of execution as my editorial duties may appear, they have really involved no inconsiderable amount of embarrassing responsibility. In the case of each individual entry or transcript, I was obliged to decide on the novelty or originality, as well as on the inherent value or interest, of the narrative, description, or reflections comprised in it. Thackeray used to say that, when *Punch* was first established, there was a member of its staff who knew every joke that had been made since the beginning of all things. It would require an editor equally well versed in *Ana*, or anecdote literature, to declare where and when (if ever) each of the stories or traits of character preserved by Miss Wynn had been in print. All I could do was to refer to the likeliest repositories, and having done so, boldly to take for granted that what was still new to me would prove new to the majority of readers. As she professedly copied the details, or wrote them down from memory, and did not

---

* Daughter of the late Colonel and Mrs. Shipley, and wife of Colonel the Honourable R. T. Rowley, M.P.

invent, it stands to reason that they were once as well known to others as to her; but it does not follow that a striking incident should be kept back from the existing generation because it may have been familiar to the last. It is also obvious that a fresh and well authenticated version of a received anecdote may prove highly valuable to the biographer or historian.

Besides endeavouring to supply as succinctly as possible the information required to explain the allusions or show the bearings of the statements, I have done my best to remedy the frequent deficiency of dates.

A. H.

8 ST. JAMES STREET:
April 25, 1864.

CONTENTS.

	PAGE
The Dead Alive	1—2
The Wynyard Ghost Story	2—5
The Innocent Convict	5—10
A Convent Tragedy	10—13
Mr. Burke's Ghost Story	14—17
Execution of Charles I.	17—20
Earthquake at Naples	20—25
The Emperor Alexander	25—26
Extracts from Letters from Germany	26—30
Last Moments of Louis XVI.—Escape of the Ducs D'Angoulême and Berry	30—38
Sir Walter Scott's Stories	39—40
Buxton Letter	41—43
The Tyrone Ghost Story	43—54
The Duke of Marlborough—Admiral Barrington—The Gunnings	55—58
Account by a Lady of a Visit to Princess Dashkow	58—64
Lord North	64—65
Account of a Hurricane in Jamaica	65—70
Napoleon on Board the 'Northumberland'	70—76
Napoleon and his Brothers	76—78
The Pretended Archduke	79—86
Anecdotes of Denon	87—89
Early Impressions of Celebrated Men—Pitt, Fox, Lord Wellesley, and Windham	89—94
Imperial and Royal Visitors in 1814—Visit to Oxford	94—99
The Stage : Miss Farren, Mrs. Siddons, Miss O'Neil, Kemble, Talma.	99—108
Pistrucci, the Improvisatore	108—110

PAGE

The Rev. Edward Irving . . 110—120
The Queen of Würtemberg, 'née Princess Royal of England'—Napoleon at Würtemberg—George the Third's Insanity . . 120—123
God Save the King, and Hyder Ally 123—124
Improvisatori . . . . 124—127
Literary Gains . . . . . 127—129
Napoleon at St. Helena . . 129—134
Execution of the Rebel Lords in 1746 134—137
Dream of the Duchess de Berry . . . 137—138
Cannibalism in Sumatra . . . . 139—145
Spinetto on the Pastoral Drama . . . 145—147
Balloons and Diving-Bells . . . 147—152
Conversations with General Alava . 152—159
Deaths of the Emperors Alexander and Paul 159—166
Duchesse D'Albany . . . . 167—169
An Archbishop on False Pretences 170—171
The Duc de Berri . . . . 171—173
Christophe, King of Hayti . 173—181
Louis XVIII. and the Fortune-Teller 182—183
Revenge . . . . . . 183—186
Queen Caroline . . . . 186—188
Extracts from the Works of Francis Egerton, Earl of Bridgewater . . . . 188—193
Letters from Bishop Heber . . . 193—201
The Ricketts Ghost Story . . 201—210
Insanity of George III.—Sir Henry Halford and George IV . . . . 210—215
Countess Macnamara.   The Bourbons 216—219
The Old Woman of Delamere Forest 220—233
Madame D'Arblay . . . . 233—235
Sir Walter Scott . . . . . 235—237
Party Feeling in France . . . . 237—240
Manuscripts of Tasso . . . . 240—243
Duchesse de Berry . . . . 243—245
Louis Philippe . . . . . 245—247
Léontine Fay 247
Charles Kemble . . . . . 248—249
Mr. Coesvelt's Pictures . . . . 249—250

PAGE

Balloons . . . . . 250—251
Mr. Davidson's Eastern Stories . . . 251—256
Eastern Magic . . . . . 256—260
Jerome, King of Westphalia . . . 261—262
Dr. Playfair's Patient . . . 262—263
Baron Osten's Account of his Escape from the Jaws of
   the Lion in 1827 . . . . 263—265
Mexican Morals and Manners . . . 265—267
Authorship of Junius . . . . 267—272
Good Sleepers: Mr. Pitt—The Duke of Wellington 272—279
Death of William IV.—Accession of Queen Victoria 279—282
Macready's Lear . . . . 282—284
Chantrey's Studio . . . . 285—287
Macready's Coriolanus . . . . 287—289
From the Orders of Charles II. for the Household 289—290
The Pretender at the Coronation . . . 290—293
Queen Anne . . . . . 293—295
Old-Fashioned Manners . . . . 295—296
Touching for the King's Evil . . . 296—299
The Emperor Nicholas . 299—300
Catherine of Medicis . . . . 300—303
Impressions of Ireland in 1840 . . . 303—307
Lady Morgan . . . . 307—309
Anne of Austria . . . . . 309—311
The Baron Geramb and La Trappe 311—314
Louis Philippe 314
Henry the Ninth of England . . . 315—316
Kean . . . . . . 317—320
Lady Hester Stanhope . . . . 320—329
Clairvoyance . . . . . 329—335
Faustine . . . . . 335—337
Addendum to the First News of Waterloo, and the
   Meeting of Wellington and Blucher 338—341
Addendum to the 'The Tyrone Ghost' . 341—342
Epitaphs, Epigrams, and Inscriptions . 343—359

DIARIES

&c.

———◆———

THE DEAD ALIVE.

London: March 17th, 1803.—WE passed the evening with the Grimstones, talking about the Duke of Bridge-water, who, it was then thought, might very possibly be brought to life again, though he had been dead above a week. They told me the following extraordinary story:

Many years ago, a Mrs. Killigrew was supposed to have been dead above a week; when she was to be put into her coffin, her body was so swelled that it was found impossible to get her diamond hoop-ring off without cutting the finger; this her husband would not consent to; accordingly, she was buried with the ring.

The sexton, who had observed this, determined to steal the ring that night. Having forced open the coffin, he proceeded to cut off the finger, but the first gash of the knife brought Mrs. Killigrew to life again. The sexton, frightened, ran away, leaving his lanthorn, which she immediately took, and walked to her own house. There her appearance, of course, created great consternation among the servants; no one would venture to open the door; fortunately the rumour reached the ears of her disconsolate husband, who went directly to receive her. After this event she lived ten years, and in the course of that time had two children. A maid who belonged to Mrs. Killigrew, after her death lived with Mrs. Walters, grandmother to the Grimstones: from her they had this story.

THE WYNYARD GHOST-STORY.*

Buxton: Oct. 16*th*, 1803.—I returned from Blithfield.†
The night before my departure, the conversation hap-

---

* No ghost story is more frequently mentioned in society than this, but the amount of accurate information concerning it may be estimated from Sir Walter Scott's version: 'The story of two highly respectable officers in the British army, who are supposed to have seen the spectre of the brother of one in a hut, or barrack, in America, is also one of those accredited ghost tales which attain a sort of brevet rank as true, from the mention of respectable names as the parties who witnessed the vision. But we are left without a glimpse when, how, and in what terms, this story obtained its currency; as also by whom, and in what manner, it was first circulated; and among the numbers by whom it has been quoted; although all agree in the general event, scarcely two, even of those who pretend to the best information, tell the story in the same way.'—*Letters on Demonology and Witchcraft*, p. 349.

The late Sir R. Peel had a fixed impression that he had seen and spoken with Lord Byron (then ill at Patras) in 1810, in the streets of London.—*Moore's Memoirs*, vol 6, p. 14.

† The seat of Lord Bagot, in Staffordshire.

pening to turn on ghost stories, Lord Bagot mentioned the following, as being very curious from its uncommon authenticity.

During the American war, Major Wynyard (who afterwards married Lady Matilda West), Gen. Ludlow, and Col. Clinton, were dining together in a mess-room at New York. In this room there were but two doors, one of which led to a staircase, and the other to a small closet, or rather press, without either door or window. A man entered at the door, when Gen. Ludlow, the only one of the gentlemen whose head was turned to the door, exclaimed, 'Good God, Harry! what can have brought you here?' The figure only waved its hand and said nothing. At his friend's exclamation Major Wynyard turned round, and his astonishment at seeing a brother whom he had left in England was so great, that he was unable to speak. The figure stalked once round the table, and then disappeared through the closet door, pulling it after him, without fastening it. One of the gentlemen rose immediately to open the door, but the figure was already vanished, and no trace of any mode of egress was found in the closet. Col. Clinton, who had never seen Mr. H. Wynyard, and was less horrified than his friends, proposed that they should mark both the day and the hour on which they had seen this strange apparition, believing that they should never hear of it again, but at the same time, thinking it might be a satisfaction to know the precise time of so extraordinary an occurrence. The next mails which came from England brought news of the death of Mr. Henry Wynyard, which had taken place at the same hour, two days after that on which his brother had seen the figure.

Some years after this, as Col. Clinton and Gen. Ludlow were walking together in London, Col. Clinton exclaimed: 'There is the figure which we saw in America.' Gen. Ludlow turned round, and saw a man (whose name Lord Bagot had forgot) so famous for being so like Mr. H. Wynyard, that he was perpetually mis-taken for him. This man never had been in America. All these facts were told to Lord Bagot by Col. Wynyard, in the presence of either one or both of the gentlemen who were with him at the time that this extraordinary adventure happened.

Another curious fact I heard at Blithfield. The Bishop of Carlisle told Lord Bagot that, in examining the papers of the late Duke of Bridgewater, in the midst of some useless papers which they were burning, they found two original warrants signed by Queen Elizabeth, one for the execution of the Duke of Norfolk, the other for that of Essex. Both warrants bear exactly the same date. Norfolk's is signed in a fine strong hand; that of Essex in one so trembling, that it is hardly legible.*

---

* In Park's edition of Walpole's 'Royal and Noble Authors' (vol. 3), is a fac-simile of the so-called original warrant in the

At **Blithfield** is preserved the cap which Charles I. wore on the day of his execution, and which he sent to Col. Salusbury, an ancestor of the Bagots. The cap is made of crimson satin, richly embroidered with gold and silver. I saw likewise a letter from Charles to Col. Salusbury. It is published by Pennant, but he does not mention where the original is to be found.

***

THE INNOCENT CONVICT.

Nov. 18*th*, 1803.—We left Buxton in the midst of a deep snow, and after a very cold and wretched journey arrived at Elton* the next day. During the time we were there, I heard the following story, which appeared to me very interesting :

Some years ago some passengers in a vessel bound for Botany Bay, were very much struck by the appearance of a female convict who was on board. She was a very beautiful woman, and appeared to be only 18 or 19 : her elegant manners were as striking as the beauty of her person. To these charms, she added one still more powerful—great modesty and strict propriety of deportment. It was this quality, so extraordinary in this most abject situation, which first called forth the

Stafford collection, and the signature is clear and firm. There are three flourishes which could not have been executed by a trembling hand.

* Elton Hall, Oundle : the seat of the Earl of Carysfort.

attention of her superiors.   The captain of the vessel
was requested to examine the register which was sent
with every convict, detailing their offence and their
sentence, and inform the passengers what had been the
crime of a creature who appeared so lovely.   He found
that her name was Mary Green, and that she had been
convicted on the clearest evidence of stealing a card of
lace from a shop in Oxford Street.

During a long passage her continued good conduct
gained her so much respect that, a maid-servant belonging to one of the officers having fallen sick on
board, his wife took Mary Green to supply her place ;
she found very soon that she had gained by the change:
the more she saw of Mary the better she liked her.   At
last she tried to persuade herself that her favourite was
innocent of the crime laid to her charge.   She questioned her as to her former situation, and as to the
reasons which could have induced her to the commission
of a crime which seemed so foreign to her nature.   Mary
replied, as she had to all her former enquiries, that no
power upon earth could make her reveal any part of her
story.   She added that she was perfectly resigned to her
fate, and determined to pass the rest of her days in New
Holland, as she never could revisit her native land.
Still, in spite of the mystery which hung about her, she
rose every day in the good opinion of her mistress, who,
after some time, placed her about her children ; then
only she discovered that, in addition to all her amiable

qualities, Mary possessed, in a superior degree, all the talents and accomplishments which belong to an exalted situation. She spoke several modern languages, and understood both painting and music. In short, she soon became the favourite companion of her mistress, who could no longer treat this superior being as a servant. Still, however, Mary resisted her urgent entreaties to discover her former situation; she owned that it had been superior to that rank in which she now found herself; confessed that her present name was assumed; added that she had been very unfortunate, but would never add to her other misfortunes that of thinking that her relations and friends were blushing for her.

About three years after this time, the chaplain of the settlement was called upon to attend the death-bed of an old female convict who was lately arrived. Though an old offender who had grown up in the paths of vice, this woman felt in her last moments great con-trition, and made a full confession of all her crimes. She said that what laid the most heavy on her conscience was the recollection of her having laid one of her of-fences to the charge of an innocent young woman. She said, that having gone in one day to a shop in Oxford Street at the same time with a very young girl who appeared to be fresh from the country, she had spoken to her; and after having stolen a card of lace she followed the young woman out of the shop. Soon after, hearing the cry of 'stop thief,' she made a pretence of her clog being untied to ask the assistance of the young woman, who was still close by her, and while she was stooping had contrived to slip the lace into her muff, and to escape herself before their pursuers reached them. She said she had afterwards heard that the poor girl had been convicted of an offence of which she knew her to be perfectly innocent.

This account immediately brought to the chaplain's mind the Mary Green who had excited so much curiosity. He went immediately to her, asked for her story, and received from her the usual answer, refusing all intelligence on this subject. He, however, pressed her, told her that it might be of the utmost importance to her to confide in him, as some circumstances had lately come to light which he hoped might lead to her exculpation if she would give him all the particulars of her case. She burst into tears, told him that she was the only daughter of a respectable merchant of Birmingham, but still refused to tell the name: she said that at eighteen years of age she had gone to London for the first time, to an uncle who lived in Newman Street; that a day or two after her arrival she had, in the dusk of the evening, gone to a haberdasher's shop, to which she had been directed as being only a few steps from her uncle's house. On coming out of the shop she had heard a cry of 'stop thief' and had hastened home to escape the mob, by whom she had been very much hustled. On the steps of her uncle's house she was arrested, the piece of lace was found upon her, and she was immediately carried into confinement. She said that she thought that it was hardly possible that any testimony of her character could avail against the positive evidence brought against her, more particularly as her only defence was that she knew not how the lace came in her muff. She therefore determined to conceal her name and never apply to her family. This happened just before the time of sessions. Mary's trial and condemnation ensued so soon after, that her relations had not had time to make all the enquiries which they afterwards sent in vain all over the kingdom.

These circumstances tallied so exactly with the old woman's confession that the chaplain ventured to tell Mary that he had no doubt of her acquittal. He informed the Governor of the whole transaction, who promised to transmit this information by the first ship to the English Government, and said that her innocence appeared to him so clear that, without instructions, he would venture to say that she should no longer be considered as a convict, but as a planter. In England the strictest enquiry was made, and every circumstance exactly tallied with Mary's deposition. The next ship brought her complete acquittal and conveyed her back to her disconsolate parents, who had not ceased to lament the unaccountable disappearance of their beloved child. Soon after her return she married extremely well to a young clergyman, who had a very good living.

I was told that this story was perfectly true in every part; and there can hardly be a stronger instance of virtue and innocence triumphing over the most unfortunate false appearances. It was the virtue and modesty of Mary's behaviour which were the first cause of bringing her innocence to light. Had she not been so distinguished, the chaplain never would have thought of her, but an unjust accusation of theft naturally brought her to his mind. Perhaps it may be said that her beauty contributed in some degree to the celebrity which she obtained, and consequently to her acquittal.

A CONVENT TRAGEDY.

*Extract from a Letter from Mr. Southey to Charles W. Wynn, dated January 8, 1805.**

JANE POWER was placed in the Irish Nunnery at Belem, near Lisbon, when but a child; she grew up there and took the vows. Shortly after there came over a young Irish woman (Louisa Bourke, by name), who went through the year of her probation resolutely, and took the veil. She had left her own country, and then abandoned the world, in a fit of jealousy: her lover at length traced her, followed her, and spoke with her at the grate. A reconciliation ensued: they corresponded and

---

* A great many letters to Mr. Charles Wynn from Southey have been printed by his son and his son-in-law, but this particular letter is not amongst them.

resolved to try to get her out by means of dispensation. The scheme was discovered; its success would have been a great misfortune to the convent, as the large fortune which Louisa had brought must in that case have been refunded. It was said that she had died very soon after. At this time, Jane Power was ill; after her recovery, being in a remote part of the convent which was not in use, she heard Louisa's voice, which seemed to proceed from within the wall; she thought it was her spirit, and much alarmed, asked if she should order any services for her soul. Louisa replied she was still alive, and requested her friend to come to her, giving her at the same time directions to find an entrance to her place of confinement. It was a small cell on a higher story, matted round, and so entirely remote from all the inhabited part of the convent and from every ear, that she was even allowed a musical instrument there. She had that day got down by finding some means of slipping back a bolt or lock, and by the same means Jane was enabled to visit her, which she did regularly every night for some months. Once she stayed later than usual, because her friend appeared more depressed than she had ever seen her. In consequence of this delay, her lamp was exhausted and went out in the cloisters. She was afraid that in the dark she might mistake her cell and thus be discovered; she therefore sat herself down to wait for daybreak. When the dawn came, she thought she would go back to tell Louisa how she had passed the night; she knocked and received no answer; after some time she pushed the door, but found something against it. Having at last succeeded in opening the door, she saw her wretched friend lying on the floor with her throat cut from ear to ear. Jane Power fainted, and in this state was found lying on the bleeding body of the unfortunate Louisa by the nun who brought food to the prisoner. She was carried before the abbess, who made her take the most solemn vow never to reveal what she had seen.

She continued several years longer in the nunnery; the horror which the scene she had witnessed had left upon her mind, made her situation dreadful. Her prospect brightened a little upon the arrival of our troops. Her sister's husband, whose name is either Heatley or Headley, had a civil appointment in our army there. During his stay, the frequent visits of her sister and of her English friends, made her life more cheerful than that of a nun usually is. When the troops were moving, she complained bitterly to her sister, and Headley determined to carry her off; he conveyed boy's clothes to her, and gave her his watch that she might know the hour at which to make her escape. In order to secure her from interruption from any of the male servants of the convent, he made them all drunk. When Jane, in her disguise, came to the door, the key creaked in the lock. She had resolution enough to return to the dormitory and dip it in a lamp. Still she was before the

hour appointed; for never having had a watch, she had
not wound it up; and when at last the time came, she
flung the watch over the wall instead of a stone. However, she effected her escape.

Still there remained a difficulty; the captain of the
packet, after having promised to take her, repented
and refused after she was out of the convent. She was
got on board by the management of Col. Trent's wife,
who went in the same packet; and the captain of a
frigate, who was acquainted with her story, convoyed
the vessel out, declaring at the same time that if Todd
(the master of the packet) would not take her, *he* would
run all risks and carry her to England himself, rather
than that she should be forced to return to the convent.
There came on rough weather, and poor Jane whispered
that perhaps it was sent because of her. However, she
reached Falmouth in safety, and the last I heard of her
was that her friends were endeavouring to procure from
the Pope a dispensation of her vows.

I give you this story as Mrs. Trent gave it me. Mrs.
Trent is a very extraordinary woman. Her husband was
among the persons stopped in France; she went over,
obtained his liberty, and smuggled home the son of
Hoppner the painter.

When Jane Power saw the mail coach, she said the
king was coming; and the first thing she asked for,
when she was safely housed, was a looking-glass; for,
since she was five years old, she had never seen her
own face.

MR. BURKE'S GHOST STORY.

December, 1804.—I became acquainted with Mrs. (wife of Colonel) Dixon, first at Acton, afterwards here. From her conversation I gained much amusement, and, I hope some instruction. One or two stories that she told us I am determined not to forget.

At a meeting of the Literary Club, at which Dr. Johnson, Mr. Burke, and several other eminent characters of the day were present, it was observed that an old gentleman, who had never missed one of the meetings of the society, was that day absent. His absence was considered as the more extraordinary because he happened to be president that day. While the company were expressing their surprise at this circumstance, they saw their friend enter the room, wrapped in a long white gown, his countenance wan and very much fallen. He sat down in his place, and when his friends wondered at his dress, he waved his hand, nodded to each separately, and disappeared from the room without speaking. The gentlemen, surprised at this circumstance, and determined to investigate it, called for the waiter, and asked whether anybody had been seen upon the staircase which led to the room where they were sitting. They were answered that no person had been seen either to enter the house or to mount the stairs, and that both the staircase and the entrance had been

---

* Acton Park, Wrexham: the seat of Sir R. A. Cunliffe Bart.

constantly filled with comers and goers. Not satisfied
with this, they sent to the house of the gentleman
whom they had just seen, to enquire whether he had
been out. His residence happened to be very near the
coffee-house where they were, and their messenger
immediately returned with the following melancholy
intelligence: their friend had died about ten minutes
before, of a violent fever, which had confined him
entirely to his bed for several days.

Some of the most eminent men of the club gave
themselves great pains to discover the imposition which
some thought had been practised upon them; others
firmly believed that their friend's ghost had actually
appeared to them; and the latter opinion was confirmed
by the total failure of all enquiries. All their efforts
proved vain to remove the veil of mystery which
hung over this transaction. At last they determined to
remove the club to another part of the town, entering
at the same time into an engagement never to reveal
the circumstance which had occasioned this change.
They wisely thought that such a story, supported by the
evidence of such men as Johnson, Burke, &c., might do
much mischief while the causes remained unexplained.

Many years afterwards, as Mr. Burke was sitting at
dinner with some friends at his own house, he was told
that a poor old woman, who was dying in an obscure
garret in the midst of the greatest wretchedness, had
just said that she could not die in peace unless she could

reveal a most important secret to Mr. Burke. This summons appeared so like a fraudulent means of extorting money, that Mr. Burke refused to go. In a short time, he received a second message still more pressing, and at the same time, such an account was given of the extreme poverty and misery of the poor expiring object, that his compassion was excited, and he determined to go, in spite of the earnest entreaties of his friends, who still feared for his safety. They accordingly watched in the little obscure alley, saw him ascend the staircase which led to the garret in which he was told that the poor woman was lying, and reminded him that succour was at hand.

Mr. Burke soon returned. He told his friends that he had found everything as it had been represented; that the old woman had died after telling him a very extraordinary circumstance, which had given him great satisfaction; he then related all the former part of this story, and added that the dying woman had confessed that she had been guilty of a neglect which had cost an unfortunate man his life. She said that upon her death-bed, she was determined to make all the atonement in her power, confess her error, and had therefore requested his presence, knowing him to be the most intimate friend of the deceased. She said that some years before, she was nurse to a gentleman who was ill of a dangerous fever, and named Mr. Burke's friend. She said that on a particular day—which she named—she was told by the physician that the crisis of the disease was that day to be expected, and that the ultimate issue of the malady would very much depend upon the patient's being kept perfectly quiet at that moment; which could only be done by incessant watching, as the delirium would probably run very high just before. In that case the physician directed that the patient should be forcibly detained in his bed, as the least cold would prove fatal. He therefore ordered the nurse not to leave the room upon any account the whole of the day. The nurse added that in the afternoon of that day a neighbour had called upon her; that, seeing the gentleman perfectly quiet, she had ventured to leave his room for ten minutes; when she returned, she found her patient gone. In a few minutes he returned and expired immediately. When she heard the enquiries made, she was well aware what had given birth to them, but was at that time prevented by shame from confessing the truth ! *

EXECUTION OF CHARLES I.

Jan. 18*th*, 1805.—I went to Llangollen; the ladies gave me a paper of which the following is the copy :—

---

* If anything of the kind had occurred at the Literary Club, it could hardly have escaped Boswell. Sir Walter Scott relates a similar story, the scene of which is ' a club of persons connected with science and literature ' at Plymouth.

Copy of an old MS. found behind an ancient engraving of Charles I., in the Parsonage House at Inkberghe, in the County of Worcester.

' Dr. Rd. Smallbrooke, Bishop of St. David's, informed me that, when he was chaplain of Archbishop Tennison, yᵉ Archbishop told him as follows concerning the person that executed King Charles.'

' When the Archbishop was rector of St. Martin's, he was sent for to pray by a dying man in a poor house in Gardner's Lane, Westminster. He made haste, but found the man just expired. The people of the house told him that the man had been very anxious to see him, and to confess to him that he was the executioner of King Charles; that he was a trooper of Oliver, and that, every man in the troop having refused to do that office, Oliver made them draw lots, and the lot falling upon him he did the work in a mask, and that he immediately mixed in the crowd, hiding the mask ; that he had never been easy in his mind since. He had lived some time in their house, was poor and melancholy, and much distressed for want of consolation from Dr. Tennison. Dr. Tennison was in great esteem for his good offices about dying persons. Charles lay one night, Saturday, May 10th, 1645, at the Parsonage at Inkberghe.' *

Assuming this story to have any foundation in truth, the penitent must have been William Hulet, who was tried on the 15th Oct. 1660, for regicide. Evidence was given that he, and one Walker, were the two men who officiated in disguise on the scaffold; but which of them cut off the king's head, and which

Extract from a Gazette, entitled 'Every-day Journall,' collected by J. Walker Clerc, and published by a particular Order of Parliament.

Feb. 1*st*, 1648.—The gazette begins with an account of King Charles' trial and condemnation, and after the sentence passed on him follows this paragraph :—' If the King had been guiltless of the charge, who is so weake to think he would have suffered the sentence of death to have passed on him for want of pleading ?   He pleaded the jurisdiction of the Court, wherein he strikes at the people's privileges to question tyrants.'

Jan. 30*th.*—' This morning a letter was brought from Prince Charles to the King, by one of the gentlemen belonging to the Dutch ambassador, delivered to the captain of the guard, who acquainted the King therewith, but the King refused to receive it, and desired that it might be returned back again.'

Then follows the King's speech from the scaffold, as given in all the histories, ending with his requesting

---

held it up, with the exclamation, ' This is the head of a traitor,' was left in doubt.   Hulet was found guilty, but pardoned on the recommendation of the judges, who disapproved the verdict. Various other persons—Lord Stair, Colonel Joyce, &c., &c.—have been named ; and the question, ' Who cut off Charles I.'s head?' has been as eagerly discussed as ' Who was the man in the Iron Mask?' or, ' Who wrote Junius?'   The weight of evidence is in favour of Richard Brandon, the common hangman, who died in 1649.   See the *State Trials* for 1660 ; Ellis's *Original Letters, New Series*, vol. iii. 340, and *Notes and Queries*, passim.   The index to that valuable compilation makes all its treasures easily available.

Colonel Hacker to 'take care they did not put him to paine.' The gazette then proceeds,—'after some other circumstances, the executioner severed his head from his body.'

'Those of the King's line that now are, or hereafter shall be, may sadly lay it to heart, and not aspire to monarchy, considering what sad successes their predecessors have had. King Charles is beheaded; his brother was poisoned; his sister put to exile; his eldest son exiled, her eldest son drowned; his father strongly suspected to be poisoned; his grandfather murthered and hanged on a tree; and his grandmother beheaded.'

N.B. This gazette was read by Lord Grenville to the King and the Prince of Orange, a few days after the execution of the unfortunate Louis XVI., to prove to them that, even in committing a great crime, the English preserved more of decency and humanity than the French. It was melancholy to read the last paragraph to the dethroned Prince of Orange, who, as well as George III., is the immediate descendant of Charles.

EARTHQUAKE AT NAPLES.

Extract of a Letter from Naples, giving an account of the Earthquake.

Naples: July 26th, 1805, 12 o'Clock at night.—We have had a most dreadful earthquake; it took place about a quarter-past ten. I was at the theatre, where I found myself suddenly rolling about in my chair, and the whole house apparently falling: judge of the confusion it occasioned. Everybody rushed to the door, and I was fortunate enough to be one of the first; several houses had been thrown down, and many lives lost. The front of the house next to Mr. Elliot fell down, and killed a man who was passing. On my return to my house I found the walls cracked, and in many places quite opened. As the mountain remains quiet, only throwing out flames occasionally, we are afraid of a second shock. Elliot and his whole family mean to pass the night in their carriages on the sea-shore: most of those who have carriages have followed his example; the squares are crowded with them. I am not determined what I shall do.

2 o'Clock, a.m.—The streets are crowded with processions: nothing is heard but the howling of the lazaroni; everybody calling on St. Ann, for what reason I have not yet been able to learn. I believe the worst thing to do is to go to bed.

July 27th.—We have had no return of the earthquake. I have been assured by several grave people that we are indebted to St. Ann's interposition for this, as she seems to be in the secret: a heretic may be pardoned in saying she might as well have prevented the first shock. Joking apart, we have had a very narrow escape. The shock was excessively severe, and lasted nearly a minute: had it continued with equal violence a few seconds longer, we should have had a repetition of all the horrors of the Lisbon earthquake in 1755. There is scarce a house that has not been damaged more or less. There was nothing in the heavens that indicated the approach of this commotion; the day had been sultry, and was succeeded by one of those fine Italian nights unknown in the north; there was not a cloud to be seen in the horizon, nor a breath of air stirring. During the shock, and for some time afterwards, partial eddies of wind brought with them immense clouds of dust, but they were soon dispersed; and the remainder of the night was as fine as the former part, nor is there a cloud to be seen this morning.

July 28*th.*—The whole town passed last night in the squares and open places, as a return of the earthquake was expected. It was the most horrible sight I ever beheld. Notwithstanding the immense crowds, a perfect silence prevailed, interrupted only by the crying of women, and the singing of children, who paraded the streets in processions with flambeaux in honour of the Virgin. Not a smile was seen on any countenance; the fierce looks of the lazaroni increased the horror of the scene. The havoc is infinitely greater than was at first imagined. The houses destroyed are estimated at five millions of piastres; whole streets are in ruins. The shock was so strong that the crew of the 'Excellent,' anchored at two miles from the shore, supposed that the ship had struck against the earth, and all the officers and men were upon deck *en chemise.* It is supposed that not more than ninety people have been crushed at Naples.

July 29th.—All remains quiet, but we are daily receiving reports from the environs that are truly distressing. Half of the town of Averca is destroyed. At Capua the barracks fell in, and killed or wounded seventy-three soldiers. The towns of Isernia (about sixty miles from hence) and Campo Basso are entirely destroyed. At Aventino they have lost eight hundred persons. At another town (the name of which I have forgot) the loss is upwards of one thousand. I will write again by the next post, that you may not be uneasy on my account. I am, however, in great hopes that all danger is over.

Naples: August 6th, 1805.—We have fortunately had no return of the earthquake: the slightest, in the present ruined state of the town, would bring the whole about our ears. The shock has been sufficiently great; 'tis said twelve thousand persons have perished, though the government allows but five thousand. Forty-two towns or villages have suffered more or less, some of which are entirely destroyed. The town of Boiardo has totally disappeared, and a lake has been formed in its place. A new volcano is said to have burst out in the chain of the Apennines which runs behind Isernia; a fortunate event, which has, perhaps, saved us from the renewal of the earthquake by giving vent to the volcanic matter,

which from some secret cause had set in agitation the
bowels of the earth.   You may form some idea of the
violence of the shock, from the circumstance of some
persons being affected by it as by sea-sickness. The
children of Sir Grenville Temple, who, from being ignorant of the danger, cannot be supposed to have been
influenced by fear, were affected in this manner in
common with several grown people. I myself did not
feel any sensation of this sort, perhaps from having been
constantly in motion: the same cause prevented my
feeling the second and third shocks, which took place at
eleven and one o'clock the same night; but if my imagination does not deceive me, the earth has never ceased to
tremble ever since the great shock. One wing of the house
in which I live has been declared uninhabitable: my
part has not suffered so much ; but it will be necessary
that it should undergo a thorough repair, being cracked
from top to bottom, and the walls open in several places.

August 13*th.*—At seven o'clock last night we had a
most furious eruption of Mount Vesuvius. The lava, a
mile and a half in breadth, ran down to the sea a distance of seven miles in three hours, destroying vine-
yards, cattle, houses—in short, everything it met in its
passage. The damage it has done is immense. The
effect it produced when it came in contact with the
sea was truly sublime; for one hundred yards round
you might have boiled an egg in the water, so violent a
heat did it communicate. Seven or eight old people only

have perished. Notwithstanding the destruction it has occasioned, I cannot but look upon it as a fortunate circumstance, as it has probably saved us from a repetition of the earthquake.

THE EMPEROR ALEXANDER.

Wynnstay: Oct. 1806.—I heard a curious trait of the character of the Emperor Alexander. At one of the great national festivals of St. Petersburgh, where he was greeted by multitudes almost innumerable with the most violent applause,—every one seeming to vie with his neighbour in the mode of best expressing their enthusiastic fondness for their Emperor,—he turned to the Duke of G. who was standing near him, and said he could not look at that immense populace without shuddering when he considered them as absolutely dependent upon the will of one man; adding that he should never feel completely happy till he saw introduced into Russia, a limited monarchical government similar to that of England *. . . The Duke of G. spoke much of the violent detestation expressed by all orders of men for the Archduke Constantine. It seems strange that such statements can be loudly professed with impunity under the government of a son of the Emperor Paul; but one

* Alexander is said to have replied to Madame de Staël, when she spoke of his beneficent rule, that he was only a happy accident.

fact which the Duke of G. said was related to him by Alexander, is much more so. The Emperor was one day reproving Count Pannin, his favourite, for expressing so freely his opinion of Constantine. He told him that he must consider it a want of respect to himself when his brother was treated in such a manner: besides, added he, consider what may be the probable consequences to yourself; remember that, if anything should happen to me, Constantine becomes your Sovereign.* Pannin replied that no one was more anxious than himself to avoid anything which might appear like disrespect to His Majesty, and therefore would for that reason avoid expressing his opinions on this subject; adding that, as to the other argument, that had no weight with him, ' for Sire,' said he, ' if anything was to happen to you, I wish Archduke Constantine to know, and beg you will tell him from me, that he shall not reign twenty-four hours.'

EXTRACTS FROM LETTERS FROM GERMANY.

August: 1800.—On the morning before Ratisbonne was taken, a grand and solemn ceremony was performed in the cathedral, of which the band and organ are reckoned the best in Germany. At one passage of the

------

* Pannin might have remembered the reply of Charles II., when the Duke of York (afterwards James II.) reproached him with not taking precautions against assassins: ' Depend upon it, James, no one will kill me to make you king.'

Latin service, the fears of the inhabitants of a siege and bombardment seemed to be expressed in the words, ' Jerusalem, Jerusalem, thou shalt be made desolate !' The prophecy was chanted by a shrill single voice, like one from the dead, at the further end of the long echoing cathedral. A dreadfully sublime pause succeeded, and then the whole thunder of the organ, drums, and trumpets, broke in. I never thought terrific music could have reached so high. Two hours after an alarm was given, and the Hungarian infantry were called out to support their defeated countrymen. This music, though less sacred, was also perfect in its kind. Its effect was heightened by the sound of artillery coming nearer and nearer, and the flash of carbines from the neighbouring wood, where they were skirmishing in small parties. The sight of men and horses passing, gave a serious aspect to the scene, and convinced the spectator that he was not hearing the drums of a holiday parade.

Sept. 1*st*, 1802.—He gave me an account of the demolition of the strong castle of Ehrenbreitstein, which human force had never conquered; but the destruction of which was a stipulated article in the German Treaty of Peace. The task is not even yet fully accomplished. He was present at the springing of the principal mine. It must have been a sight terrible and magnificent in the extreme.

The mighty structure, compacted and cemented by

the skill of early ages, did not immediately separate,
but rose at the explosion in one great mass, slowly and
sullenly, to the distance of four feet from the ground;
for a moment it remained in the air in awful equipoise,
visibly balancing from side to side, as if in doubt
which way to deal devastation; at last, with resistless
impetuosity, and with a crash that rent the air, it forced
its way down a shelving precipice of 800 feet into the
valley beneath. Near the river's brink was an ancient seat
of the Elector Palatine, which had long been desolate
and uninhabited. Against this the bastion, still entire,
rushed with all its augmented and accelerated force.
Feeble was the resistance; but feeble as it was, the
sudden collision loosened all the component parts of the
destructive engine, and the tower and the palace form
one blended shapeless heap of indiscriminate ruin.

Mentz: 1802.—This unfortunate city thrice changed
its masters during the war. Custine first took it; then,
after a most severe bombardment, it fell into the hands
of the Prussians; and again it reverted to the French
amid the tide of their splendid victories.

Its public buildings are all ruined and destroyed; its
religious houses demolished; the trees which formed a
magnificent avenue on the ramparts are felled to the
earth; the palace of the Elector and all the adjacent
villas so entirely done away, that their place knoweth
them no more; the stately cathedral, once the pride
and glory of ecclesiastical sovereignty, presented to the

view little more than a broken dilapidated mass of complicated destruction.

Here my melancholy walk ended: the evening was
far advanced, and there remained just enough light to
relieve the dark shadows which the projections of tombs,
chapels, and arches threw forward. Except a few
wanton mutilations, the superb monuments all remain
as in their pristine state: they chiefly consist of busts
and statues of the successive Electors, in the purest
white marble, from the fifteenth to the middle of the
eighteenth century. Amid these splendid specimens of
art, the traveller sees in the great aisle a shapeless heap
of forage: near the pulpit, all glittering with coloured
ornaments, a depôt of straw in trusses; in the choir,
which neither war nor sacrilege could entirely deprive
of its enrichments, two or three miserable cabriolets;
the western chapel, once embellished by all that wealth,
ingenuity, or devotion could prompt or suggest, turned
into an occasional stable. It was a second Babylon in
ruins; full of doleful creatures, profaned, desecrated,
devastated. The pavement, formerly in rich mosaic,
exhibits evident proof of that furious zeal which ran-
sacked the mansions of the dead in order to fabricate
engines and weapons of death. The leaden coffins were
too valuable objects of military consideration to escape
the hands of those whose hearts nothing could soften.

As my dubious feet were feeling their way along, and
it was only not totally dark, my guide, a savage-looking

ruffian fellow, suddenly and violently seized my arm.
I was straining my eyes to catch a glimpse of a gigantic
figure in marble elevated to a considerable height against
one of the pillars.   I had insensibly prolonged my stay,
rapt in musing and meditations congenial to the scene;
but when I met with this unexpected attack, and as I
deemed assault, it took not a moment to bring me to
myself.   The man, in his rude jargon between German
and French, soon explained to me his kindness and my
own danger: at my feet was a hideous chasm through
which in the siege a bomb had forced its way into a
spacious vault that had ever since remained open; one
moment more, and it would have received another
visitor.*

LAST MOMENTS OF LOUIS XVI.—ESCAPE OF THE
DUCS D'ANGOULÊME AND BERRY.

Stowe: January 9th, 1807.—This morning I have
been very much interested by an account given us of some
of the horrors of the Revolution by the Duke de Sirent.
He read to us a history of the last moments of Louis
XVI., written by Abbé Edgeworth, at the request of the
brothers of that unfortunate Monarch.   In the history
there was little that we did not know before from Cléry's

---

* I rather think that Sir R. Wilmot Horton was the writer of
these remarkable letters.

and other publications : but every particular became doubly interesting—first, from being so authenticated, but still more from the extreme emotion of the reader. This was peculiarly striking when, in describing the anxiety expressed by the King respecting the fate of the clergy, the abbé says he informed him of the kind, hospitable reception they had met with in this country, upon which the King forcibly expressed his gratitude towards the English for the protection they had afforded to his unfortunate subjects. At these words the poor óld man's voice faltered, and his eyes filled as he looked towards Lady B.

The most striking circumstance mentioned by Edgeworth is a speech of the Deputy of the National Assembly, who was ordered to accompany him in the fiacre which carried him from the National Assembly to the melancholy abode of the condemned Monarch. After very little communication on indifferent subjects, the man suddenly exclaimed, ' *Mon Dieu, quelle tâche nous avons à remplir ! Quel homme ! quelle résignation ! quel courage ! Il faut qu'il y ait la quelque chose de surhumain.*'* After this speech the abbé had the pru-

---

* It was the Minister of Justice (Garat) who accompanied the abbé on his way to the Temple, and his soliloquy is thus reported in the *Dernières Heures,* as printed ;—' " Grand Dieu ! " s'éoria-t-il, après avoir levé les glaces de sa voiture, " de quelle affreuse commission je me vois chargé ! Quelle homme ! " ajouta-t-il en parlant du Roi, "quelle résignation ! quel courage ! Non, la nature toute seule ne saurait donner tánt de forces ; il y a quelque chose de surhumain."

dence to preserve perfect silence; he thought that, though he might be able to work on the mind of this man, it was still more likely, considering the short time they had to pass together, that he might only exasperate him, and be denied the permission of seeing the unfortunate King. The behaviour of Louis in these last trying moments exhibits proofs not only of his uncommon piety, resignation, and meekness, but also of fortitude and resolution, which appear little to accord with the general weakness and indecision of his character. In reading this melancholy history, it was singular to see that the duke appeared to be most affected by some trifling instances of degradation, which we might otherwise have overlooked. For instance, when Louis was described as receiving the sacrament *sans prie-Dieu, sans coussin,* in a small bed-room * without any furniture but *trois mauvaises chaises en cuir,* he was deeply affected, probably from the having so frequently been an eye-witness of all the splendour which used to attend this ceremony.

Afterwards, the duke gave us the account of his escape from Paris with the sons of the Comte d'Artois,—the Duc d'Angoulême and the Duke de Berri. These children

---

* According to the printed copy of the narrative, it was the King's cabinet, 'où il n'y avait ni tapisserie ni ornemens; un mauvais poële de faïence lui tenoit lieu de cheminée, et l'on n'y voyait pour toute meuble qu' une table et trois chaises de cuir.' It was in the adjoining chamber, the King's, where 'le Roi entendit la messe à genoux par terre, sans prie-Dieu ni coussins.'

were entrusted to him not only by their father, but by the King, who both seem on this occasion to have given evident proofs of indecision and weakness of mind. The Comte d'Artois (now Monsieur) having told the duke that he wished him to escape with his sons, whose governor he was, everything was prepared for their departure that night. The father seems to have little troubled himself with any arrangements, saying to the duke, ' *Je m'en repose sur vous, ce sont vos enfants,*' and refusing even to name the place or country to which he was to take them. At last, upon his representing that they were *enfants de l'état,* he promised to get from Louis an order empowering the duke to remove them. Very late at night, not having received this order, Monsieur de Sirent determined to follow Monsieur to the queen's supper, where he knew him to be. He says he never can forget the appearance of deep dejection and consternation which he saw in the faces of all the royal family, assembled after supper in the state bedchamber of the queen. In a window stood the King and the Comte d'Artois, in earnest conversation. Monsieur de Sirent endeavoured once more to obtain further orders; representing that from various political circumstances, of which he was ignorant, there must be reasons for preferring one country to another for the refuge of the royal children. After a pause, both brothers, nearly in the same words, assured him of their perfect confidence in him, and re-fused to give any further orders; thus shifting all the weight of responsibility from their own shoulders upon his. They gave, however, one much stronger proof of pusillanimity; when the duke repeated his request for a written order from the King, His Majesty said, '*à propos, il vous en faut un assurement*,' and put into his hands a folded paper. His dismay must have been great when, on his return home, he found this to be only an order to furnish him with post-horses; in short, a sort of safe conduct for himself, without any mention of the young princes. He had, therefore, to set out on his perilous enterprise with the additional horror of knowing that, if the princes were missed soon enough to be overtaken by the emissaries of the National Assembly, he had no permission to show; and, therefore, the whole blame would fall on his devoted head. Besides, it seemed but too probable that they might work on the mind of the weak monarch so far as to make him wish to recall the princes; in which case, he would never avow that he had permitted their departure. Neither of these fears were expressed by M. de Sirent, but from the circumstances, it was easy to imagine what he must feel.

At last, in the middle of the night, they set out; the duke, his two pupils, a surgeon, and a servant in one carriage, followed by one in which were the duchess and her daughters. The children had no idea where they were going; they were told they were going to see the departure of a regiment of hussars which they had much admired. The hairbreadth escapes of this journey made one's blood run cold. Monsieur de Sirent describes the villages as *ne finissant point,* particularly one near Paris filled with laundresses, who poured upon them the most violent torrent of abuse. After some hours' travelling, it became necessary to give the children some breakfast, which he thought might be safely obtained at the seat of the *Garde des Sceaux,* M. de Massieu (I think). He was absent; but from an old *concierge,* who knew Monsieur de Sirent to be an old friend of his master, they got breakfast. While the children were eating, the duke was examining the old *concierge.* Finding that he had lived 20 years with Monsieur de M., he ventured to [tell him that his visitors were the sons of the Comte d'Artois, asking him to procure them horses. In this he succeeded, and for some time they travelled prosperously, the innkeepers too much occupied by passing events to trouble their heads about *un simple particulier voyageant à Spa pour sa santé avec sa femme et ses enfans.*

At the town of Buonavite, where they intended to sleep and expected to find a *bon gîte,* they found the streets full of populace, who collected round the carriage, calling them *aristocrats,* and by every other abusive term which seemed to follow of course. They were actually beginning to pull off the papers which were stuck on to conceal the arms on the carriages, when the courier, to whom, fortunately, their intention of stopping had not been communicated,

announced the horses to be put to, and they set off again
not very sorry to lose sight of the good people of Buonavite.   At the next stop they found only a wretched post
house, but the master promised to get them some eggs
for supper, and the cushions of the carriages were taken
out to make a sort of bed for the princes and the ladies.
While they were resting, the duke sat himself down in
a corner of the kitchen chimney, trying to warm himself; for, though worn out with anxiety, he found it
impossible to sleep.   The post-master sat down by him,
and begun to talk of the news of the day, of the
wretched condition of the country, of the disturbances
hourly expected in the next town of Peronne, &c.   On
these subjects his sentiments were such as the duke himself might have expressed, and more effectually warmed
his heart than the kitchen fire.   At last, having agreed
with his host in everything, he asked him how he might
prosecute his journey to Spa with most safety and least
disturbance.   The man replied: *Monsieur, il faut,
enfin, que les coquins dorment comme les honnêtes gens,
je vous donnerai six bons chevaux à chaque voiture, et
vous serez loin d'ici avant qu'ils ne soient eveillés.*

They accordingly proceeded without obstacle through
the deserted streets of Peronne, which by ten o'clock the
next day was in a state of insurrection.   During this
day's journey they were overtaken by the Prince de
Condé, and had the mortification of seeing the horses
which had been put to their carriage taken off for his.

When he discovered them, he wished to prevent this, but the duke wisely thought that a little delay would be less dangerous than the suspicions excited by such a mark of respect. At last, on the third night of their departure from Paris, when they were within a few miles of Valenciennes, where the duke knew Monsieur would meet them, he informed his pupils of their real destination. Hitherto they had been kept in perfect ignorance. After the story of the hussar regiment, he had invented others to account for their travelling incognito. M. de Sirent took this opportunity to inform them fully, and in the most solemn manner, of the melancholy situation of their father, their King, and their country; expressing at the same time his fears as to their future fate. He then told them that now they must depend upon themselves, they must become from that hour not only men but heroes.

All this appears perfectly natural if the princes had been, as we thought when we heard all this, only eight or ten years of age; but the fact is that these *children*, kept so perfectly in the dark, delighted with the idea of seeing a hussar regiment, and believing that such a journey was caused and all the apprehensions which they could not but see in M. de Sirent excited by some trivial occasion—these *children* (as he called them) were, one near sixteen and the other near fourteen. They stayed only a few days at Valenciennes, and then proceeded to Spa; nor was M. de Sirent at ease about them till two months and a half afterwards, when they reached Turin, and were placed under the care of their maternal grandfather.

Madame de Sirent, who was *dame d'atours* to Madame Elizabeth, and had only left her, thinking that she should rather impede than assist her flight after the disaster of Varennes, determined to return to her post. Immediately on her return to Paris, she and her daughter were imprisoned, and were only released at the death of Robespierre, fourteen months after. Her life was during this time preserved by singular means: one of the inferior agents of Robespierre was highly bribed, and through his hands passed the awful orders of execution. They were given each decade on ten loose sheets of paper, one for each day; whenever the name of Madame de Sirent appeared upon the paper, he slipped that sheet underneath, and proceeded to the next. Afterwards she attached herself to the unfortunate niece of Madame Elizabeth, and is now with her at Mittau, while her husband, from the same sense of duty, is here with Monsieur and the Duc de Berri.

N.B.—In 1814 I saw Madame de Sirent, a little hump-backed old woman, a stray lady of the bedchamber to the Duchesse d'Angoulême, at the reception, or sad mock drawing-room, which she held in South Audley Street, in a small two-roomed house which the Comte d'Artois had hired. A few days after they departed for Paris.

SIR WALTER SCOTT'S STORIES.

April, 1807. Mr. Scott, the author of the ' Lay,' told us some curious border histories. We were much pleased with the conclusion of the history of Wat Tynlin. When he was grown old and blind, one of the agents of the Lady of Branksome, in her absence, called upon him for the rent of a small tower which he inhabited; part of which is standing to this day. Wat, incensed, replied he never had paid rent, nor would at that age. At last he delivered his bow to the steward, and said he would pay the rent to the man who could draw that bow; the bow was certainly tried, but we will hope that the lady would never have obliged such a man to pay his rent. However, certain it is that some vain attempts were made to draw his bow, and that Wat never paid his rent.

Mr. Scott spoke of one story which might make an excellent ballad, but he said he could not write it, as to do it justice much humour, a *quality he never possessed,** was required. Scott of Harden, one of his

---

* (*Note by Miss Wynn.*)—When in 1815 Scott published Paul's ' Letters to his Kinsfolk,' in which the attempts at humour so entirely failed, I lamented his having forgotten this declaration. *Now,* in 1824, when he is considered as the undoubted, though unacknowledged, author of so many admirable novels, containing more humour than could probably be found in all the other authors of this century collected together, I wonder at his having made it. I see that when I tell this story nobody believes me, and I feel I should doubt my own recollection if the above had not been written on the very day that I saw Scott, in 1807.

ancestors, was a famous border thief, and at one time, when he had either spoiled the neighbouring English of all their cattle or had frightened them all away, he began to fear that from disuse he might become less expert at the honourable trade he pursued ; and to keep his hand in, amused himself with driving the cattle of one of his own countrymen and neighbours, Murray of Elibank, an ancestor of the present Lady Elibank. Murray soon found means of revenging himself, and brought Scott, his followers, his cattle, &c., &c., all prisoners to Elibank Castle. On the walls was sitting his wife, who, perceiving the train that followed him, asked what he meant to do with Scott. ' Why, hang him, to be sure,' was the answer. The more prudent wife exclaimed, ' What ! hang such a winsome mannie as Harden, when we have three such sorry damsels at home ? ' Murray was persuaded by his wife, and sending for one of his daughters, whose ugly face and immense mouth had acquired her the name of *Mag o' mouth Murray,* proposed to Scott to marry her, leaving him no other alternative but a halter. The unfortunate prisoner most ungallantly refused the lady ; and the tradition says that it was not till the rope was tied to the tree, and he began to feel it tighten, that he repented. He was married, and sorrowfully bent his steps homewards, taking with him his ugly wife.

BUXTON LETTER.

Extract of a Letter from Dr. J——n, at Buxton, to his friend. J——s B——ll, Esq., in Scotland. (By Pepper Arden, afterwards Lord Alvanley.)

Fortune often delights to exalt what nature has neglected, and that renown which cannot be claimed by intrinsic excellence is frequently derived from accident. The Rubicon was ennobled by the passage of Cæsar, and the bubbling up of a stream in the middle of a lime quarry has given celebrity to Buxton. The waters in which it is agreed that no mineral properties reside, and which seem to have no better claim to superior heat than what is derived from comparing them with the almost Siberian atmosphere that surrounds them, are said, however, to possess a spirit which, though too volatile and unknown to receive a name from the chymists of graver ages, have, in this fanciful era, when Macaroni philosophers hold flirtation with science, taken the lead of all the other elements, and those whose nerves have not found any relief in change of sky and variety, seek for a refuge here in fixed air.

It is, indeed, amazing to see the avidity with which mankind seek after that health which they have voluntarily alienated, like Methodists who hope for salvation through faith without works. Invalids come here in hopes of finding in the well the vigour which they have lost in the bowl, and of absorbing in the bath the moisture which evaporated in the ball or the masquerade. For this purpose they venture to this dreary spot, which contemplates with envy the Highlands of Scotland, surrounded by barren mountains, beaten by storms almost perpetual. Scarce an inhabitant is to be seen unless when the sun, whose appearance is justly considered as one of the wonders of the Peak, draws them out from a curiosity natural to man who wonders into what cavern the storm has retired.

Yet this is summer; and if the winter hold its natural proportion, the inhabitants of the hall—which is not thirty yards distant from the well—must pass months without any communication with it. Yet here, the same folly which created the disease for the cure of which so much is suffered, obstructs the operation of the remedy from which so much is hoped. Animated by the appetite, which even the diluent powers of common water, assisted by the vibrations of diurnal exercise and the collisive hilarity of reciprocal salutation, would give to a body obstructed by gluttony and rest—they devour with deleterious hunger a farinaceous sponge, the interstices of which are inundated with butter, which might smile at the peristaltic exertions of an elephant, and of which the digestion would be no less an evil than the obstruction. If obstructed, it convulses the stomach with rancid exhalations; and if by its gravity it finds its way to the bowels, it tumefies them with flatulent paroxysms by its detention : in both it becomes acrimonious and mephitic, and while its fumes arise and salute the brain with palsy, its *caput mortuum* descends and lays the foundation of *fistula*.

Very providentially, however, the evils of breakfast are not aggravated by dinner. Dinner is rather a ceremony here than a repast, and those who are delicate and sick, acquire popularity by disseminating among the multitude that food which nothing but rude health, both of body and mind, can digest. When it is finished, however, the chaplain calls upon the company to be thankful for what they have received ; and the company, remembering they have breakfasted, join in the thanksgiving.

The evils of the day are likewise happily alleviated by the early hour of retiring to bed ; and if sleep forsakes the pillow, even fancy itself cannot charge it on the supper. There are, notwithstanding, here upwards of two hundred people, who, by talking continually of how much nature has left undone, and how little art has done for the place, increase the spleen they come to cure.

THE TYRONE GHOST STORY.

Lord Tyrone and Lady Beresford were born in Dublin. They were left orphans in their infancy to the care of the same person, who brought them up in the principles of Deism. Their guardian dying when they were about fourteen, they fell into very different hands, and every means was tried to convince them of the truth of revealed religion, but in vain. Though separated, their mutual affection remained unalterable. After some years they made a solemn vow to each other, that whichever should die first, would (if permitted by the Almighty) appear to the other and declare what religion was most approved by God. Lady Beresford shortly after married Sir Martin Beresford. One morning she came down unusually pale with a black ribbon round her wrist. Sir Martin asked whether she was ill, and whether she had sprained her wrist: she replied she was well, and conjured him never to enquire the cause of her wearing the ribbon. She expressed anxiety for the arrival of the post. Sir Martin asked whether she expected letters. She said she expected to hear that Lord Tyrone was dead; that he died last Tuesday at 4 o'clock. Sir Martin tried to comfort her, and assured her she was deceived by some idle dream. The letter arrived conveying the intelligence of Lord Tyrone's death, which had happened at the precise time Lady Beresford had specified.

She then informed Sir Martin that she had to announce to him that she should shortly give him a son, an event he had long and ardently desired. In some months Lady Beresford was delivered of a son; she had before given birth to two daughters. Sir Martin survived this event but four years. After his death Lady Beresford shut herself very much up, she visited no family but that of the clergyman of the village. His family consisted of himself, his wife, and a son, who, at the time of Sir Martin's death, was quite a boy; to this son, however, she was in a few years married. He behaved to her in the most scandalous manner. After having given birth to two daughters, Lady Beresford insisted on a separation from her profligate husband. After a few years she was induced by his entreaties to pardon and once more live with him, and in time became the mother of another son. The day she had lain in a month, she sent for Lady Betty Cobb, her intimate friend, requesting her and a few friends to spend the day with her, as it was her birthday; among others, was the clergyman by whom she was baptized. Having observed that she was forty-eight that day, the clergyman assured her she was only forty-seven: telling her he had had frequent disputes with her mother on the subject, and had a few days before searched the register, which proved him to be right and her only forty-seven instead of forty-eight. 'You have signed my death warrant,' said she, and requested the company to leave her, as she had many things to settle before she died. She requested that Lady Betty Cobb and her son by Sir Martin (who was about twelve years old), would come to her, as she had something to communicate to them.

When the attendants were withdrawn, she said, ' I have something to communicate to you both before I

die, a period which is not far distant. You, Lady Bett
are no stranger to the friendship which always subsiste
between Lord Tyrone and myself; we were educate
under the same roof, and in the same principles of Deisn
When my friends afterwards tried to persuade us t
embrace the revealed religion, their arguments, thoug:
insufficient to convince, had power to stagger our forme
faith. In this perplexing state of doubt, we made a vo\
to each other that whichever died first should (if per
mitted) appear to the other and declare what religion wa.
most acceptable to the Almighty. Accordingly, while Si:
Martin and I were asleep, I woke suddenly and foun(
Lord Tyrone sitting by the bed-side. I screamed, and
endeavoured to wake Sir Martin. " For Heaven's sake,"
said I, " by what means, or for what purpose, came you
here at this time of night?" " Have you forgot your
promise?" said he; " I died last Tuesday, at four o'clock,
and have been permitted by the Supreme Being to appear
to you to assure you that revealed religion is the only
true faith and the only means by which we can be
saved. I am further suffered to inform you that
you are with child of a son who shall marry my
daughter. Not many years after his birth, Sir Martin
will die; you will be married again to a man whose ill
conduct will make you miserable; you will bring him
two daughters and afterwards a son, in childbed of
whom you will die in the forty-seventh year of your
age." "Just Heaven," I exclaimed, " and cannot I pre-

vent this?" "Undoubtedly, you may," said he, "you are a
free agent, and may prevent this by resisting every temp-
tation to a second marriage; but the passions are strong;
hitherto you have had no trials; you know not their
power. More I am not permitted to say; but if, after
this warning, you persist in your infidelity, your lot in
another world would be miserable indeed." "May I not
ask," said I, "if you are happy?" "Had I been otherwise, I should not have been permitted to appear to
you." "I may then infer that you are happy; when
the morning comes, how shall I be convinced that your
appearance has been real, and not the phantom of
my imagination?"— "Will not the news of my death
be sufficient to convince you?" "No," returned I,
"I might have had such a dream, and *that* dream
by accident come to pass. I wish to have some
stronger proof of its reality." "You shall," said he;
then waving his hand, the bed-curtains, which were
of crimson velvet, were instantly drawn through a
large hook of ivory, by which the tester of the bed,
which was of an oval form, was suspended. "In
that," said he, "you can't be mistaken; no mortal arm
could have done this." "But we are sleeping, and
people have much greater strength then than when
awake. I may fancy I have done it in my sleep. I shall
still doubt." "You have a pocket-book, on the leaves of
which I will write; you know my handwriting." He
wrote. "Still," said I, " I may in the morning have my

doubts; though waking I cannot mistake your hand writing; sleeping I may." "You are hard of belief. I must not touch you; it would injure you irreparably it is not for spirits to touch mortal flesh." "I do not regard a slight blemish." "You are a woman of courage, hold out your hand." I did; he touched my wrist: his hand was cold as marble. In an instant the sinews shrank up, every nerve withdrew. "Now," said he, "while you live, let no mortal eye behold that wrist; to see it would be sacrilege." He stopped: I turned to him again; he was gone. During the time I conversed with him, my thoughts were perfectly calm and collected; but the moment he was gone, I felt chilled with horror; the bed trembled under me; I endeavoured to awake Sir Martin, but in vain. In this state of horror and agitation, I lay for some time; when, a shower of tears coming to my relief, I dropped asleep.

'In the morning Sir Martin arose as usual without perceiving the situation in which the curtain remained. When I awoke, I found Sir Martin already gone. I went into the gallery adjoining our apartment, and took from thence a very large broom used for sweeping the cornices: by the help of this, though not without difficulty, I took down the curtain, as I imagined this extraordinary appearance would excite enquiries among the servants which I wished to avoid. I then went to my bureau, locked up the pocket-book, and took out some black ribbon, which I bound round my wrist. When I came down, the agitation of my mind had left an impression on my countenance too strong to pass unnoticed by Sir Martin. He enquired the cause of my visible disorder. I told him I was well, but informed him that Lord Tyrone was no more; at the same time entreated him to drop all enquiries about the black ribbon round my wrist. He kindly desisted from all importunity, nor did he ever after enquire the cause. *You* were born, my son, as had been foretold, and four years after your ever-to-be-lamented father expired in my arms.

'After this melancholy event, I determined, as the only means by which I might avoid the dreadful event of the prediction, for ever to abandon society, and pass the remainder of my days in solitude; but few can endure to exist long in a state of perfect sequestration. I commenced an intercourse with one family only, nor could I foresee the fatal consequences that afterwards ensued. Little did I imagine that their son, their only son, was the person intended by fate for my undoing. In a few years I ceased to regard him with indifference; I endeavoured by every means to conquer a passion the fatal consequences of which, if ever I should yield to its impulse, were too well known; and I fondly imagined I had overcome its influence, when the event of one fatal moment undermined my fortitude, and plunged me into that abyss I had so long determined to shun.

'He had frequently solicited his parents for leave to go into the army, and at length obtained their permission. He came to bid me farewell before his departure: the moment he entered the room he fell on his knees at my feet, told me he was miserable and that *I* alone was the cause. At that instant my fortitude forsook me. I gave myself up for lost, and considered my fate as inevitable; and without further hesitation consented to a union, the result of which I knew to be misery, and its end death. After a few years were passed, the conduct of my husband amply warranted my demand of a separation, and I hoped by this step to avoid the fatal accomplishment of the prophecy; but, won over by his strong entreaty, I was prevailed on to pardon and once more to reside with him, though not till after I had, as I imagined, passed my forty-seventh year, but I have this day heard from indisputable authority that I am but forty-seven this day. Of the near approach of my death I entertain not the least doubt, but I do not dread its arrival: armed with the prospects of Christianity, I can meet the King of Terrors without dismay, and without a tear bid adieu to the regions of mortality for ever. When I am dead, as the necessity of its concealment closes with my life, I could wish that you, Lady Betty Cobb, would unbind my wrist and take from thence the black ribbon, and let my son and yourself behold my arm.'

Lady Beresford here paused for some time, but

renewing the conversation she entreated her son to behave so as to merit the honour he would in future receive from a union with the daughter of Lord Tyrone. Lady Beresford then expressed a wish to lie down on the bed, and endeavour to compose herself to sleep. Lady Betty Cobb and her son called the attendants to watch their mistress, and, should they observe the slightest change in her, instantly to let them know. An hour passed; all was silent: they listened at the door; everything was still, but in about half-an-hour the bell rang violently. They flew to the apartment, but before they reached the door they heard the servant exclaim, ' Oh she is dead, my mistress is dead.' Lady Betty sent the servants out of the room; she approached the bed of Lady Beresford with her son; he knelt by his mother's bedside. Lady Betty lifted up her hand, unbound the black ribbon exactly in the state Lady Beresford had described,—every sinew shrank up, and every nerve withered.

N.B. Lady Beresford's son, as had been predicted, is married to the daughter of Lord Tyrone : the black ribbon and pocket-book are in the possession of Lady Betty Cobb in Ireland, or Marlborough Buildings, Bath : who, together with the Tyrone family, will assert its truth, and by whom the above narrative is stated, and was transcribed at Tallerig, on July 24th, 1794, by the Honourable Mrs. Maitland. (*Copy of a Copy taken in 1801.*)

Real particulars of the preceding story dictated to me by Lady E. Butler and Miss Ponsonby (the ladies of Llangollen), who had frequently heard them from many of Lady Beresford's and of Mr. Gorges' descendants, with some of whom they are intimately connected and related.

Miss Hamilton, a rich and beautiful heiress, was early married to Sir Martin Beresford: it was supposed that both before and after her marriage she had been too intimately connected with Lord Tyrone. Some time after her marriage, in the year 1704, it was agreed that Lord Tyrone, Sir Martin and Lady Beresford, should pass one Christmas at Colonel Gorges' house, called Kilbrew, in the county of Meath. One night, after the family were all retired, Lady Beresford was surprised to see the door of her chamber open, and Lord Tyrone walked in, dressed in his *robe de chambre*. She exclaimed 'Good God, what brings you here at this time of night?' He walked up to the bedside and replied, 'I left Corraughmore with an intention of coming here. I was taken ill on the road, and have just expired. I am come to you for the ring which I gave you.' Lady

---

* It is amusing to compare these two versions, each professing to rest on the same quality of information, and with equal pretensions to the title of 'real particulars.' The internal evidence, however, is in favour of that furnished by the ladies of Llangollen. The story is not mentioned by Dr. Ferrier, Dr. Hibbert, or Sir Walter Scott. Mrs. Crowe ('Nightside of Nature') merely alludes to it as well known and well authenticated.

Beresford, horror-struck, pushed Sir Martin to wake him.
'He cannot wake while I am here,' said Lord Tyrone.
'He will die; you will marry the gentleman of this house;
you will die in childbed of your second son, but you
shall see me again; give me the ring.'

Lady Beresford, extremely agitated, could not immediately get it off her finger; he seized her hand,
and the ring appeared to her to roll off upon the
floor.   The next morning Lady Beresford tried to
persuade herself that the whole of this scene was the
effect of imagination, but on her wrist she found the
mark of Lord Tyrone's hand; each finger left a black
mark as if it had been burnt.   On a desk which
stood near the bed, and on which Lord Tyrone had
leant, the same trace of five fingers was found.   That
on Lady Beresford's wrist never was effaced, and to
her dying day she wore a black ribbon bracelet to
conceal it.   The ring was likewise missing; nor could it
after the most diligent search be ever found, though
every board of the floor was taken up the next day.   In
the course of time Sir Martin died, and Lady Beresford
did marry Colonel Gorges.

By Sir Martin she had one son, born in 1694; by
Colonel Gorges, three daughters, one of whom married
Lord Howth, and another Lord Desart.   After these she
had a son. Colonel Gorges, fearing that his birth might
prey upon her mind, still strongly affected with the recollection of the vision, persuaded her that her child was

a girl. She was got so well after her confinement, that the carriage was ordered for her to take the air. Meanwhile, she unfortunately enquired of a housemaid who came into her room, how her child was ; the maid replied, '*He* is very well.' '*He*!' said Lady B. ; 'it is then a son,' and she burst into tears. Her husband and friend at length succeeded in persuading her that, after having been so long brought to bed, all danger must be over, and she proceeded to take the air as she had intended. As she was going down stairs, she exclaimed, 'There is Lord Tyrone; I see him on the landing-place !' She fainted, was carried to her bed, and died a few days after.

Some years after, in 1717, her son, Sir M. Beresford, married Lady C. de la Poer, the daughter and heiress of Lord Tyrone, and was the grandfather of the present Lord Waterford.*

---

* It is difficult to reconcile the names and dates as stated in Lodge's ' Irish Peerage' with either of the versions. According to this authority (confirmed by Burke), Sir Tristram (not Sir Martin) Beresford, third baronet, born 1669, married, 1687, Nicola Sophia, youngest daughter and coheir of Hugh Hamilton, Baron of Glenawly ; and by her (who remarried with Lieut.-General Richard Gorges, of Kilbrew, county of Meath) had issue one son, Sir Marcus, created Earl of Tyrone in 1746, having in 1717 married the Lady Catherine Poer, daughter and heir to James Earl of Tyrone, who died in 1704. Sir Tristram died in 1701, three years *before* Lord Tyrone.

THE DUKE OF MARLBOROUGH—
ADMIRAL BARRINGTON—THE GUNNINGS.

April 1810.—Looking at the fine full-length portrait of John, Duke of Marlborough, Lord Braybrooke told us some interesting and curious anecdotes of him. When this great man, at a very advanced age, was called to attend a council on the best mode of defence from a threatened invasion, he gave his opinion with his usual firmness and penetration. Afterwards he said that for above fifty years he had served his country and should be happy to do so still, but that he was aware his faculties were impaired. At present, he added, he was fully conscious of his deficiency, but he feared the time might soon come when he should be no longer aware of it. He, therefore, made it his earnest request that he might never more be summoned to council, and that if elsewhere, on any occasion, he expressed an opinion, no importance should be attached or deference paid to it.

It is melancholy to reflect how low became the degradation of that mind, whose decaying powers were equal to such an act of magnanimity. After having had everything to gratify—first, as the finest, gayest man in Europe, then as its greatest general, and afterwards as its greatest negotiator and statesman—after all this, in a state of complete imbecility, an absolute driveller, he was actually exhibited by his servants to all who chose to give an additional fee after having stared at all the magnificence of Blenheim. *In this manner my grand-father (then a lad just entered at Oxford) beheld the wreck of this great man, and has often described the melancholy spectacle to Lord Braybrooke.**

A similar instance of conscious decay and of mag-nanimity, perhaps even superior to the Duke of Marl-borough, was at the same time mentioned. The late Ad-miral Barrington, being called upon by the Admiralty to take the command of the Channel fleet, refused it, saying that his mental powers were so weakened that he was no longer equal to a situation of such importance, but that he thought himself still very well able to act under an-other, though not to command ; he therefore requested to be second. In the course of the following year his weakness had so increased, that he quarrelled with the Admiralty for not placing him in that very situation for which he had himself told them he was unfit.

Some anecdotes were mentioned a few days before of a person who, in a very different way, could boast of a superiority as prominent as the Duke of Marlborough's, I mean the celebrated Lady Coventry. From old Sheridan (the father of Richard Brinsley) Lord Bray-brooke heard some curious anecdotes of her early life. Mrs. Gunning (her mother) consulted Sheridan as to what she should do with her two beautiful but penni-less daughters. He recommended that they should be

---

* ' In life's last scene what prodigies surprise,
Fears of the brave, and follies of the wise !
From Marlborough's eyes the streams of dotage flow.'

presented at the Castle ; here a great difficulty occurred: by what possible means were they to procure court dresses? this Sheridan obviated : he was at that time manager of the Dublin Theatre, and offered them a loan of the stage dresses of Lady Macbeth and Juliet. In these they appeared most lovely ; and Sheridan, after having attended the toilet, claimed a salute from each as his reward. Very soon after this, a most diabolical scheme was formed by some unprincipled young men they invited Mrs. Gunning and her two daughters to dinner, and infused strong narcotics in the wine, intending to take advantage of the intoxication which must ensue to carry off the two young women. Fortunately, Sheridan discovered their base designs, and arrived just in time to rescue the ladies. He lived to see one of these girls Duchess of Argyle, and the other Countess of Coventry ; and, it is melancholy to add, lived to see his application for admission to their parties rejected.

Lady Coventry enjoyed one very singular triumph. Having one day casually mentioned to the king, that she could not walk in the Mall because the crowd who came to gaze at her pressed round her in a way that was quite alarming, his Majesty gallantly exclaimed that the finest woman in England should not be prevented from gracing the Mall. He desired that whenever she wished to walk she would send notice to the captain upon guard, and at the same time ordered that she should be attended by a sergeant's guard. She walked several times with this train: of course, the crowd increased ; but they were prevented from pressing upon her, and her vanity, which was excessive, must have received the highest gratification in this singular distinction.*

ACCOUNT BY A LADY OF A VISIT TO PRINCESS DASHKOW. ·

Since cold is the order of the day, you may make this passing remark, that habit has no power of reconciling one to the inclemency of the climate: at least my sister says that she felt the second winter like the evaporation of saltpetre on the skin compared to the first which she scarcely minded, and now she is covered with wadded cloaks, when I need no additional clothing and the Princess is utterly unconscious it is not a summer's day. . . . Russia is yet barbarous enough to be distinguished by her hospitality. She has many other nationalities, no doubt, but my experience has not been able to distinguish any except among the lower orders of the

---

* These stories of the Gunnings might be amply confirmed from contemporary accounts of them. Walpole states that they borrowed court dresses to attend a drawing-room at the Castle, Dublin, from Peg Woffington, and writes thus of them in 1751 : 'There are two Irish girls of no fortune, who are declared the handsomest women alive. I think their being two so handsome, and both such perfect figures, is their chief excellence, for, singly, I have seen much handsomer figures than either: however, they can't walk in the park, or go to Vauxhall, but such mobs follow them that they are therefore driven away.'

people: for, with respect to the higher, I am sorry to say they imitate the French in everything; and though the manners of the French are appropriate to themselves, I cannot endure the *singerie* of *Bruin* when he frolics like the monkey on his back. Instead, therefore, of the dignified salutation of former days (namely, of bowing seriously to one another till their crowns met together), you are kissed on both the cheeks with an appearance of transport, and are told mechanically how enchanted they are to make your acquaintance, &c. The dress, too, is an imitation of the French, and they have universally adopted their language. . . . In the midst of all this adoption of manners, customs, and language, there is something childishly silly in their reprobating Buonaparte, when they cannot eat their dinner without a French cook to dress it, when they cannot educate their children without an unprincipled adventuress from Paris to act as governess, when every house of consequence (that I have seen at least) has an outcast Frenchman to instruct the heir-apparent; in one word, when every association of fashion, luxury, elegance, and fascination is drawn from France, and, in the midst of this obliteration of themselves, a dying squeak against Buonaparte redeems them in their own eyes from this social and political suicide.

How I abhor these *general* observations arising from circumscribed experience; as mine, I don't know how, induces me to depart from the detail of gossip. Strange

to say, this same gossip would lead me to talk of Princess
Dashkow's character (as I know more of her than of any
one else), which is diametrically opposite to all *singerie*;
for if ever there was an original upon the face of the
earth, it is herself.   Though she uniformly behaves to us
with the greatest kindness and attention, she exacts
(from imperial habits, I suppose) a sort of deference,
that surprised one excessively at first sight, from her own
country people.   For example, no man, though covered
with stars, attempts to sit down in her presence without
being desired, and not always even when requested.   I
have seen a dozen Princes stand out a whole visit.   Once
I saw them *bowed* out of the room (when she got deadly
tired of them); and after she had given them her hand
to kiss, they departed.*   It never enters into her head
or heart to disguise any sentiment, and therefore you
may guess what a privileged sort of being she is: and
lucky it is that she has sensibility, and gentleness of
nature; otherwise she would be a pest or scourge.
She is the first by right, rank, sense, and habit in
every company, and prerogative becomes such a matter

---

* The late Sir Robert Adair used to relate that, during his
mission to St. Petersburgh, he and the French Ambassador were
sitting with Potemkin when an *aide-de-camp*, a young nobleman,
brought him a disagreeable note or missive of some sort. Potemkin
started up, and actually kicked the innocent messenger out of the
room.   The Princess Dashkoff was once equally high in the
Empress's favour, and might have indulged her passions or caprices
with equal impunity.

of course that nothing appears extraordinary that she does.* . . .

I believe I never mentioned a fine place the Princess has made herself, situated in the midst of sixteen villages belonging to her. Three thousand peasants ('my subjects' as she calls them) live most happily under her absolute power; and of all the blessed-hearted beings that ever existed, she is the most blessed, excepting Mrs. C. There are 200 servants (taking in all denominations, inside and outside) belonging to the establishment; more than 100 horses, 200 cows, and everything else in proportion. The house is enormous, and has wings at either side which are only connected by balconies raised on iron railings to the second story. Twenty bearded men

---

* She was the third daughter of Count Worowzow, and was married at sixteen under characteristic circumstances. The Prince Dashkow having made a compromising proposal to her, not *pour le bon motif*, she affected to treat it as a proposal of marriage, and communicated it as such to her family. The prince married her, as the only or best way of getting out of the scrape. He owned her first child, but demurred to the second. She played a leading part in the intrigues and conspiracies which made Catherine the Second Autocrat of all the Russias; but the gratitude of her imperial friend and mistress did not keep pace with her expectations, and a coolness grew up between them which estranged her from the court. The first reward she claimed was the colonelcy of a crack regiment. This Catherine refused, but made her Director of the Academy, and she is said to have proved fully equal to the post. She was popularly supposed to have been intrusted with the momentous duty of subjecting the empress's male favourites to a kind of competitive examination or test; whence her name of *l'éprouveuse*.

are now busily employed in making a temporary wooden
passage, as in winter (strange to say) they had provided
for no internal communication: so much was sacrificed
to the beauty of the outside. There are a hundred
whimsical and most ridiculous peculiarities of custom;
such as, letting you provide your own bedclothes in a
palace even. We have our own sheets, blankets, and
quilts; and they would think one as extraordinary in
expecting that the *house* was to provide for these things,
as *you* would if, in your house, I laid myself up, and sent
for your gown to use as a matter of *right*. In fact, this
system of each person having a separate little establishment, is observed in more ways than that; for sauce-
pans, candles, candlesticks, tea and coffee equipage, and
a hundred etceteras, are regularly found in the care of
the *femmes de chambre*. *I* might lock *my* castle door,
or my sister's, or Anna's, and we have provisions to keep
the citadel a week in flourishing health. The system
of hoards is therefore without bounds, and presents
appropriate to this comical system are perfectly the
fashion. The Princess sent us a pair of silver candlesticks and a store of wax candles on our arrival here. I
expected a spit or a gridiron next; but though not
exactly so, we got presents of iron pans the following
day

In the midst of this immense establishment, and in
the centre of riches and honour, I wish you could see
the Princess go out to take a walk, or rather to look

over her 'subjects.' An old worn-out great-coat, and a silk pocket-handkerchief worn to rags about her neck, form her dress ; and well may it be in rags, for she has worn it eighteen years, and will continue to wear it as long as she lives, because it belonged to Mrs. Hamilton. Her originality, her appearance, her manner of speaking, her doing every description of thing, altogether give me the idea of her being a fairy; for she helps the masons to build walls, she assists with her own hands in making the roads, she feeds the cows, she composes music, she sings and plays, she writes for the press, she shells the corn, she talks out loud in church and corrects the preacher if he is not devout, she talks out loud at her little theatre here and puts in the performers if they are out in their parts.

She is a doctor, an apothecary, a surgeon, a farrier, a carpenter, a magistrate, a lawyer ; in short, she hourly practises every sort of incongruity, corresponds with her brother who holds the first place in the empire on his trade, with authors, with philosophers, with Jews, with poets, with her son, with all her relations, and yet appears as if she had her time a burden on her hands. She is unconscious whether she speaks English, French, or Russ, and mingles them in every sentence. She speaks German and Italian equally well, but her pronunciation is not clear, which takes from the pleasure I should otherwise receive from her conversation. I have just finished reading Voltaire's, Diderôt's, Garrick's, and the Abbé Raynal's letters to her. She has promised me the Empress Catherine's: and it is highly necessary to qualify oneself with the knowledge of public affairs and characters in Russia since the time of Catherine, for she alludes to them perpetually; and her mind wanders back so naturally to the court, study, toilette, and boudoir of Catherine, that I am beginning to fancy *I* recollect her habits of life and conversation, and that I was a party concerned in the Revolution. By-the-by, the principal reception-room at Troitska is ornamented with an immense picture of Catherine on horseback in uniform, taken the *very day of her husband's destruction,* and (the Princess says) a perfect resemblance. Besides this, there are portraits of her in every room. . . . Don't irritate me by saying, you suppose I am beginning to speak the language. No, let that satisfy you for ever. I feel my powers of *duncishness* increase daily, my powers of idleness, and of helplessness in everything that is good. So adieu, &c.

W. Wilmot.

Troitska, Sept. 1805.

LORD NORTH.

Among the many anonymous letters which daily poured in upon the late Lord North, he received one announcing to him the arrival of a box, which was exactly described. He was warned not to open this box, as it was so contrived that, upon opening the lock, a loaded pistol which the box contained should be discharged. On the following day (which I forgot to say was the time specified) Lord North received a box exactly answering to the description. Without mentioning the circumstance, he took the portentous box, and, concealing it under his great-coat, went immediately and threw it unopened into the Thames.*

ACCOUNT OF A HURRICANE IN JAMAICA.

Extract from a letter dated, ' Chester Coffee Estate, three quarter way up the Blue Mountains (Jamaica), from the side of a large wood fire; thermometer $58\frac{1}{2}°$, the mountain winds blowing almost a hurricane, and the rain descending in Equinoctial torrents.—15th October 1815, 10 A.M.'

As soon as I was sufficiently recovered from the effects of the yellow fever to bear the journey, I was brought to this invigorating climate, and wonderful its effects have been in eleven days.

This is a higher situation than any I have yet visited, higher even than Mount Atlas. The house is superb, th fireplaces in every room, and the climate that of the south of France. There is a large and beautiful

---

* This story was related by Mr. T. Grenville.

garden, where grow side by side, in the utmost luxuriance
and full of fruit, the mangan, cinnamon, and nutmeg
trees of the East, the apple, pear, and nectarine of England, and the pine-apple, orange, cocoa tree, guava, &c.,
of the West. In no other part of the world, perhaps,
could you see assembled the productions of so many
countries; and this is from the unvarying temperature
of the climate, being neither influenced by the seasons
nor ever getting too warm for European plants or too
cold for those of the tropics.

Kingston, Nov. 5, 1815.—Little did I expect, when I
sat down so comfortably at Chester Hill to write to you by
my snug fireside, what danger and misery were awaiting
me. It was then, as you may see by my date, blowing very
strong, but we expected nothing further. I was interrupted
at twelve o'clock by a summons to luncheon; in the
midst of it we were suddenly alarmed by seeing the
fine mangan tree in our garden torn up by the roots,
whisked into the air, and carried out of sight; this
made us apprehend what soon succeeded—a violent
hurricane. After this first gust of wind, fresh ones
attacked us, each with increased violence; not one of
the beautiful trees was left standing; cedar, orange,
apple, and all the large trees being torn up, and the
cocoas, cabbages, &c., snapped in the middle. The wind
continued raging with tremendous force; and next, we
were terrified beyond description by the whole wing of
that part of the house we had just quitted, walls and

all, giving way, though a most substantial stone building; the roof entire, without loss of a shingle or beam,
being carried up into the air, the walls falling in with a
tremendous crash; and the beams, boards, &c., of the
two floorings were seen flying with amazing velocity
through the air, knocking down all that came in contact
with them. It was with the utmost difficulty that, on
hearing the walls shaking and cracking, we saved ourselves, and got into the farther end, or rather division,
of a double house. Here, however, we had not been
ten minutes before the wind getting under the remain-
ing part of the roof (since the fall of the wing, totally
unprotected) tore it up too, throwing down on us the
ceilings and some of the beams, by one of which I was
knocked down and hurt.

However, we contrived to rush out, expecting that
the walls, now unroofed, must follow; and being
unable to stand upright from the fear of being
taken off our legs, we crawled into the kitchen, an
outhouse which, being very low and nearly circular,
we hoped might stand. We were disappointed; for
after our seeing the coffee-store, coffee-works, overseer's
house, all the negro houses, and every possible place of
shelter, blown down; not a tree standing; beams, trees,
branches, and wooden shingles with large nails in them
flying about in every direction, with certain death to
every living thing they encountered; night coming on
and the gale increasing—the kitchen gave way, injuring

us all more or less, and, I fear, maiming one negro for life   I only received another hard blow.

As a last resource and almost forlorn hope, we betook ourselves to a cellar under the ruins of the house, trying to hope that, if the walls fell in (and we heard stones dropping from them every instant), they might not beat in the floor of the dining-room over our heads and crush us with their fall.   That they would fall, we had no doubt, and a very very slender hope that the flooring would withstand them, and no possibility of escape. This was about eight in the evening, when the night was just setting in.   Our cellar was about nine feet square; up to our knees in water from the torrents of rain falling through the unroofed ruin above us, under a constant shower-bath in that cold climate that very cold night, in the instant expectation of being crushed to death or horribly mangled, we remained the whole of that dreadful night.

Our party consisted, besides myself, of Mr. A., Dr. M., the overseer, the bookkeeper, four black men, and four black women with their six children.   What I suffered from cold, and the bruises I had received, exceeded in mere bodily suffering anything I have ever felt or expect to feel—far worse than the surgeon's knife searching for the bullet; and I certainly never felt the *passion* of fear before, at least nothing resembling my sensations that night.   At about two in the morning one of the walls fell in, luckily so that the wind blew the stones

&c., *from* instead of *on* us; still a great part fell over
our heads on the flooring, of course on boards, with a
tremendous crash. We conceived it was the whole
house, and the screams of the poor women and children,
the (as they supposed) dying prayer of the men, were
horrible beyond anything I can conceive. I rose up
from sitting on an empty barrel, hoping the beams
might strike my head first, and end my sense of suffering
for myself and my companions. For that the beams
were falling, and that death seemed inevitable, was
evident; but after many alarms of this sort and constant
dread, the gale abated at sunrise, after the longest night
I ever passed.

At 6 A.M. the rain and wind had entirely ceased,
and we were able to walk out of our dungeon and
witness the scene of destruction. Not a house, a
tree, a negro hut or shed, left standing; large trees
thrown down or torn away; small snapped off close to
the roots; all the beautiful garden destroyed; one of
the four walls of the house levelled, a wing entirely
down, the remainder unroofed: and we had no means
of communication with our neighbours, as every rivulet
was swelled to an impassable river. At the end of three
days, however, we got to the nearest neighbour's house,
which had not suffered so much; and a week after, the
roads and rivers admitted of my return here safe and
sound. Kingston has suffered much less than the
mountains . . . The hurricane has cooled the air, and

now the temperature of Kingston is tolerable even after leaving the Blue Mountains.

NAPOLEON ON BOARD THE 'NORTHUMBERLAND.'

Extracts from letters from an officer of Marines.

H.M.S. NORTHUMBERLAND : *Aug.* 5, 1815.

It is my guard, and I have to sit in the antechamber of Napoleon, to prevent communication between him and the ship's company, and also to be a check on his own domestics ; it is now *one*, and I must keep awake till *six*. . . . . Napoleon gets very sulky if he is not treated with that deference and respect to which he is accustomed : his own followers treat him with the same respect as if he was still emperor.   Beattie, my captain, was at Acre : Buonaparte learnt this in conversation ; seemed quite pleased, caught hold of his ear and gave it a good pinch (which is his custom when pleased), and seems to have taken a great liking to him. He is sometimes very communicative : to-day he mentioned the project he had formed for invading England in 1805 ; declared it to have been his intention to lead the expedition himself, and said it might have succeeded. The plan was this : he sent his fleet to the West Indies for the purpose of drawing our fleets there, which it did, Lord Nelson and Sir Robert Calder both following

Villeneuve there; he was to return immediately to the Channel, and Napoleon said he calculated that Ville-neuve would be in the Channel at least a fortnight before our fleets could get back. His army *was* embarked (200,000 he says), but the plan was disconcerted by Villeneuve's going into Cadiz instead of coming to the Channel. His words were, 'He might as well have been in the East Indies as at Cadiz;' and he then declared that if Villeneuve had obeyed his orders he should certainly have invaded England, be the result what it might.*

Bertrand is the only one that seems to feel his situaation; he speaks of Napoleon often with tears, and is extremely agitated when conversing on the state of France. He says Napoleon did not calculate upon fighting the English and Prussians at Waterloo. The Prussians were beaten on the 16th, and it was not supposed they could have been up to take part in the battle of the 18th. He thinks the French would have been victorious if the Prussians had not come up; but circumstances were not favourable. The French soldiers fought very well; the officers did not. I asked him what became of the French army after the battle, why they did not retreat in some sort of order? He said, with a shrug, they were annihilated, there were none

---

* His plan, as described by M. Thiers, was much more complicated, and required a concurrence of events on which it was preposterous to rely.

left; yet, notwithstanding these admissions, they break out gasconading about their victories.

Napoleon's spirits are better; he enters into conversation very freely on different parts of his life. The other day he was speaking of Waterloo: he said he had not the least idea of fighting on the 18th : he did not suppose Wellington would have given him battle; he so fully expected Wellington to retreat that he had not even made preparations for battle, and was a little taken by surprise; 'but,' said he, 'I never was so pleased as when I saw he intended to fight. I had not a doubt of annihilating his army; it was the only thing I could have wished. I expected him to abandon Flanders, and fall back on the Russians; but when I found he gave me battle singly, I was confident of his destruction. My soldiers behaved well; my generals did not.' He says it was dusk when his army was thrown into confusion ; that if he could have shown himself, they would have rallied and been victorious ; but that the rout was so great, he was carried away in the throng. He went to Paris to try to save the honour of France, but found he could not.

He positively asserts that, previous to the battle of Waterloo and after his return to France, Austria proposed to him to abdicate in favour of Napoleon II., and promised to support him. His followers, too, have mentioned so many particulars respecting this, that I do not doubt the fact. This proposition had nothing to do with the forged letter of the Duke of Bassano, which they also speak of as a falsehood: none such was shown to him by Murat.

He has been talking this evening about his turning Mahometan: he said it was a long time before he could persuade them that he was a true Mussulman; but 'at last I persuaded them that Mahomet was wrong in some things and I was right, and they acknowledged me to be the greater man.' He says that in his retreat from Acre he lost nearly half his army.

Yesterday he remarked that Madame Bertrand was in much better spirits than when she attempted to drown herself, and added, 'a man of true courage will bear up against misfortunes, and finally surmount them, while common minds will sink under them.' He converses sometimes on the subject of his making away with himself, and calmly reprobates the idea of his being supposed capable of it.*

I believe the object of the guard is to prevent communication with the crew. Napoleon told the admiral that he did not doubt he could get many to join him if he tried; and indeed they are a set of as mutinous rascals as I ever heard of; though I don't think they would assist him to escape. What I am going to state must, for the credit of the country, be a secret: they mutinied, and refused to get anchor up at Portsmouth: the

---

* He seems to have forgotten his own attempt to poison himself at Fontainebleau. clearly proved by M. Thiers.

Artillery company, the 53rd, and ourselves, were under arms for three hours—that is to say, till we had sailed. About twenty of the principal seamen were seized and confined, but sent away from the ship; and the conduct and language of the sailors now is beyond everything; they think nothing of striking the midshipmen.*

St. Helena.—We arrived at this barren horrid island yesterday, after a passage of ten weeks. In my former travels in these latitudes everything seemed animated; the sea swarming with fish, water brilliant and phosphoric, sky without a cloud. Now everything has been the reverse: since we left Madeira, the sun has been constantly obscured with clouds, the weather even on the equator as cold as you can have had it in England: scarcely a fish to be seen ; and what is still more extraordinary, the trade winds, which in the tropics are calculated upon as certain, have blown almost from the opposite quarter to what they were expected, and thereby opposed our progress. We crossed the equator on the 23rd September, the same day as the sun; the greatest height of the thermometer was then only 75°, with a vertical sun ; since it has been as low as 66°: today it is only 70°. Napoleon has been in pretty good health and spirits all the voyage, conversing on every subject without the least hesitation. [Here follows the

---

* This state of things appears to have been carefully concealed from the public.

well-known justification of the poisoning of the sick at Jaffa; execution of the Duc d'Enghien, &c. &c.]

I have dined three times with Napoleon. I cannot say I think his manners have much of that elegance which might have been expected from a person of his ci-devant rank. He has a particularly disagreeable grunt when he does not understand what you say, and desires a repetition. He converses freely, but not at table, with the Frenchmen; and takes no more notice of the ladies than if they were a hundred miles off. I have not heard him speak once to Madame Bertrand at table, and seldom elsewhere. Napoleon landed on the 17th of October; he appeared a good deal affected at leaving the ship, and spoke so.

Did I tell you that the band, who used to play every day, struck up of their own accord, a few days after we left England, *Vive Henri Quatre* upon Buonaparte coming after dinner? Thinking it might hurt his feelings, we stopped them immediately; but he had heard enough to know what it was, and requested they would play that or any other French tune, as he liked it much; and afterwards they played the loyal and revolutionary airs indiscriminately. Of the Duc d'Enghien's business he said, not a fortnight ago (December 1815)—and you may rely upon he did say, though I did not hear it—it was in dictating to his secretary, Las Casas—that two days after the Duc was executed, he received proofs of his innocence, and that the Duc even solicited employment in his service, stating his poverty; but that the application was not received till after his death. This Buonaparte certainly said; for I do not think his secretary would say so if it was not true; and he said he had it from Napoleon's mouth, as part of papers which he was dictating the day before I had it.*

NAPOLEON AND HIS BROTHERS.

Lady H. has been telling us some of the conversation which passed at Walcot † while Lucien Buonaparte was there. He was very communicative on the adventures of his own and his brother's life, and anecdotes so authenticated are worth remembering.

When Lucien was living at his villa on the Lago Bracciano, near Rome, he was requested by his brother Joseph, then King of Naples, to come to him on business of great importance. Joseph told him he wished to consult him on a letter he had just received from Napoleon, offering him the crown of Spain, and desiring him to come and receive it at his hands. Joseph professed himself very much inclined to decline the new honours offered him. This resolution Lucien did his utmost to confirm; he

---

* Mr. Warren stated in his printed letters that he had seen a copy of the alleged letter from the Duc d'Enghien in the possession of Las Casas.

† Walcot, Salop; a seat of the Earl of Powis.

reminded Joseph of all the difficulties he had found in establishing himself on the throne of Naples. Those were overcome, and the Neapolitans were now perfectly tranquil under his government. In Spain, he would have the whole to go over again, and would probably find the Spaniards much more disinclined towards him than the Neapolitans had ever been. Joseph accordingly wrote to Napoleon, respectfully declining the crown offered him, and expressing his gratitude for that he already possessed, and his perfect satisfaction. Unfortunately for himself (much against the advice of Lucien) he added, that ' *il se rendrait aux ordres de sa Majesté,*' and set out to meet Napoleon. He, to use the words of Lucien, ' *prépara un de ces grands coups qu'il aimait tant et qui lui ont si souvent réussi.*' Bayonne was the appointed place of meeting, but Napoleon went farther, met Joseph on the road, and got out of his carriage to be the first to congratulate the King of Spain. In one moment Joseph found himself surrounded by the numerous suite of his brother, and had received their homage almost before he knew where he was. This public ceremony having taken place, it was no longer possible to retract.

In those days, when crowns were literally going a begging, Lucien (by his own account at least) seems to have shown great firmness in rejecting them, not only for himself but for his family. At one time, Napoleon sent for one of Lucien's daughters, offering to marry her to the Prince of Spain (Ferdinand) or to the Prince of Wirtemberg (Paul). Lucien determined to refuse both: ' *L'un*,' he said, ' *était fou, l'autre était pire que fou, mais il falloit obéir aux ordres suprêmes de mon frère; et j'envoyai Charlotte à Paris, suivie de ses femmes seulement et de l'abbé B.'* I have forgotten the name, but he was the nephew of Lucien's first wife, and was present when the story was told. When the poor victim arrived at St. Cloud, where the Emperor was, she was immediately presented to him; and when she knelt to pay her obeisance, he said, ' *Levez-vous, Princesse.*' She had the courage to reply, ' *Non, Sire, je ne suis pas Princesse; je ne suis que Charlotte Buonaparte: permettez-moi, Sire, de retourner chez mon père.*' This permission was granted, and the intended Queen of Spain (afterwards Princess Gabriella) was, when this story was related, living with her parents at Ludlow.

On the day of Napoleon's coronation, Garnerin sent up a balloon to make the news fly. This balloon landed near Lucien's Roman villa, in twenty-six hours exactly from the period at which it was launched from Paris. Yet speedy as this communication appears, it might have been still more so; for, at its first setting out, the balloon was impelled quite in another direction. How soon it took its south-eastern course cannot of course be known.*

In the journal of De las Casas this circumstance is mentioned as related by Napoleon, who speaks of the time as ' *en peu d'heures.*'

THE PRETENDED ARCHDUKE.

I have heard this evening a strange wild romantic story from Mr. Bankes, almost too improbable for a novel, and yet the leading facts seem established beyond a doubt.

A stranger, with one attendant only (I think), arrived some years ago at the house of a man of the name of Contessini, then British Consul at Jaffa, who was obliged, on seeing some passports and papers, to bestow a bed and a dinner. The latter was bad enough, but the stranger gave the servants of the consul a gratuity three or four times as large as any they had ever received before. Old Contessini, according to the custom of the East, took this fee from his servants; being an honest man, and being impressed with a strong idea that the liberality of the stranger bespoke a person of consequence, he very much improved his fare on the second day. On the third, the stranger began to open a little; he asked Contessini whether he was not consul for Austria as well as England, and received a reply in the affirmative. 'Well,' says he, 'you need not hoist the Austrian flag, but I will confide to you a secret of the greatest importance, under the seal of the most inviolable secrecy. I am travelling in the strictest *incog.*, but I am the Archduke John, the brother of the Emperor of Austria.' The poor consul was overwhelmed with confusion : he got up from the dinner-table at which they were sitting, insisting upon serving behind the chair of his illustrious guest, who had great difficulty in persuading him, partly by the force of arguments drawn from the necessity of concealment from the servants and partly by that of his arms, to resume his chair.

In this state things remained some days : the old consul was delighted to see that the archduke took great notice of his son, a fine lad. One day the boy, coming into the stranger's room, found him occupied in taking some things out of a trunk in which were fine uniforms embroidered most richly and covered with stars and orders. The boy told his father of the fine things he had beheld, and not being under any promise of secrecy, repeated his story to every person he met. Suspicions began to be excited as to the rank of the stranger; the old consul looked mysterious, and began to whisper his secret. This made the residence of Jaffa very unpleasant to the prince : he talked of prosecuting his journey through the Holy Land, and asked Contessini whether there was any person in Jaffa from whom he could procure money. 'I fear,' replied the old man, 'there may not be a sum sufficient to supply the occasions of your Imperial Highness; but if such a sum (naming something about 100l.) is sufficient, I can easily find it.' The money was produced : the archduke gave his note, disguised himself as a monk, and proceeded on his journey to Nazareth, where there was a large convent; and Contessini, after much importunity, obtained leave to acquaint the prior by letter of the real name and rank of the stranger.

He took up his abode for some time in the convent: every respect was shown to him; the prior kept the secret for some time; but much curiosity and many suspicions were excited by the uncommon liberality of the stranger. He evinced this chiefly by giving at the mass, which he attended with the most exemplary regularity, a contribution for the wants of the convent, which, though it was nearly ten times as much as they were in the habit of receiving from the most liberal of their contributors, was in fact very small. By this and various other means he so established his character without betraying his rank, that the prior made not the smallest difficulty in advancing a large sum from the funds of the convent on his word only, and on his promise of obtaining various immunities and advantages for the convent from the Emperor of Austria. He returned to his old friend the consul at Jaffa: expressed a wish to fit out a vessel to convey him to the coast of Italy, for the purpose of performing a pilgrimage to Loretto. The attendant or cameriere suggested to the consul that he was mad not to try to take advantage of the partiality which the archduke expressed for his son to try to obtain for him a situation in his household. The permission was given for young Contessini to attend the archduke, and many very vague promises of future protection were made. In return

for this the consul could do no less than take upon himself all the trouble of the purchase of the vessel, and of
course he made himself responsible for all the expenses.
He was also persuaded by the cameriere to embark
several bales of cotton, which the young man, his son,
would sell to great advantage.

One of the next adventures of this great personage
was at one of the Turkish ports.   He was lodged
in the house of the Austrian consul, to whom he
carried a letter from old Contessini declaring his
rank, but still with injunctions of the greatest secrecy.
A few days after his arrival the Turkish fleet, with the
Captain Pasha (the third man in the empire) on board,
anchored in the port.   The consul with great difficulty
obtained from his guest permission to declare his rank
to this great personage ; an invitation ensued to visit
the fleet; every royal honour and observance were paid;
and very large presents of jewels, &c., offered, and of
course accepted, by the prince.   He then went (I forget
where) to another Eastern convent, where he was received
with still greater distinction by the archbishop.   Here,
however, his career seemed very near a close ; the notes
or bills had all been protested, and a rumour of the
fraud spread very soon after his arrival.   He was the
first to tell the story to the old archbishop, to inveigh
against the tricks of swindlers, and at the ingenuity of
one who, having discovered him to be travelling *incog.*
in the East, had ventured to personate him ; then

followed a dozen stories of exactly similar personations, &c., but he ended in stating, that though loaded with passports, letters of credit, &c., from the emperor, which were all in his vessel, he should be very averse to the appearing publicly in his own character. He said his journey, or rather his pilgrimage, had been undertaken from motives of religion only, very much against the consent of the emperor, who would be still more incensed when he discovered the fraud which had ensued from the circumstance of his travelling *incog.* It became, therefore, his duty to guard his secret more strictly than ever. Upon this pretence he once more obtained a large sum to enable him to perform his pilgrimage to Loretto, and once more he resumed his travels.

When he reached the Continent he professed himself surprised to find the emperor more incensed than ever: the cameriere was dismissed, and young Contessini, who was enthusiastically devoted to him, was persuaded that the life of his illustrious master depended upon his secrecy. After various adventures, hair-breadth escapes, daring frauds, &c., he reached Hamburgh. There he contrived by various forgeries to raise a sum of money, on credit, to charter a vessel for America. This was wrecked somewhere on the British coast. The adventurer and his faithful Contessini arrived in London. The latter, from whom Mr. Bankes had the whole detail, described with the most beautiful simplicity, in his bad Italian, the effect produced in his mind by all that he saw, and especially by the *grande bellissimo superbo* hotel where they were lodged, and which, with some difficulty, he at last explained to be the Saracen's Head.   Among its various merits, he did not enumerate that of its being a peaceful abode.   Englishmen were not so easily to be taken in as consuls, pashas, and archbishops in the East.   The various frauds and forgeries of the adventurer were soon brought to light, and the *bellissimo* hotel full of officers of justice in pursuit of him.   However, he contrived once more to escape them by getting out of a garret window upon the roofs of the neighbouring houses.   Such was the extraordinary simplicity and credulity of his faithful attendant that even at this moment, after all that he had witnessed, he described himself as perfectly convinced that his master was going straight to St. James's, meaning at last to avow his rank and resume his native splendour.   Judge, then, what must have been his dismay when he found himself safely lodged with the archduke in Newgate.

From the extreme ignorance of the narrator it was impossible, Mr. Bankes said, to gain a clear idea of this part of his adventures.   By some means they got out of Newgate, and very soon after were sent to a lock-up house.

Here the story of the impostor closes, not, as might be expected, by his obtaining the due reward of all his iniquities, but by his seducing the wife of the keeper of the lock-up house, carrying off with her every valuable in the house, and contriving to elude every pursuit. Poor Contessini was now left alone to stand his trial, and Mr. Bankes said nothing could be more curious than his admiration, his simple gratitude for his extraordinary good fortune in having been taken before the most upright, the most humane, the greatest of judges, the only one man in the whole world who would not have hanged him because he had been imposed upon by a rascal, never having had any share in the transactions which made him amenable to justice. A subscription was collected to enable this poor creature to return to his own country, which he did not reach without having been once more wrecked.

When Mr. Bankes was at Jaffa, he heard repeatedly of the adventurer, who had imposed himself upon so many persons, and raised large sums of money, as the Archduke John. He was one day questioning the British Consul on the subject, who, from common report, related many of the leading particulars, especially the reception by the Captain Pasha. He added, ' As you seem very curious, if you wish it, I will send for the son of my predecessor Contessini, who for some time followed the fortunes of this adventurer.' He came. Mr. Bankes was so pleased with his extraordinary story, and with his mode of relating it, that he took the man as his servant, though he had little else to recommend him.*

---

* Mr. Bankes's story is substantially confirmed by Sir William Gell, who says in his *Memoirs,* ' We had been told that one of the Austrian archdukes was passing through Greece at this time, and that he was now (1804) at Modon, giving out that he had quitted Vienna on account of some disagreement with the Austrian imperial family, and was travelling *incog.* . . .

' A few months after, we heard of an unpleasant accident which happened quite unexpectedly to his Imperial Highness. After he had resided some time at the house of the poor consul, a Polish nobleman, Prince Sapieha, landed at Modon. As he was well acquainted with the Austrian imperial family, he flew to the house of the consul, as soon as he heard the archduke was there. He entered hastily the room where the consul and his guest were dining, eagerly enquiring for his friend the archduke. The consul, distressed at the arrival of a person whom he doubted not was despatched from the court to reclaim the wandering prince, and hoping that the messenger was not personally acquainted with his imperial guest, thought it better to hesitate, and gave no answer till Prince Sapieha demanded with more eagerness to be shown to the room of the archduke. During this time, the adventurer said not a word, and the consul was at length induced to confess that his Imperial Highness was present. Of course Prince Sapieha needed no further explanation, left the room, and soon quitted Modon, not without having had the charity to advise the owner of the house where he lodged to inform the Austrian consul that he was ruining himself for an impostor. The adventurer was not, however, routed by the unfortunate visit of the prince, for he succeeded in persuading the consul, who was alarmed, and began to expostulate, that he knew Sapieha well, but was so disgusted at the impertinence of his abrupt entrance during dinner, instead of sending in due form to know when his company would be agreeable, that he did not condescend to acknowledge him.'

ANECDOTES OF DÉNON.*

Mr. Bankes told me that, one morning while he was breakfasting *tête-à-tête* with Dénon, a servant brought in a packet from the mint containing a medal just struck. Dénon laid it flat on his hand, considered the reverse, then exclaimed, '*Nous sommes seuls, mon ami: parlons à cœur ouvert; voilà le comble de la flatterie ;*' then he read, '*Mousé oum resta uratoum—et puis* (turning the medal and showing the head of Louis XVIII.), *voilà cet homme qui a tout fait pour le détruire.*' When one recollects what Dénon and his old master had done for the Museum ; when one remembers how soon under the new régime he was turned out ; when, besides, one looks not only at the Louvre, which the fate of war has stripped of its finest ornaments, but at the various collections, at the *Jardin des Plantes,* which from neglect and want of encouragement have suffered nearly as much ; when, most of all, one looks at what was the *Musée des Monumens,* now totally destroyed and dispersed by bigotry — when one thinks of all these circumstances, one wonders that, speaking *à cœur*

---

* Dénon was the most celebrated of the *savans* who accompanied Napoleon in the Egyptian expedition, of which he published a scientific and illustrated account in 1802. He was Directeur Général des Musées under the Emperor, and was displaced on the Restoration. Lady Morgan speaks highly of his conversational powers in her " *France.*"

ouvert, Dénon could express himself so moderately on the subject.

One day Mr. Bankes said he expressed to Dénon a strong wish to see Roustan, the Mameluke, who is now keeping a small shop. Dénon's reply did him honour. ' You will certainly do as you please, but you must allow me to say that, from the moment you condescend to seek such a wretch as that man, I shall consider our acquaintance as ended, and you must not wonder if my doors are closed against you.' Mr. Bankes said he certainly would not incur such a penalty, but remonstrated, alleging that he was far from admiring the character of Roustan, very far from defending his ingratitude towards Napoleon, but that he should have much pleasure in learning from his mouth some of the lesser particulars of the domestic life of his master, which have been so variously represented. Dénon allowed the truth of all this, but said that if any Englishman of name was known to go to Roustan's house, he would soon be followed by several of his countrymen; money would flow in, and the wretch would soon be raised from the state of well-deserved contempt and degradation which was the natural consequence of his ingratitude.

It seems he was given to Napoleon by one of the pachas, as a thing of much less value than an Englishman would consider a dog. Napoleon took a fancy to him, loaded him with favours, kept him always about his person, gave him the means of marrying, and in the most trying moments of his life, when he considered himself as going into the greatest dangers, his last thought always seems to have been that of making an additional provision for Roustan. Even on the eve of leaving Paris in the campaign which terminated his career of glory, he thought of Roustan. After having thus fattened on Napoleon's prosperity, after having so closely attended on him as always to sleep across the door of his tent or his room, he forsook him in adversity and refused to follow him to St. Helena.

EARLY IMPRESSIONS OF CELEBRATED MEN — PITT, FOX, LORD WELLESLEY, AND WINDHAM.

I have often thought, in reading Lord Orford's ' Reminiscences,' that almost anybody might make, by writing down theirs, a book which would at least be sure of giving entertainment to the writer when the recollections it records becomes less vivid. Upon that hint I write, and first I mean to record those sights which are gone and past, and which never can greet my eyes again. Without ever having read Lavater or any one else who has written on physiognomy, I have, as most people probably have, delight in tracing character in countenance, and therefore there are few recollections I love better than those of the faces of the great men whom I have seen at various periods. I can now laugh at the recollection of my excessive disappointment in the first great man I remember seeing—in society at least. I was about sixteen or seventeen when, at Dropmore*—where I was with Lord and Lady Grenville only—Mr. Pitt arrived for a visit of two days.   First, I was disappointed in that turned-up nose, and in that countenance, in which it was so impossible to find any indication of the mind, and in that person which was so deficient in dignity that he had hardly the air of a gentleman. After this first disappointment my every faculty seemed to me to be absorbed in listening. If not tropes, I fully expected the dictums of wisdom each time that he opened his mouth.   From what I then heard and saw, I should say that mouth was made for eating; as to speaking, there was very little, and that little was totally uninteresting to me, and I believe would have been so to everybody.   I was certainly not capable of a very accurate judgment, but I was as certainly in a mood very much to overrate instead of underrating what fell from the great man, and to be quite sure that what I did not understand must be mighty fine.

On the second day arrived Lord Wellesley,* whom I thought very agreeable ; partly, I fancy, from his high-bred manners, and still more from his occasionally

---

* It appears from Lord Wellesley's Correspondence, that he spent some days at Dropmore in the spring of 1797, and this must have been the visit in question. He left England for India in the November of that year, and did not return till January 1806, when Pitt was dying.

saying a few words to *me*, and thus making me feel treated as a reasonable creature. After we had retired for the night, I heard from the library, which was under my room, the most extraordinary noises—barking, mewing, hissing, howling, interspersed with violent shouts of laughter. I settled that the servants had come into the room, and had got drunk and riotous; and I turned to sleep when the noise had ceased. Never can I forget my dismay (it was more than astonishment) when next day at breakfast I heard that my wise uncle and his two wise guests, whom we had left talking, as I supposed, of the fate of Europe, had spyed in the room a little bird; they did not wish it to be shut up there all night: therefore, after having opened every window, these great wise men tried every variety of noise they could make to frighten out the poor bird.

At a later period, in the year 1805, I found myself for nearly a week at Stowe, with Mr. Fox; but as there were above fifty others in the house, with the Prince Regent at their head, the whole thing was a formal crowd, and I could only gaze at the countenance of the one whom I should most have liked to hear talk. Certainly in this mixed society he hardly ever was heard to speak, but occasionally with some one individual one saw him entering into an animated whispered conversation, and it was curious to watch the sudden illumination of a countenance which, when silent, had to my fancy a heavy, sullen look. How far it might even then have been altered by malady, I cannot judge; but I know that the next time I beheld Mr. Fox, not six months after, at Lord Melville's trial, I thought I never had seen the ravages of illness so strongly marked in any human countenance. All its animation had disappeared, the leaden eyes were almost lost under the heavy eyebrow, even that appeared to partake in the extraordinary change which all the colouring seemed to have undergone, the pallid or rather livid hue of the complexion deepened the sable line of the dark brow, and the whole countenance assumed a lethargic expression. He lived scarcely three months after the time I mention.*

In my recollection, no person appears to have possessed the power of making conversation delightful, as much as Mr. Windham. His peculiar charm seems to me to have been that sort of gay openness which I should call the very reverse of what the French term *morgue*. To all, this must be agreeable, and it is peculiarly delightful to a young person who is conscious of her own inferiority to the person who condescends to put her perfectly at ease. During the party at

---

* This account of Fox's appearance in his latter years is confirmed by contemporaries. But, according to Sir William Napier, Pitt retained till within a year and a half of his death a boyish love of frolic, and (in 1804) was once actually engaged in a struggle to prevent the blackening of his face with a cork, whilst two of his colleagues were kept waiting in the anteroom.—*Bruce's Life of Napier*, vol. i. p. 31.

Stowe to which I have alluded, I found myself embarked for the morning's or rather day's amusement, in a carriage with Lady King, Lord Braybrooke, and Mr. Windham. My mother was in some other carriage, my two sisters in a third. When we all met in our own rooms, they with one accord voted they were a little tired and very much bored. I, though much more liable to both these complaints than any of the party, could only say I had been highly amused the whole day. The fact was, they had no Mr. Windham to listen to, and I had; and yet, truth to say, when I was asked how he had contrived to amuse me so much, I had very little to tell even then; and now after so many years that little has passed away.

I do recollect, however, one singular circumstance. Junius happened to be mentioned, and on that old subject Mr. Windham ventured what was to me at least a quite new guess. Gibbon was the person he mentioned as the only man of high talents living at that period in obscurity which might effectually have concealed him. Soon afterwards I mentioned this conjecture to Charles (the late Right Hon. Charles Wynn), whose accurate memory immediately produced a proof of its fallacy. He said, ' I cannot help thinking that, at the period of the publication of Junius, Gibbon was not in England.' Upon referring to the letters of Gibbon, it proved that he was in Switzerland during the greater part, if not the whole, of the appearance of Junius. It seems most

singular that Mr. Windham should even mention a
conjecture which he had not brought to this obvious
test.*

IMPERIAL AND ROYAL VISITORS IN 1814—VISIT TO
OXFORD.†

Of the mob of kings, and princes, and foreign generals, whom the events of 1814 brought to London, I
believe I did not miss seeing one, nor had I ever any
opportunity of doing more than staring at them.
Upon the whole, though the appearance of the theatre
at Oxford was most striking, still, the scene which
made the deepest impression upon my mind, was the
entrance of Louis XVIII. into London. We stood in
Lord Dudley's balcony; there were few there, and
those few not inclined to talk: so one had time to muse
over all the strange occurrences of the day, and over

* Miss Wynn and her brother must have been under a mistaken impression as to the period during which the Letters of
Junius appeared. The letters under that signature began in January
1769, and ended in January 1772. Gibbon returned to England in
1765, and did not leave it again to reside abroad till 1783; but
his habits and turn of mind, as developed in his autobiography, to
say nothing of his political opinions or his style, completely pre-
clude the notion of his being the author of Junius. He had been
often started as a candidate.
† To bring together her reminiscences of historic personages,
Miss Wynn passes on at once to 1814, when London was crowded
with them. It will be remembered that the exiled royal family of
France had frequently partaken of the splendid hospitality of
Stowe, and that she went to Oxford in the suite of her uncle,
Lord Grenville, the Lord High Chancellor of the University.

all the historical recollections it naturally suggested. I cannot say that I quite liked to see the British Guards decorated with the white cockade. I was amused at seeing the Prince Regent sitting backwards in the landau. He had, of course, given the front seat to Louis and the Duchesse d'Angoulême. I wondered how a position so unusual would agree with him; since the days of absolute childhood, when he might have gone with the king and queen, he never could have found himself in such a one, and I thought of the possibility of an interruption most undignified to the procession.

The reception of James II. by Louis XIV. was certainly far more splendid; but I am inclined to doubt whether, to a feeling heart, the magnificence of St. Germains — which, by-the-bye, I believe from what remains could have existed only in the imagination of Frenchmen—could be nearly as gratifying as the popular feeling so powerfully excited and so freely expressed on this occasion. I was then, or rather soon after, very much astonished to hear from Lord Arthur Hill, who was in the balcony with us, and afterwards at Paris, how much more tranquil, more tame, had been the entrance of Louis into his own capital. I had then taught myself to believe the French a very demonstrative race, and did not know how much more difficult it is to excite popular feeling among the mercurial Frenchmen than among the phlegmatic English.*

---

* Miss Wynn appears to have forgotten that the popular feeling was far from favourable to the restored dynasty.

I was not well enough to go to the drawing-room
which Louis held at Grillion's Hotel, but I went one
evening to the Duchesse d'Angoulême's, in Monsieur's
dark two-roomed house in South Audley Street.* It
was literallv hardly possible to see across the room, and
the whole thing was, if one could have entertained
such a feeling, a burlesque upon royalty. The sour,
ill-tempered, vulgar countenance of the blear-eyed
Duchess was a great damp to the interest one was prepared to feel in one whose fate had been more melancholy than that of any heroine of romance. The little
crumpled Duchess de Sirent might easily be fancied
the good fairy whose wand had produced the wondrous
change; but she had not, like the godmother of Cinder-
ella, changed the dusty dirty abode into a palace, or
even converted into cloth of gold the dingy brown dress
of her *protégée.* ' Waverley ' was not; yet published,†
but when I read there the account of Charles Edward's
drawing-room at Edinburgh, I could think of nothing
but the dark rooms in South Audley Street.

---

* No. 72. Madame d'Arblay gives a curious account of the
confusion that prevailed both there and at Grillion's during the
royal receptions. (*Diary*, vol. 7, pp. 22–39.) In a letter of July
9th, 1814, Sir Walter Scott writes : ' The Duke of Buccleugh told
me yesterday of a very good reply of Louis to some of his attendants, who proposed shutting the doors of his apartments to
keep out the throng of people. "Open the door," he said, "to
John Bull ; he has suffered a good deal in keeping the door open
to me." '

† *Waverley* was published in 1814.

At Oxford it seemed to me that there was a great want of dignity of manner among the assembled grandees. Even the dandy Alexander seemed to want it; though he was much better than any of his compeers, excepting, perhaps, our own king when he happened to be in good humour, which was not always the case during his visit to Oxford. As to the King of Prussia, he looked as stupid and as vulgar as I believe he really is. When complimented, he never could look otherwise than *embarrassé de sa personne,* bored to death, and could not even make a tolerably gentleman-like bow. His two sons looked fine animated boys; the eldest was said to have accompanied the army, and, it was added, had scarcely been prevented by those around him from exposing himself most gallantly. They seemed to look at everything with the genuine happy feelings of their age, and are said to have expressed great delight when the measles seemed likely to prove an impediment to their quitting this country, but they got well much sooner than they wished.

It did not at that time occur to me as *possible* that these sovereigns might not understand one syllable of the elegant classical orations made in compliment to them. I have since heard from Dr. Crichton — a Scotch physician belonging to the household of the Empress dowager, who accompanied one of her grandsons, the brother of Alexander — that neither this young prince nor any one of a numerous suite, excepting one man, understood a word of Latin or Greek.

H

I think the illumination of the High Street of Oxford was by far the finest sight of the kind I ever beheld. From the difficulty of getting a sufficient number of coloured lamps, they were obliged to put candles on every window and on every part of every building which would bear them.   By this means, the light, instead of intersecting and twisting through all the ornamental part of the architecture, followed the fine broad lines, gave a magnificent contrast of light and shadow, and made that which is naturally so beautiful, much more so. One church was illuminated.   It seems very difficult to find an inscription short enough to be read in lamps; if it is long, the beginning is burnt out before the end is lighted.   The difficulty was much increased by the necessity of making this appropriate to a church.   I never heard who had the merit of suggesting the beautifully simple '*Our prayers are heard.*'

The night was beautiful, uncommonly calm and warm. From my window, which looked down upon the High Street, it seemed as if one could really have walked upon the moving mass of heads.   In one moment, almost without any previous notice, at least without any that could call the attention of the mob which was so fully occupied, a tremendous storm of thunder and rain came on.   The effect was really more like the dissolving of the enchanted spell and the changes of scene in a pantomime, than anything I ever did see or ever expect to see again in real life.   The High Street, which was one blaze of light, and one unceasing hum of happiness, became in the course of five minutes quite dark and quite deserted : nothing was heard but the thunder and the torrents of rain. Where all the multitude could find shelter, I never discovered. I heard afterwards that many who had walked miles from their abodes to see the show, slept upon chairs and tables in the small houses in the suburbs of Oxford. Amidst that crowd in the High Street were, I am told, Alexander and the Grand Duchess,* who, as soon as they could get away from the great dinner in the Radcliffe library went out to walk *incog.* This was on the 14th of June. It is curious to remember that the season was so backward that on this day there was the greatest difficulty in procuring one small dish of strawberries to deck the royal banquet, the forced strawberries being all over and the natural not ripe.

THE STAGE : MISS FARREN, MRS. SIDDONS, MISS O'NEIL, KEMBLE, TALMA.

The transition from princes and statesmen to actors and actresses, was natural enough in the first quarter of the

---

* The Grand Duchess of Oldenburg, who attracted great attention by her showy person and dress. The Oldenburg bonnet speedily became the rage. It was remarkable for the length of the poke and the height of the crown. By way of caricaturing it in the pantomime, Grimaldi appeared with one of the old-fashioned coalscuttles on his head and a chimney-pot on the top. When the restored princes re-entered Paris in 1814, the Duchess of Augoulême gave offence by her quiet style of dress and flat bonnet, supposed to be a servile adoption of English fashions.

century, whatever it may appear now. The stage was an
important part of the intellectual life of the contemporaries
of the Kembles, Kean, and Miss O'Neil. A striking illustration is given by Dr. Doran, who states that, on one evening
in 1804, when young Betty played *Hamlet*, 'the House of
Commons, on a motion by Pitt, adjourned and went down to
the theatre to see him. Charles Fox read ' *Zanga* ' to the little
actor, and commented on Young's tragedy with such effect
that the young gentleman (then in his 14th year) never
undertook the principal character.'* The stage divided the
attention of the literary world with poetry and romance. The
appearance of Joanna Baillie's ' De Montfort,' Milman's 'Fazio,'
Maturin's 'Bertram,' or Shiel's ' Evadne,' was an event little
inferior in interest to the publication of ' Marmion ' or 'The
Corsair.' In assigning so prominent a place to the acting
drama, therefore, Miss Wynn simply reflects the opinion of
the time.

Nothing appears to me more difficult than even to
preserve an idea of the pleasure one has derived from
good acting. I am quite convinced no description
can give the least idea of that which one has not seen.
After having heard and read so much as I have of
Garrick, I have often looked at the picture in St.
James's Square,† and fancied I had some idea of him; but
then, when I saw Mr. Angerstein's picture of Garrick
between Tragedy and Comedy, I found it so different
that all my ideas were overturned.

---

* *Their Majesty's Servants: Annals of the English Stage*, vol.
ii. p. 416.
  † No. 18, the town house of Sir Watkin Williams Wynn.

I certainly recollect Miss Farren on the stage, and remember very clearly her taking leave of it, but nothing remains upon my mind which would lead me from my own knowledge to say that she was an excellent actress. I know I was told so; but in the part of Lady Teazle, in which I saw her frequently, I could not point out one prominent part which has left on my mind an impression of excellence. Perhaps the absence of prominent parts may, to a certain degree, be considered as the characteristic of that never-failing elegance and ease which marked her performance. Perhaps, too, it is just the sort of excellence which is the least likely to strike and captivate the imagination of a very young person. I recollect (*not* the admirable acting in the famous screen scene *but*) the circumstance of seeing Lord Derby leaving his private box to creep to her behind the scene; and, of course, we all looked with impatience for the discovery, hoping the screen would fall a little too soon, and show to the audience Lord Derby as well as Lady Teazle.*

Mrs. Siddons in her prime is certainly a bright recollection, but I did not feel for her acting quite the

---

* Dr. Doran states that Miss Farren took her final leave of the stage in Lady Teazle on the 8th April, 1797, and was married to Lord Derby on the May-day following, his Countess having died on the 14th of the preceding March. In allusion to the earl's attachment to the actress, Horace Walpole writes to Miss Berry in 1791 : 'I have had no letter from you these ten days, though the east wind has been as constant as Lord Derby.'

enthusiasm that most people profess. It was too artificial
for my taste : her attitudes were fine and graceful, but
they always seemed to me the result of study : not like
Miss O'Neil, who always was graceful merely because she
could not help it, because it was impossible to throw
those beautifully formed limbs, and especially that neck,
into any position that was not beautiful. At the same
time I must say, in Isabella, and in Jane Shore, Miss
O'Neil struck me as very inferior indeed to Mrs.
Siddons. She never excited that deep thrill of horror
which made my blood tingle at my fingers' end. I was
melancholy, and that was all.

Miss O'Neil had sense enough to refuse the character
of Lady Macbeth, conscious that her powers were inade-
quate to it. I never saw Mrs. Siddons with a good
Macbeth ; for Kemble I never reckoned tolerable ; nor
did I feel I knew what the character was till I heard
Mrs. Siddons read the play. Certainly, in that reading,
some speeches of Macbeth's, and almost the whole of the
witches', were the parts that struck me most. Probably
Lady Macbeth, however excellent, had by frequent repetition lost some of her power ; certainly (I felt) in
that part Mrs. Siddons could no longer surprise me. Yes,
she did though. I looked with impatience for the grand
sleep-walking scene, and thought I would take advantage of my position, which was very near her, to watch
the fine, fixed, glassy glare which she contrived to give

to her eyes. Alas! that was quite gone, whether the diminution of the natural fire of the eye presented this effect, or whether the muscles were grown less flexible from age and want of constant practice, I know not, but I feel quite certain of the fact. It struck me when I saw her once more, in one of her frequent re-appearances, act Lady Macbeth on the opera stage. Then, **my** pleasure in seeing her was increased by my delight in watching the effect she produced on the very eloquent though plain countenance of Madame de Staël, who sate in the stage box, literally wrapped up in the performance.

Mr. Greathead, who had been in the habit of hearing Mrs. Siddons read Macbeth even (he said) from the period of her being his mother's maid,* before she had appeared on any stage up to the present moment, told me he was struck with a great difference in her manner of reading the witches' scenes after the appearance of 'Guy Mannering.'† He said it was quite clear to him that Meg Merrilees had explained to Mrs. Siddons, Shakespeare's idea in the witches. This he told

---

When Mrs. Siddons, then Sarah Kemble, was very young, she left her parents in a pet, because they would not let her marry Mr. Siddons, and entered the service of Mr. and Mrs. Greathead, of Guy's Cliff; whether as reader, nursery maid, or lady's maid, has been disputed, and matters little. Mr. Campbell says her principal employment was to read to Mrs. Greathead (*Life of Mrs. Siddons*).

† *Guy Mannering* was published in 1815.

me upon my observing with delight upon their totally
altered appearance on Drury Lane Theatre, which I ascribed to the same cause.   I consider this as one of the
most singular and at the same time the most glorious
triumphs of the genius of the Great Unknown, as it is
now the fashion to call him. I can hardly conceive anything finer than the expression which Mrs. Siddons gave
to the simple reply, ' *A deed without a name.*' *   It
seemed full of all the guilty dread belonging to witchcraft ; and it is just this idea of guilt which seems to me
so difficult to convey to *our* minds, which are so
engrossed with the folly of the whole thing that we do
not recollect it was a sin.

My delight, my astonishment, when I first saw Kean
in most of his great parts, I recorded at the time and
therefore do not mention here.   Miss O'Neil gave me
great pleasure, but it was altogether a lighter sensation
than that excited by Mrs. Siddons or Kean.   There was
none of that thrill which more exactly answers the idea
of *pleasing pain* than anything I ever felt, and I can
hardly attach any other meaning to the words.   She
was sometimes very affecting, always graceful, pleasing,
but I think never great, and certainly never offensive.
I am, upon recollection, inclined to doubt whether her
scene with Lord Hastings in ' Jane Shore ' might not

---

* *Macb.* How now, you secret, black, and midnight hags !
        What is 't you do?
All. A deed without a name.

deserve the epithet of *great*: in the last scene she fell very far short of Mrs. Siddons. I could imagine a person looking at those features, which, though handsome, are certainly very deficient in expression, and asking how could that face succeed on the stage? She must have painted her eyebrows, for how could there be any expression in a face so entirely without brow as hers? I should be puzzled to answer these enquiries, but I believe both Miss O'Neil and Kean (in a lesser degree) may be adduced as instances of expression without features, and may show how much feeling may be betrayed by the human frame, independent of the face.

Still there certainly was a powerful charm in the evanescent hue of Miss O'Neil's delicate complexion. I saw her once in Mrs. Haller give interest to the dull scene in which old Tobias pours forth his tedious gratitude; her rosy blushes showed how unmerited she felt every commendation bestowed on a creature so guilty. In the whole of this part she appeared to me absolute perfection; one trait of nature enchanted me. In the last scene, after having been pleased by her appearance of deep contrition, her painful consciousness of degradation, I anticipated with pain the sort of disgust which I had always experienced at the return of the jewels. The whole incident seems to me too trifling, and becomes ludicrous when Mrs. Haller, looking to see whether they are all right, makes an oration on each

article.* With these feelings what was my delight
when Miss O'Neil, who had kept her eyes steadily fixed
on the ground and appeared really sinking into it, in
taking the box from the stranger looked at him for the
first time, and by that look told us more than by words
how he was altered, her fears, her love, &c. &c. In
short, I looked at her face and quite forgot the jewels,
which, even the first time the play was ever acted,
nearly made me disgrace myself by laughing in the
midst of the tears and screams which Mrs. Siddons
called forth.

Talma has extremely delighted me. I never go to a
French tragedy expecting that close and sober imitation
of nature which one looks for on the English stage:
one might as well look for it in the midst of opera
recitative as in the jingle of rhyme. Still it is pleasure,
and great pleasure too, though of a different nature.
I think Talma superior to every performer I ever saw
in the expression of bitter scorn, especially when it is
mixed with irony. Still, I think he never gave me as

---

* *Strang.* And now I may at least desire you to take back what
is your own—your jewels.   (*Gives her the casket.*)

Mrs. Haller (*opens it in violent agitation, and her tears burst upon
it*). How well I recollect the sweet evening when you gave me
these! That evening, my father—joined our hands; and joyfully
I pronounced the oath of eternal fidelity. It is broken. This
locket you gave me on my birthday. This bracelet I received
after William was born. No! take them—take them! I cannot
keep these, unless you wish that the sight of them should be an
incessant reproach to my almost broken heart. (*Gives them back.*)

much pleasure on the stage, as he did in Lady Charleville's drawing-room, where I heard him talk over
English and French acting, express his wish to unite
the merits of both, and deprecate the horrible accuracy
with which the last mortal throes are often represented on
our stage. He spoke of Kemble's Macbeth, wondered at
his tameness—especially immediately after the commission of the murder, and said that his whole frame ought
to have spoken of the horrid deed. Thus far everybody
must have agreed with him; but when the very natural
question, *Qu'auriez vous fait?* was put to him, and he
proceeded to act his feelings, I, for one, thought it most
absurd, because then my ideas were screwed to the pitch
of Macbeth and nature. Probably I might have admired
if I had been screwed up to the pitch of Oreste and
French rant. Much ought to be allowed for the super-
abundance of action which the French bestow on the
relation of the common events of life, and in ordinary
conversation.

What would I give to have been present at a scene
related to me that evening by Sir J. B. Burgess. He
had, a few days before, introduced Talma to Lady
Charleville.* After a little commonplace, Talma was

* Catherine, Countess of Charleville, wife of the first earl, a
woman of many and varied accomplishments, and of masculine
strength of understanding. She died at an advanced age in 1849.
The translation of Voltaire's *Pucelle*, still frequently ascribed to
her in book catalogues, was always indignantly denied by her. It
was executed and printed for private circulation by her second

drawn on, as if electrified by finding in her a kindred admiration of his hero, Napoleon; and related all that passed on the last memorable day of departure from Fontainebleau. He gave the speeches of Talleyrand, of Napoleon, of a physician who acted a conspicuous part, with such an accurate imitation of their several manners, that Sir James told me he felt as if he too had been present at the scene.

This evening Talma recited to us Hamlet's soliloquy, in English; he has been for so large a portion of his early life in England, that the thing was upon the whole much less absurd than might have been expected; there was no very striking gallicism, excepting the word consû-mātion.

PISTRUCCI, THE IMPROVISATORE.

Last night I heard Pistrucci, the improvisatore, for the third time, and my account of him will be far less favourable than if I had written it after the first or second time of hearing him. Even now I cannot believe that it is solely because the charm of novelty is past, and the edge of curiosity blunted, that my feelings are so changed. That this is partly the case I am aware, and feel also, that the more one hears him, the more one becomes aware of the very large

---

husband, the Earl of Charleville, prior to their marriage, and was not at all in her style. She delighted in refined wit and detested coarse humour.

proportion of absolute commonplace which pervades his verses. Still, with all this allowance, I cannot but believe that his performance last night was really inferior to what I had heard before.

Last night I liked him best in the return of Coriolanus to Rome: two attempts were downright failures; the one was Sancho, in his government of Barataria, the other the destruction of Pompeii. The first proved to me that he does not possess one particle of humour; but perhaps I may be wrong, if the total ignorance of the story which he professed be genuine, and if he really took his cue only from the little related to him at the moment. No such excuse can be made for his failure in Pompeii; the subject was necessarily well known to him, and had he succeeded I should not have given him much credit concerning it—one which must have been so frequently given before. As it was, I own I can even now hardly believe anyone could have been so very tame on a topic so inspiring. There was nothing in this evening's performance to convince one of the reality of his impromptu talent; at his public performance, he seized so many of the circumstances arising at the moment, that the most incredulous could no longer doubt his power of versifying quite instantaneously; but I should not say that he rises with his subject. Till I heard him fail in Pompeii, I was inclined to ascribe much of his failure to ignorance of the subject. On one occasion, he gave a new view of a threadbare theme, Waterloo: he took

the rising of the third sun on a field of blood, described finely the cannon obscuring his brightness,
&c. &c.

THE REV. EDWARD IRVING.

The familiar instance of the Rev. Mr. Spurgeon may help
to convey a notion of the more extended popularity and more
durable influence of the Rev. Edward Irving, the founder of
a sect which is still in full vigour.   His successful career as
a London preacher commenced in 1822, and lasted till 1832,
when he was displaced by the Presbytery for preaching
doctrines which they reasonably enough deemed heterodox.
In July 1823, Lord Eldon writes to Lady M. Bankes: 'All
the world here is running on Sundays to the Caledonian
Chapel in Hatton Garden, where they hear a Presbyterian
orator from Scotland, preaching, as some ladies term it,
charming matter, though downright nonsense.   To the shame
of the King's ministers be it said, many of them have gone
to this schism-shop with itching ears.   Lauderdale told me
that when Lady —— is there the   preacher never speaks
of a heavenly mansion, but a heavenly *Pavilion*.   For other
ears, mansion is sufficient.   This is a sample.' *

The reviewer of an excellent 'Life of Irving,' by Mrs.
Oliphant, states that the little church of Hatton Garden was
not only crowded, but filled, with the very audience after
which he had longed, ' with imaginative men, and political
men, and legal men, and scientific men, who bear the world

----

* Twiss's *Life of Eldon*, vol. ii. p. 483.

in hand. The Duke of York (continues the reviewer)' had been already interested in him at his first outset; Wilkes soon found out and appreciated his powers; Brougham is reported as one of his early auditors, and to have taken Mackintosh, who repeated to Canning an expression which he had heard Irving use in prayers, of a bereaved family being thrown on the fatherhood of God — an expression that so struck the statesman that he, too, was drawn to hear him, and to allude to his marvellous eloquence in the House of Commons.' *

It was about this time that Miss Wynn heard him, and her description of his oratory gives a much better impression of it than could be collected from his printed Orations, in which the imagery is chastened and the extravagance toned down. He was a very tall man, with impressive features, and he wore his hair long and parted in the middle, in obvious imitation of the pictures of Christ. Like Balfour of Burley, he 'skellied fearfully with one eye,' if not with both, but lost no favour on that account. When Wilkes's obliquity of vision was objected to him, an enthusiastic partisan vowed that he did not squint more than a gentleman ought to squint; and the 'angels' of the Irvingite creed seemed to think that a certain obliquity of vision was becoming in a saint. He died in 1834, in his thirty-ninth year.

The contradictory opinions of the press gave rise to an amusing squib, entitled, 'The Trial of the Rev. Edward Irving;' in which the different editors and critics appeared as witnesses.

June 29th, 1823.—I am just returned from hearing, for the first time, the celebrated Scotch preacher Irving,

---

* *Edinb. Rev.* for Oct. 1862, p. 441.

and highly as my expectations were raised, they are more than satisfied. At first, I own I was very much disappointed: his first extempore prayer I did not at all like; his reading of the 19th chapter of John (for he never gave to any of the Apostles the title of Saint) would have been very fine if its effect had not been frequently spoilt by extraordinary Scotch accents. He spoke of the *high-sup*, of being *crucifeed, scorged,* &c. &c. For twenty minutes, he went on talking of the enemies of our faith as if we had been living in the ages of persecution and of martyrdom, of *himself* as if he were our only teacher and guide, and of the *good fight* as though it were real instead of being metaphorical. Indeed, his action might almost have led one to suspect that he considered it a pugilistic contest. I thought all this part vulgarly enthusiastic, self-sufficient, dogmatical. Disappointment is not a word strong enough to describe my feelings, which nearly amounted to disgust. Then he told us that the intention of the *following* discourse would be to show from the page of history what man had been through all ages, in all countries, without the light of revealed religion. My brother whispered me, 'We have been twenty-three minutes at it, and now the sermon is to *begin*.' I felt exactly with him, and yet after this expression, I can fairly and truly say that the hour which followed appeared to me very short, though my attention was on the full stretch during the whole time.

Irving began with comparing the infancy of nations to the infancy of individuals; told us that was generally supposed to be the season of their greatest innocence : took as examples the early ages of Persia, Greece, and Rome. He reprobated the false arguments of those who, in speaking of heathens, adduce such men as Solon, Socrates, &c., as general examples; as well might we, said he, take the heaven-inspired Milton as the test of the republicans of his day; the noble-minded Falkland as a specimen of the cavalier soldiers; Fénelon as one of the Court of Louis XIV.; D'Alembert as one of the wicked pernicious *cotry* (as he called it) whose aim was the subversion of all order civil and religious; or Carnot as the model of that hellish crew of republicans who destroyed all religion and deluged their country with blood. Then came a splendid burst of eloquence on the vices of the ancients. He appealed to their vases, especially to those intended for the sacred purpose of containing the ashes of the dead; to the sculpture, still adorning the doors of their temples, as records of such vice as is not known in the most depraved of modern times. He asserted that if it were possible that social virtue, that self-government, could be attained without the aid of Christianity, Greece, which had discovered perfection in almost every branch of art, and had gone so far in science, would not have remained without these attainments. From them he proceeded to the Eastern nations, of whose vices he gave a still more disgusting picture, and especially those of the *mild* Hindoo, as false sentiment and philosophy have termed them : their language does not even possess words to express many of the virtues most revered among us, chastity, temperance, and honesty.

Having stigmatised most of the heathen nations of ancient and modern times with the vices uniformly found to degrade all savages, he proceeded to speak of those who have been considered as the brightest examples, and first of the Stoics. In the difficult task of self-government, they seem to have made much progress; but in steeling the heart against some temptations of passion, &c., they also steeled it against every kindly affection, made its every feeling centre in self. If, he said, stoicism may be said to have enjoyed what he termed the *man*hood of the soul, it had none of the *woman*hood, none of the feelings that adorn, comfort, or endear human nature. He proceeded to draw a beautiful parallel between the state of the Stoic, and that of Adam before it had pleased the Almighty to bestow on him a helpmate. He asserted that, in argument, in reasoning, the modern philosophers were very superior to the ancient, and added, that many very commonplace writers were, in this respect, very far superior to the most celebrated ancients, even to Cicero

---

* This is a mistake. There are Hindoo words for each of these virtues, and chastity has been deified. The Hindoo name for the Goddess of Chastity is Arundadi.

himself.* This superiority, which by-the-bye I am a little inclined to doubt, he ascribed entirely to the influence of Christianity, and spoke of its effect, even on those who deny its truths and exert their talents to write against it. How, he said, can a man who has sucked with his mother's milk the Lord's Prayer and the Ten Commandments, whose mind has been nurtured with the sublime poem of Milton, with the Pilgrim's Progress, nay, even with the plays of Shakespeare — how can this man be said to be free from the effects which Christianity produces on the mind?

He told us he conceived the spirit of religion to be even yet quite in its infancy; he trusted that we might see it make the greatest progress. If the rulers of the state would be governed by the plain rule of Christian duty, instead of the rules of worldly policy and expediency— if the more graceful part of the creation who govern the manners of this great city, would add the Christian graces to their other graces, would consider themselves as the spouses of Christ — if the critics who govern its literature would attend as much to the rules of Christianity as to those of human learning — what might not be the effects?

It was quite impossible to look at Lord Liverpool and Lord Jersey, placed immediately opposite to the

* The moderns, in this respect, have been compared by an admirer of the ancients to a dwarf standing on a giant's shoulders, and thus seeing farther than the giant.

preacher, and not fancy that the first and second of these appeals were addressed to them. As to the third, if Mr. Brougham and Sir James Mackintosh were not in the church, the preacher was likely to have prepared for them, as they have been there very frequently of late.

After having written so much about this *oration* (*sermon*[*] I cannot call it), it is quite unnecessary to say that I admired it extremely, at least in parts. I am conscious that there were great faults, even n the latter part, in which were also transcendent beauties. Want of simplicity is the greatest; even all Irving's energy could not give earnestness to such invariably figurative language. With this was occasionally mixed vulgarity bordering on coarseness in the images, excess of action, and occasional repetitions. Still there is extraordinary power, power which makes me feel I never knew what eloquence was till I had heard Irving, and at the same time leaves me with the most eager desire to hear him again on Sunday, in spite of all the impediments of crowd, heat, distance, and hour.

His reading the lesson was very fine, but what delighted me most was the solemn, simple, energetic manner in which he gave the blessing. The prayers did not please me: he prayed for *our own* ancient simple *painstaking* Church; then for the Established

---

[*] *Note by Miss Wynn.*—It is singular that I should chance to use the very word by which Irving himself called these compositions, when they were published soon after (in 1823).

Church, that her dignitaries may be *dignified*, and may be enabled to take due care of the widely-extended districts committed to their charge. The plain psalm-singing, in which the whole congregation joined, particularly delighted me; parts of the version seem to me very fine; but what I like most is the custom of reading the whole psalm first from the pulpit; it gives real devotion to a part of the service which, in our Liturgy, is generally the unintelligible squalling of a parcel of charity children, screaming that which nine-tenths of the congregation cannot follow, and of the other tenth a considerable part are disgusted by the absurdity of the version.

July 6th.—I have once more heard Irving, and I know not whether it is because the novelty is over that the impression is weakened, but I feel much less displeased, and at the same time much less pleased, than I was last Sunday. I am quite sure the arrogance, the self-sufficiency, the dictatorial spirit, though still but too evident, were much less striking than in the oration of last Sunday. The coarseness and vulgarity were also in great measure avoided, but the metaphors were still very superabundant, and also were generally pushed much too far. It appeared to me that this oration was deficient in clearness, but perhaps my understanding, as well as my hearing, was dulled by the various inconveniences of the situation in which I found myself; close to the door, far removed from the preacher, and separated

only by the thin partition of the pew from a crowd
who squeezed and made incessant noise. Even when
one did not hear some voices crying for mercy and
others for silence, the crowd pressed against the pew till
they made every board creak, and kept one in continual
apprehension that at last they would give way. During
the last hour of the oration the people were more quiet;
some servants, who I believe came for the fun of pushing
about, were turned out, and we heard better.

The general outline of the subject was still to show how
inefficacious was mere morality to constitute the happiness
of man in this life. He said he had purposely omitted
drawing any argument from the *future* state, as he was
anxious to prove his facts from those truths which are
admitted even by unbelievers, but he must address one
observation to those who, believing in a future state,
lived as if they thought of this world only. He said
their conduct was like that of a mother who, in bringing
up an infant, could fancy that it was always to remain
in the same state, was always to be fed as a nursling, to
be swathed, to be led like an infant. This simile, though
a happy one, was spun out to a length which destroyed
its effect. Soon after followed a beautiful burst of
eloquence on that power of Christianity which could
bend the rebellious stubbornness of the heart, strengthen
the tender heart, prop the weak, and enable it to tear
itself from those affections which are dearer far than a
right eye. Nature would teach a far different doctrine,

an eye for an eye ; nature and the world we live in are setting their adverse currents against the proper course of the human heart. Where, but in Christianity, is to be found the electric spark which is to repel them? Where, but in her, is to be found the mighty trident to stem these storms and currents?

One assertion of Irving's was not a little startling : he told us he considered Hume as one of the most powerful advocates of revealed religion who has ever appeared. That able metaphysician has, he said, proved the inefficacy of mere human reason, &c. &c. I own I could not help thinking while he made this strange assertion that it was not unlikely that some one of my neighbours in the aisle would, upon the recommendation of their pastor, take the first opportunity of edifying themselves by a perusal of the works of this powerful advocate of Christianity. I am sure that from his oration they could never have discovered that this was not a plain matter of fact.

He gave us a beautiful illustration of Jacob's ladder, calling it emblematical of the Christian dispensation which had opened the communication between heaven and earth : the angels ascending he called the human affections drawn up to heaven, and those descending the divine Spirit shedding its consoling influence in return. An exhortation (which appeared to me very commonplace) to those who were leaving the crowded city for the beautiful scenery of nature, concluded the oration.

The concluding prayer was the best I have heard from
Irving, but it is in this part that the want of simplicity is most apparent, and totally destroys all the
earnestness which he vainly tries to supply by vehement
gesticulation. Some expressions (and those not the·
best) were repeated from the prayer of last Sunday;
we had again 'ennoble the nobles,' 'dignify the dignitaries,' to which he added, 'with the dignity of religion
and virtue.' In the first prayer we had this strange expression, 'Clear our souls from the *obscuration* of sin.'

THE QUEEN OF WÜRTEMBERG, ' NÉE PRINCESS ROYAL OF ENGLAND '—NAPOLEON AT WÜRTEMBERG—GEORGE THE THIRD'S INSANITY.

Stuttgard: Oct. 1823.--In the midst of the incessant
gossip of the Queen Dowager, the subject of which is
almost always herself and her family, some curious
grains may be collected from a quantity of useless chaff.
There is no topic on which she seems to me to show
such good sense as in speaking of Napoleon. I heard
her say, ' It was of course very painful to me to receive
him with civility, but I had no choice; the least failure
on my part might have been a sufficient pretence for
depriving my husband and children of this kingdom.
It was one of the occasions on which it was absolutely
necessary to *faire bonne mine à mauvais jeu*. To me

he was always perfectly civil.' I have since heard that he gave her facilities for correspondence with her own family at the time that the state of Europe would otherwise have made it nearly impossible.

The Queen, who is always trying to puff off the con- jugal tenderness of her husband, told my mother that he left it to her option whether she would receive Napoleon. She said, 'I could not hesitate; it was my duty.' I do not give her any credit for a determination so perfectly natural; few women *would*, I think, have hesitated under the same circumstances, even if the option given her was not an order given in a more polite form. I do give her much credit for the honest candour with which she *now* speaks of the fallen conqueror, though perfectly aware that it is very disagreeable to most of the members of her own family, and especially to the King. The Queen of Bavaria was not as wise, and upon some occasion when Napoleon was incensed at some slight from her, he said she should remember what she was but for him, *la fille d'un misérable petit Margrave* (Baden), and imitate the conduct of the Queen of Würtemberg, *la fille du plus grand Roi de la Terre.*

The Queen said that the great preparations made in the palaces at Stuttgard Louisbourg for the reception of Napoleon, were not with her approbation, and that she said to the king, ' *Mon ami, vous devriez faire le pauvre au lieu d'étaler vos richesses, si vous ne voulez pas avoir des fortes contributions à payer.*' It was ridiculous enough to hear her say how, when Napoleon admired the Lyons embroidery and said, ' I cannot have such at the Tuileries,' she told him it was her work, adding, ' God forgive me, that was a lie.' When he made the same observation on some other instance of magnificence, she told him it was all done by the ' *Duc, mon beaupère*,' and in relating this, added the same corrective. She said the manners of Napoleon were extremely *brusque*, even when he was making the civil. She had seen both Josephine and Marie Louise with him, and seems to have been less pleased with the manners of the former than most persons who saw her.

Napoleon used to play at whist in the evening, but not for money, playing ill and inattentively. One evening when the Queen Dowager was playing with him against her husband and his daughter (the Queen of Westphalia, the wife of Jerome) the King stopped Napoleon, who was taking up a trick that belonged to them, saying, ' *Sire, on ne joue pas ici en conqué-rant.*'

The Queen spoke much of her father, of his recovery from his first illness: mentioned the story one has often heard of his wish to read ' King Lear,' which the doctors refused him, and which he got in spite of them, by asking for Colman's works, in which he knew he should find the play as altered by Colman for the stage. This I had often heard, but the affecting sequel was quite new to me; and fatiguing as the visits to Louisbourg are, I wished I had been there to have heard it from the Queen's own mouth. When the three elder princesses went in to the King, he told them what he had been reading. He said, ' It is very beautiful, very affecting, and very awful,' adding, ' I am like poor Lear, but thank God, I have no Regan, no Goneril, but three Cordelias.' The Queen wept in relating this; and my mother says, she felt as if she could have done the same.

GOD SAVE THE KING, AND HYDER ALLY.

June 1824.—I heard the other day from Miss Stables, a singular instance of the power of music, which I am anxious to remember because it is so well authenticated. When her father was a very young man, he followed his regiment to the East Indies. Upon some occasion (I forget what) this regiment gave a dinner to that savage tyrant, Hyder Ally, who a short time after returned the compliment by sending the greater part of those present to the far-famed Black Hole.* During dinner the regimental band played, and ended by playing *God save the King.* Hyder Ally appeared much struck, and fainted at last from emotion. Mr. Stables was one of those who

---

* This is an obvious mistake. Miss Wynn was probably thinking of the treatment experienced by the British officers and soldiers after the battle with Hyder Ally of Sept. 10, 1780.

assisted in removing him from the dining-room, and who, standing by when he recovered, heard him exclaim, 'Is your King a God that you adore him with such music as that?'

IMPROVISATORI.

June 1824.—I have heard another improvisatore, a man of the name of Rosetti, who, I am told, has pub-blished poems of great merit. His improvisazione I consider as decidedly inferior to almost all I have heard of Pistrucci's. I am inclined to believe that his lines were more harmonious; but am not quite sure that I may not have been deceived and blinded, or rather *deafened,* to any harshness of rhythm by the beauty and *musicalness* of his tones. From what I heard this evening, I am more than ever convinced that with its surprising novelty the talent of improvisazione* has lost its principal charm for me. The numberless expletive expressions which occur so frequently, and seem to fill up each pause as regularly as the accompanying music, become very fatiguing; and Rosetti very rarely relieved their sameness by any passage of spirit. The subjects chosen I thought indifferent. The first was the treachery of Cæsar Borgia, who invited five

* This is a cumbrous, awkward word in English, but I cannot, like a lady (I forget *who,* but *I heard* her), say, 'He played an *improvisatore* on the piano.'

friends to sup with him and murdered them. Very little indeed was said or sung to reprobate the treachery, but much on the tame, commonplace, threadbare subject of the lamentations of the wives, children, &c. &c. of the deceased.

The second subject I think much better, and was, therefore, more disappointed in the performance. It ought, however, in fairness, to be remembered that in this Rosetti was, by his own desire, fettered not only by a given measure, the *ottava rima*, but also by given rhymes for each stanza. The subject was Lorenzo de Medici going in person and alone, with an embassy from the Republic of Florence, to the treacherous Ferdinand King of Naples; no other Florentine daring to trust himself in the power of this cruel traitor, who is represented as quite overcome by this instance of generous confidence.

A short time ago I heard the Marchese Spinetti, in the course of his lectures on modern literature, treat the subject of improvisatores, and was amused at seeing how very much higher he rates the talent than Foscolo, whom I heard lecture upon it last year. I must say that when he enumerated the infinite variety of knowledge, of talent, of feelings, requisite to make a good improvisatore, I thought he required even more than Imlac, in his well-known definition of a poet, and longed to exclaim, like Rasselas, 'Enough! thou hast convinced me that no human being can ever be an improvisatore!' This Spinetti would have denied; and if the wonders which he related of the celebrated improvisa-trice, Corilla,* are well authenticated, her knowledge must have been fully equal to that of the Admirable Crichton. At one sitting she treated twelve different subjects; these were repeated to us, and certainly — properly filled—would have comprised a vast fund of knowledge; yet I fancied when I thought them over, I could in most discover the loop-hole by which the improvisatore so often contrives to slip out of the given subject, and glide into the beaten track of commonplace. Spinetti told us he under-stands that Rosa Taddei, now living at Florence, is supposed to be nearly equal to Corilla.

Talking on the subject of improvisazione with Prati, to whom Italian is nearly as familiar as his own language (German), I said, 'After all, it is a talent peculiar to the Italians, and depending, in great measure, upon the facility of versification which their language affords.' He assured me, not only that he had frequently heard the thing done in German, but that want of voice for singing alone would prevent him from doing it himself. Spinetti, in his lecture, spoke of a French improvisatore, who, in his own language, versified impromptu, with all the fetters of a given *subject, measure,* &c.

The Italians have been the most assiduous and successful professors of this art, but they have by no means enjoyed a

* Crowned in the capitol in 1776.

monopoly of it. Spain and Portugal have produced many much admired improvisatori ; Germany, a few; France and Holland, one or two each ; and England one, Theodore Hook, of surprising and surpassing merit in his way. Sheridan listened with wondering admiration ; Coleridge, under the combined influence of wit and punch, placed him on a par with Dante ; and Byron spoke of him as the only Englishman ever equal to the feat. His favourite mode of exhibition was a comic song, or mock opera, to which he played the accompaniment on the piano. It is worthy of remark that only one of the Italians (Gianni) has submitted his extemporised effusions to the test of print with even moderate success; and that only one (Metastasio) has acquired an independent and permanent celebrity.

LITERARY GAINS.

Dropmore: July 29th, 1823.—I heard to-day, from Mr. Rogers, that Constable, the bookseller, told him last May that he had paid the author of ' Waverley ' the sum of 110,000*l*. To that may now be added the produce of ' Redgauntlet ' and ' St. Ronan's Well,' for I fancy ' Quentin Durward ' was at least printed, if not published. I asked whether the ' Tales of my Land-lord,' which do not bear the same name, were taken into calculation, and was told they were; but of course the poems were not.

All this has been done in twenty years: in 1803, an unknown Mr. Scott's name was found as the author of three very good ballads in Lewis's 'Tales of Wonder;' this was his first publication. Pope, who had till now been considered as the poet who had made the most by his works, died worth about 800*l.* a year. Johnson, for his last and best work, his ‘ Lives of the Poets,’ published after the ‘ Rambler’ and the Dictionary had established his fame, got two hundred guineas, to which was afterwards added one hundred more.

‘ Waverley’ having been published in 1814, the sum mentioned by Constable was earned in nine years, by eleven novels in three volumes each, and three series of ‘ Tales of My Landlord,’ making nine volumes more ; eight novels (twenty-four volumes) being yet to come. Scott’s first publication (‘ Translations from the German’) was in 1796. During the whole of his literary life, he was profitably engaged in miscellaneous writing and editing ; and whatever the expectations raised by his continuing popularity and great profits, they were surpassed by the sale of the corrected and illustrated edition of the novels commenced under his own revision in 1829. Altogether, the aggregate amount gained by Scott in his lifetime very far exceeds any sum hitherto named as accruing to any other man from authorship.

Pope inherited a fortune, saved, and speculated ; and we must come at once to modern times to find plausible subjects of comparison. T. Moore’s profits, spread over his life, yield but a moderate income. Byron’s did not exceed 20,000*l.* Talfourd once showed me a calculation by which he made out that Dickens (soon after the commencement of ‘ Nicholas Nickleby’) *ought* to have been in the receipt of 10,000*l.* a year. Thackeray never got enough to live handsomely and lay by. Sir E. B. Lytton is said to have made altogether from 80,000*l.* to 100,000*l.* by his writings. We hear of sums of

500,000 fr. (20,000*l.*) having been given in France for histories —to M. M. Thiers and Lamartine, for example—but the largest single payment ever made to an author for a book was the cheque for 20,000*l. on account,* paid by Messrs. Longman to Lord Macaulay soon after the appearance of the third and fourth volumes of his history ; the terms being that he should receive three-fourths of the net profits.

NAPOLEON AT ST. HELENA.

Hastings, January 1822.—By a singular chance I have met at two consecutive public balls, first, an officer just returned from St. Helena, who was there at the moment of Buonaparte's death ; and secondly, one who was on board the 'Northumberland' when he went to St. Helena. From the first I anticipated much amusement, and expected that the second could only have bored one by repeating a tale which one has so often heard, that one feels possessed of almost all that can be told. In both instances the event proved exactly the reverse of my expectations. The first had never seen Buonaparte, and either could not or would not say any-thing about him. He told me that when he arrived at St. Helena, three or four months before the death of Napoleon, the inhabitants seemed to have entirely for-gotten him ; and that the man who so few years ago was the one subject of interest, of curiosity, of conversation through the globe, was never mentioned even within the narrow precincts of his insular prison.

As to the other officer, Captain Sweeny of the Marines, he had for ten weeks passed some part of every day with Napoleon, and was quite as ready to tell as I was to hear all that he knew about him. I first asked whether he had ever seen any instance of that violence of temper of which we have heard so much; he said, 'Never:' adding that appearing there only as a guest and for a few hours in company, there could not occur anything to provoke his passions. Still, as the narrator went on, I thought that, if the ill-temper had been so very near at hand as we have been taught to believe, there must have been occasions more than sufficient to call it forth. From his own people Napoleon continued to exact all the outward tokens of respect which they had shown to the Emperor. One day he was sitting on deck in rain such as I am told can scarcely be conceived by those who have not felt tropical rains : Bertrand, Montholon, and Lascasas were all standing round him bareheaded. My informant spoke to them, and especially to Lascasas, who has very delicate health, telling them they would make themselves ill if they did not put on their hats: they did not answer, and Buonaparte gave him a very angry look, but said nothing. He then said, 'General, you had better send for a cloak: you'll be wetted to the skin:' he very sternly replied, 'I am not made of sugar or salt.'

Napoleon always spoke in the handsomest manner of

his great rival the Duke of Wellington, and did not, like almost all of the officers who fought under his banner, attribute their defeat at Waterloo to chance, to a mistake, &c. He expressed the greatest admiration for the British navy.

It was one of the singular chances belonging to his extraordinary reverse of fortune that on board the 'President'* he found a nephew of Sir Sidney Smith. Napoleon one day in conversation with Captain Usher, after high commendation of his officers and of the treatment which he had met with from them, complained that there was one from whom he never could get anything but the shortest monosyllables in reply to all he could say to him. He added, 'I am the more provoked, as I hear Smith is a young man of great talents, who speaks French as easily as his own language, and yet I cannot draw him into any conversation.' Captain Usher remonstrated with young Smith; spoke of the respect due to fallen greatness, of the rank which Napoleon had so recently held. Smith replied that he hoped he should never be found deficient in proper respect, but he could not conceive it to be a part of his duty to enter into conversation with Napoleon; adding, that if he had enquired who he was, he thought he could not wonder at his declining any conversation with the person who had so much persecuted his uncle. When

---

* The ship in which he was conveyed to Elba.

Napoleon left the 'President' he gave a handsome snuff-box to Captain Usher, and rings to every one of his officers but young Smith, who would not accept any present, however trifling, from his hand.

Both the officers with whom I have conversed agree in speaking of Bertrand in the highest terms. They say that the only thing they could say against him is that his devotion to his master was sometimes carried so far as to border on servility; but that conduct which would have been contemptible in the servant of the Emperor, became respectable in the follower of the exile. His fidelity was the more meritorious when one recollects how many feelings of affection as well as interest militated against it. The scene which Madame Bertrand made, and her attempt at throwing herself into the sea, are well known; but I always doubted whether her repugnance might not have been acted, or rather exaggerated, to increase the merit of the sacrifice which Bertrand was making. By Captain Sweeny's account it was very genuine, and she left no efforts or blandishments untried, by which she could hope to work on his feelings as a father or a husband, to induce Bertrand to relinquish his intention of following his master. That he persisted, we all know, but I did not give him credit for being a very fond husband and father. His son, Napoleon, is I hear now as fine a boy as it is possible to behold.

Soon after they landed at St. Helena, Madame Bertrand incurred the displeasure of the fallen despot: it seems that one of the ships of the convoy was commanded by a Captain Hamilton, who discovered a distant relationship to Madame Bertrand, a Dillon by birth. Of course he showed her more attention on this account, and she received this attention like a Frenchwoman, but with perfect innocence. However, Napoleon was angry, and said to Bertrand: ' Your wife must no longer appear at my table; she has chosen to receive all the English officers, and from Captain Hamilton these attentions have been most pointed.' To this Bertrand made no answer, and submitted to the being almost entirely separated from his wife, whom he could only see for a very short period. This continued sixteen days, at the end of which time Napoleon, without another word on the subject, said, ' Tell your wife to come to dinner next Sunday.'

With all this he treated this devoted servant in a most ungracious manner, and said to him one day before all the English officers : ' As to your fidelity, I value it not; I know that it is not for my sake that you follow me, but for the sake of the credit you will gain from posterity.' Latterly it is said that Montholon had supplanted Bertrand in his master's favour, and yet he is thought in every respect his inferior. Captain Sweeny said that when, after a tedious voyage of ten weeks, the shores of St. Helena were discovered,

Napoleon seemed at first to feel the joy which animated every other person on board at the idea of leaving the ship ; but when on a nearer approach he discovered the barren rocks and desolate shore of his insular prison, the expression of despair, mingled with other feelings, on his countenance was most striking.   Napoleon left the deck, went into his cabin, and for many hours would not land.   Hopes of escape were not probably at any time entirely extinct, and enabled him to endure his wretched existence longer than could have been expected. While on board the ' Bellerophon ' he said, ' I suppose you, in England, expected me to prove a second Cato, and destroy myself after the battle of Waterloo ; but I was determined to show the world I would be a great man in adversity as well as prosperity.'

EXECUTION OF THE REBEL LORDS IN 1746.

Letter describing the execution of the Rebel Lords, in 1746, copied from the original.

'*August* 20*th* (1846).—Dear Sir,—As you and Mrs. Grimstone attended the Lords' tryal, I thought it would not be disagreàble to you to have an account of their exit or the last act of their tragedy, especially as I saw part of it, and heard the rest from one who was on the scaffold.   The sheriffs came there between 9 and 10 to

see if everything was prepared.   The scaffold was nine
feet above the ground, with a rail and black bays hanging from it.   On the floor (which was covered with saw-
dust) was fixed the block 2ft. 2in. high and 3 inches
broad : near it lay red bags to receive the heads, and
two white sheets to wrap the bodies in, and on each
side were the coffins with coronets and inscriptions, and
on the ground two hearses.   The executioner was in
blew with gold buttons and a red waistcoat (the cloaths
of Fletcher executed by him): the ax that of a carpenter.

   ' At 11 the Lords came : Kilmarnock attended by Foster and a young clergyman.   Balmerino was dressed in
blew turned up with red (his uniform).   Going into the
house prepared for them, a spectator asked which was
Balmerino, to which he replied, " I am he at your service."   Then turning to Kilmarnock he told him he
was sorry he was not the only sacrifice, and asked the
sheriffs if they were ready, for he longed to be at home,
and said he was asham'd for some of his friends, who
shed tears when Lord Kilmarnock came on the scaffold.
The bays was turned up that all might see, and the
executioner put on a white waistcoat.   My Lord had
a long discourse with Foster, who pressed him to own
there what he had told him privately,—a detestation of
the fact for which he suffered; which he did and which
Foster has advertised.

   ' The executioner was a great while fitting him for the

block, my Lord rising several times; and when down on his knees, it was six minutes before he gave the sign, when his head was nearly severed from his body by one blow: a slight cut finished the execution, and the body fell on its back.   .

'The scaffold being cleared, and the executioner having put on a clean shirt, Lord Balmerino mounted the stage, and immediately walked to his coffin, and read the inscription, and then called up a warder, and gave him his tye wig, and put on a Scotch plaid cap, and then read a paper denying the Pretender's orders for no quarter, commending him very much: but, being interrupted, he desired (briskly) to go on, and said he should lay down his head with pleasure on that block, pointing to it, and desiring those between him and it to remove. He reflected very much upon General Williamson, but said he had received the Sacrament that morning, and was told it was not proper for a person in his condition to say more of him, but referred for his character to Psalm 109, from verse 5th to 15th.   He said the Pretender gave him leave to enter our service, but, as soon as he could be of service to him, he left us.   He talked to the executioner, took the ax in his hand, and tried the block, and told and showed him where to strike (near his head), and gave him three guineas (all he had); kneeled down, and presently gave the sign.   The first blow did not strike his head off, so that the assistants were forced to lift up his body to receive a second, but the third finished him.

'I own I was a great deal more moved when I called on my friend Mr. Gill in the afternoon, and found him in great pain and given over by his Doctor, than I was with what I saw in the morning.

'The Guards attending were 1000, and I am sure the spectators were 100 to 1 of the Guards.

'I am yours and Mr. and Mrs. Grimstons

'Most obliged servant

'R. GRAHAM.'

DREAM OF THE DUCHESS DE BERRY.

A few months after the death of the Duke, the Duchess had a dream, or vision as they called it, which made a great noise at the time. Lithographic engravings were made of the scene: verses were published before we arrived at Paris in the month of July. It was about this period that the Nuncio gave to Mme (La Comtesse) Macnamara the paper, of which the following is a copy:—

'Voici le Rêve de Mad^e. la Duchesse de Berry, tel qu'il a été conté par cette Princesse à Monsr l'Evêque d'Amiens, de qui je le tiens:

'Vous connoissez le salon vert de l'Elysée Bourbon. J'y entrais. Je vis contre la cheminée qui est en face de la porte une grande figure blanche qui me fit peur,

quoiqu'elle n'eut rien de terrible.   Elle étoit enve-
loppée d'un manteau parsemé de fleurs de lys, et je
connus que c'étoit St. Louis.   Mad^e. de Gontault étoit
auprès de moi, tenant deux enfans qui étoient les miens:
l'un était ma fille agée de cinq ans, et l'autre étoit un
fils un peu plus jeune que sa sœur.   Mad^e. de Gontault
les poussoit vers la figure blanche, et moi je faisais au
contraire tout ce que je pouvois pour les retenir. Cepen-
dant elle l'emporta sur moi, et mes enfans se trouvèrent
tout auprès de St. Louis; qui posa une couronne sur la
tête de ma fille.   Je pris cette couronne et la mis sur la
tête de mon fils, disant que c'étoit lui qui devait être
couronné.   St. Louis reprit cette couronne, et la mit
sur la tête de ma fille, mais il en mit une seconde sur
la tête de mon fils et je m'éveillai.'

This dream produced so strong an effect upon the
mind of the Duchess, that the royal family, who at
first rejoiced in her deriving consolation from any circumstance, began to grow uneasy at the confidence with
which she spoke of all that she would do with her son,
just as if he had been actually there.*   Monsieur
thought it his duty to speak to her most seriously on the
subject, and to prepare her for the too probable disappointment of her high-raised expectations.   The only
reply he obtained from her was, ' *Ah! Papa, St. Louis
en sait plus que vous.*'

---

* The Duc de Berry was born in the September following.

CANNIBALISM IN SUMATRA.

March 1825.—From Sir Stamford Raffles I have heard histories of the manners and customs of the Island of Sumatra, so very strange that from any person but one who, having been many years governor of the island, was an eye-witness of some of the scenes he described, and in all had opportunity to ascertain the truth, I could not have believed one word. The first undoubted fact which he told me is, that at this time there is in a part (the north-western part, I think) of that island a population of about a million who are cannibals, and cannibals of a more horrible description than any I ever heard or read of, for they literally eat their victims *alive*. This, it seems, is the punishment for three or four great offences : one of which is adultery. An execution for this crime was witnessed by one of the white resident merchants, a person, Sir Stamford says, ' in whom he had perfect confidence,' and was thus described to him :

The criminal being tied to a stake, the executioner, armed with a very large sharp knife, asked the injured husband, who on this occasion had precedence over every person, what piece he chose : he selected the right ear ; which was immediately cut off. An assistant of the executioner placed it on a large silver salver, on which were previously arranged in heaps, salt, pepper of various degrees of heat, lemons, &c. The salver was presented to the husband, who, after having seasoned the disgusting morsel to his taste, proceeded to eat it. The next in rank happened to select the nose: the ceremony was repeated; and the executioner (being a *merciful* man), after two or three more slices, ran his sword through the body of the wretched victim, and then divided the body among the surrounding multitude, who crowded with savage ferocity to the feast.

Sir Stamford told me that, finding that some few among the principal persons expressed disgust at this horrible custom, he exerted his influence to abolish it, but he was answered as if he intended to subvert the public morals. They made use of the same arguments to defend their practice, as were used in this country to defend one less barbarous, the interment of suicides in the highway.* They said death might happen to any

---

* In 1813 the bill for omitting the embowelling and quartering in the punishment of high treason, was thrown out in the House of Commons by 75 against 60; 'so that (wrote Romilly) the ministers have the glory of having preserved the British law, by which it is ordained that the bowels of a man convicted of treason shall be torn out of his body whilst yet alive.' The judgment against Captain Walcot (concerned in the Rye House plot) was reversed, because it did not direct that the bowels of the prisoner should be taken out and burned *in conspectu ejus et ipso vivente.* Lord Russell was one of those who disputed the King's prerogative to remit the hanging and quartering in Lord Stafford's case; and when his own turn came, the King (Charles II.) said: 'My Lord Russell shall find that I am possessed of that prerogative which, in the case of Lord Stafford, he thought fit to deny me.'

man, and was not a sufficient punishment to deter from crime: circumstances to excite horror must be added; and some of those who fed on human flesh seemed to consider themselves as performing a *painful duty.*

I asked about how many executions might occur in the course of the twelvemonth, and was answered forty or fifty. Among the different villages, besides this, they are in the habit of eating their parents when they become old and useless. These are willing victims. The ceremony begins with music, dancing, and complete intoxication; and the poor old wretches are killed and roasted before they are eaten by their *dutiful children.* Latterly, however, some progress was made in civilisation: they began to feel some repugnance at eating *their own* parents; and neighbouring villages agreed to exchange their old for food. I naturally asked Sir Stamford whether he did not feel the utmost dread and abhorrence of this savage people. He said, 'Decidedly *not*: in the other transactions of life, they are a *mild*, strictly honourable people.' He gave me a proof of his opinion of them, telling me he had travelled through their district accompanied by Lady Raffles, and without any guards or means of defence. They had lodged in their huts, which are very large, and on account of the great moisture of the climate raised on large wooden piles. On one occasion, in one of these huts, above one hundred of these people slept in the same room with the Raffles' party; but this seems to have been an extraordinary occurrence, occasioned by a very stormy night which prevented many from seeking more distant habitations.

After all this, nothing is to me so wonderful as the plain historical fact, that Sumatra was discovered by the Portuguese in the year 1510, and since that period seems to have been continually the resort of eastward-bound European ships. I conclude that in this large island a remote part has been little visited by Europeans; still, that little, one should think, must in the course of above 300 years have produced some progress towards civilisation. · It seems strange, too, that a district large enough to contain a population of a million should be so cut off from all intercourse with the capital and that part of the island which has been so long inhabited by European merchants of different countries. I was astonished to hear that so near the equator a climate so temperate should be found. Sir Stamford said there was hardly a day in the year in which the thermometer did not rise above 80°, and very few in which it was higher than 84°; then, in the night and early morning, it frequently falls to 70°, and this, partly from the extreme moisture and partly from the relaxation of frame which the previous heat has produced, is felt as severe cold.

Sir Stamford says the mermaid is frequently seen on the coasts of Sumatra; but his report of her appearance is far different from, and much less poetic than, the fabulous histories I have been in the habit of hearing.

He describes her appearance as very like that of a cow, and says he cannot conceive how any resemblance to a woman can have been fancied, excepting in the position of the breasts and in the manner of nursing her young. They have very strong affection for their young, and when these are removed, call them with a loud continual moan, very discordant, and this is the far-famed mermaid's song. This moan is sometimes accompanied by tears, and a strange property is ascribed to those tears by a kind of poetic superstition. It is supposed that the tears which the mother sheds to recall her absent offspring, have the power of attracting towards the person possessing them the *one* most dear to that person. The precious drops are, therefore, eagerly purchased by lovers, as a kind of talisman to preserve and retain the affections of the beloved object.

After writing the above, I looked over Marsden's 'Sumatra;' I there find the account given by Sir Stamford of the race of cannibals exactly confirmed.* The

---

* 'These (offenders) are tried by the people of the tribe where the offence was committed, but cannot be executed until their own particular *raja* has been made acquainted with the sentence, who, when he acknowledges the justice of the intended punishment, sends a cloth to cover the head of the delinquent, along with a large dish of salt and lemons.' Amongst the many proofs addressed by Mr. Marsden to the incredulous, is the following:— 'When Mr. Giles Holloway was leaving Tappanuli, and settling his accounts with the natives, he expostulated with a *Batta* man who had been dilatory in his payments. "I would," said the man, "have been here sooner, but my *pangula* (superior officer) was detected in familiarity with my wife. He was condemned,

part of the island in which they are found is on the
N.E. coast, and is called Batta, and cannot be more
than 200 miles from Achin—the northern point where
an English factory was established early in the reign of
James I. Marsden calls the fish which he says has
given rise to the idea of there being mermaids in the
tropical seas, the Dayong. He describes the head as
covered with shaggy hair, and says the tusks are applied
to the same purposes as those of the elephant and, being
whiter, are more highly prized.

I was conversing on the subject of Sumatra with Mr.
Stanley, the Vicar of Alderley, who tells me that it is
still more strange that, in this age of discovery, most of
the islands in the Indian seas possess unexplored regions
in the interior. He instanced Borneo, Ceylon, Mada-
gasear (where there seems much reason to believe that
there exists a diminutive race, a nation of dwarfs) and
the Philippine Islands. As to the latter, he told me
that he had the authority of a captain and of a lieutenant
of a merchant vessel, who said that two young men with
tails had come to the coast from the interior of the
country; that they came on board their vessel, remained
some time, and had even consented to come to England
with them, but afterwards either repented and returned

---

and I stayed to eat my share of him : the ceremony took us three
days, and it was only last night that we finished him." Mr.
Miller was present at this conversation, and the man spoke with
perfect seriousness.'—*History of Sumatra*, p. 394.

home or died (I forget which). Mr. Stanley told me he had taken a great deal of pains in examining these men, and never could find any wavering in their testimony, or discover any circumstance which led him to doubt their veracity.*

SPINETTO ON THE PASTORAL DRAMA.

May 11th.—I went yesterday to hear Spinetto's lecture at the institution, when I found that the pastoral drama was the subject. I expected to be much tired, anticipating only a discussion on the ' Aminta ' and ' Pastor Fido,' too long and much too full of national partiality for my patience or my estimation of their merits. I was agreeably surprised. Spinetto is fully aware of the faults of these two dramas, and especially of their tremendous *long windedness,* and did not dwell upon them very long. He laughed at the attempts made in France at this species of composition, the absurdity of which must be felt by every person who has the least love of poetry or discrimination of character. The French ideas of shepherds and shepherdesses seem to me to be exactly adapted to the stiff, long-stayed,

---

* The Rev. Dr. Wolff stated positively, in the last of his publications, that a noble English family was distinguished by the same appendage as these two young men ; and that one of them had the seat of his carriage adapted for the reception of his tail. His nether garments were probably made like Satan's—

' His coat it was red, and his breeches were blue,
And there was a hole for his tail to come through.'

hoop-petticoated, powdered, full-wigged caricatures of the human form which Watteau, Boucher, &c., call by these names.

When Spinetto came to speak of the pastoral drama in England, he of course began by the 'Faithful Shepherdess' of Fletcher.* Praise of the occasional beauties of the poetry and emanations of genius throughout the performance, was nearly overbalanced by blame on occasional coarseness and immorality. He then proceeded to the 'Gentle Shepherd,' which he rated higher, adverted to the general diffusion of knowledge in Scotland, and digressing to the eternal never-ceasing topic of additional schools, wished them to prosper, neatly applying a quotation from Petrarch, ' *Quando luce il sol, ed ovvunque luce.*' We then came to ' Comus,' which I feared would scarcely be allowed to come under the denomination of a pastoral drama; but the praise bestowed upon it fully satisfied my partial feelings. The morality of Spinetto, which I own myself apt to think puritanical and over-strained, was quite in its place when he admired the skill with which the sainted muse of Milton contrived

---

* Can he have forgotten *The Passionate Shepherd* of Marlow:
   ' Come live with me and be my love.'
The same incongruity may be observed as in the French pastoral:
e. g. the damsel is to have—

   ' Slippers lin'd choicely for the cold,
   With buckles of the purest gold;
   A belt of straw, and ivy buds,
   With coral clasps and amber studs.'

to describe, or rather represent, the licentious court of Comus without contaminating herself.

Spinetto then startled his audience by telling them that we possessed a drama which might be denominated *pastoral* by a still greater poet. I was puzzled, and could anticipate only the 'Winter's Tale,' which, after all, I think should have been mentioned, though certainly not quite equal to 'As you Like it,' which he terms the most perfect pastoral drama extant. I have often thought that this beautiful play is not generally rated as highly as it deserves, and was delighted at hearing a foreigner commend it so forcibly. At the same time, I cannot go quite as far as my friend Miss Stables, who places it second to 'Hamlet' only, and above every other play. Now, in reading, I believe I prefer Othello, Lear, and Macbeth. Upon the stage, I am quite sure that the two plays from which I derive most pleasure are 'Macbeth' and 'As you Like it.'

BALLOONS AND DIVING-BELLS.

Stowe: August 1825.—Nugent (Lord Nugent) was talking to me on the subject of aerostation, and amused me very much. His sanguine mind still looks, after so many failures, to a degree of progress which may produce some useful result; and when I expressed utter incredulity, and said, 'Since the discovery of the science, so little progress has been made, that I can anticipate very little from the future,' he only replied, 'If from the first discovery of navigation you were to take thirty-five years, you would probably find that, in that period, much less progress was made than has been made in aerostation in the thirty-five years which have elapsed since the discovery.' In the first place, an argument which necessarily rests on probability only, I think worth very little; but, granting this position, I conceive that the state of science, of knowledge, &c., of that age, will bear so little comparison with that of the present day, that the parallel must fall to the ground. Though he did not convince me, he surprised me, by telling me how much had been done latterly. By observations on the different currents of wind, with the power of ascending by increasing the quantity of gas, of descending by throwing out ballast, they have acquired some little power of directing the balloon. But the most important discovery is one made by Sadler, which enables them to measure with tolerable accuracy the rate of their flight. A long log-line is thrown out, and by measuring with great accuracy, by means of a quadrant, the angle which this line makes, they can ascertain the velocity of their flight, and from observation of the compass may form a tolerable idea of their situation.

Nugent tells me that a young friend of his ascended with Graham a little time ago; it was one of the lovely bright calm days which have been so frequent this summer; still, in the elevated regions of the atmosphere, the cold was intense; but no peculiar sensation accompanied this cold. George (Lord N.) said he asked what was the appearance of the horizon of the earth: 'Cloud,' was the answer; 'the view was always caught through clouds, which formed an irregular fringe or frame to the picture.' The descent was very perilous: the young man—almost a boy—having asked Graham how high they were, and being told, I forget what, asked 'whether they could not ascend a little higher before they began their descent?' Graham said, Certainly they could, but that he was averse to the idea of expending any more gas, because a small quantity in reserve might be essential to the safety of their descent. When once the ballast is all thrown out and the descent begun, the only means of avoiding any dangerous spot on which the balloon might chance to fall, is by admitting a little more of the inflammable gas, rising, and trusting to the wind to convey the machine out of the dangerous neighbourhood. The young man still pressed for a farther ascent; Graham weakly consented; and the danger he had foreseen actually occurred.

As soon as the earth became visible through their glasses, it was evident that they had their choice of dangers only: they were coming down between the river and some lime-kilns. The kilns were certain destruction; the moment the balloon approached them the inflammable gas must have ignited, and they must have been burnt to death. The only alternative was to rise and trust to the wind for conveying them out of this dangerous neighbourhood. They had no gas left, and the only means of lightening the balloon was by cutting away the car—without the power (as George observed) of saying 'heads below'—and trusting themselves to the ropes of the balloon itself, which of course rose, having a lighter weight, made still lighter by being close to it, instead of being attached at some distance. At last they fell into the river, and, being both good swimmers, escaped.

I forgot to say that another of the modern contrivances is a pulley, by means of which the aeronaut can draw the car farther from, or nearer to the balloon: by this means the ascent or descent may be checked, and more or less advantage may be taken of the current of wind in which they may happen to find themselves. London, he says, appeared wonderfully regular at this great elevation : every smaller distinction of height disappeared : every building appeared of equal height and of dazzling whiteness.

This conversation naturally led us to the diving-bell. I found George had been down in one, in Plymouth Sound. By his account, it must have been precisely similar to that which I saw at Bordeaux. He says, when under the water, you see in the diving-bell about as clearly as you would in a carriage, when the breath has been congealed on the glasses; though you see very little without, within you can see to read the smallest print. He says, the first thing his companion did, was to direct his attention to the code of signals attached to the side of the bell, and explain them, that George might know what to do in the improbable event of his companion's being seized with a fit. The signals are given by so many strokes of the hammer against the side of the bell; the first, and most important of all, which is 'Hold fast where you are,' is given by one stroke; the second, which is, I should have thought, still more so, is 'Draw up the bell;' the others direct it to be drawn N., S., E., or W. His companion said, ' Now, you see that pointed rock, if we go on in our present course, the side of the bell must strike against it; it will be overset, and we shall inevitably be destroyed: but there is no hurry; we will go nearer and examine it.' When they approached he gave the signal to be drawn up higher; then directing the course so as to come immediately over the rock, he desired to be lowered again, and they found themselves with the point of the rock within the bell.

George describes the painful sensation in the ears exactly as the man at Bordeaux did; a buzzing and sense of pressure like that arising from a drop of water in the drum of the ear, only stronger. Cotton to deaden this sensation would be a very dangerous experiment: the compressed air would drive it in so far, it would not be got out again without some instrument. He says, that altogether the sensation is so little disagreeable, that he conceives one might remain under water for any length of time. In returning to the air, there is a disagreeable sulphureous smell, for which it is not easy to account, but which is always observed. George did not know whether this smell was experienced returning from fresh water as well as from sea water.

CONVERSATIONS WITH GENERAL ALAVA.

(Cambronne. Fouché. Spanish Legate and Aranda. The Popes. Prince de Ligne. The Empress Catherine. First news of Waterloo.)

General Alava, for many years Spanish Minister at the Court of Great Britain, is best known as the friend and companion in arms of the Duke of Wellington ; who retained through life a warm esteem for him, although political differences may have caused an occasional coolness. Alava, on his part, never wavered in his attachment. After expressing his approval of some measure of Lord Grey's Government, he suddenly turned round and exclaimed, ' But you must not think I can ever prefer this Government to the Duke of Wellington ; it is he whom I love.' Alava, says Lord Holland in his ' Foreign Reminiscences,' ' was impetuous in temper and heedless in conversation ; but yet so honest, so natural, so cheerful, and so affectionate, that the most reserved man could scarcely have given less offence than he, who commanded the respect of the many by his intrepid openness and sincerity.'

Dr. Gleig, after relating the circumstances of the wound or contusion received by the Duke at the battle of Orthes, adds: ' He was on his feet, however, in a moment, and in a condition to laugh at the Spanish General, Alava, who had likewise been wounded almost at the same instant in that fleshy and very sensitive part of the body, any accident to which is apt to excite the mirth rather than the sympathy of the looker-on.' *

No one knew better how to interpret the slightest action of his Chief. The night before one of the Duke's Peninsular victories, an officer came up to Alava and asked in much alarm, ' What will become of us? We shall have a great battle to-morrow, and Lord Wellington is doing nothing but flirting with Madame de Quintana.' ' I am glad to hear it,' replied Alava, ' if we are to have a great battle to-morrow; for it is quite certain that all his arrangements are made, if he is flirting with Madame Quintana.' Alava died in 1841.

Aix-la-Chapelle: October 9th, 1825.—I am hearing from General Alava a great deal about all those of whom history will one day talk a great deal and tell much that he could contradict on personal knowledge. For instance, he was present when Cambronne was taken, and when he is said to have made the speech so often commented upon, ' *La Garde meurt, et ne se rend pas.*' He did not say this or anything else, only screamed for a surgeon to dress his wound, having quietly surrendered.†

---

* *The Life of Arthur Duke of Wellington*, &c. p. 272.

† Siborne says that when the French Guards fell back, General Halkett, who had marked out Cambronne, dashed at him with

Alava saw the famous correspondence which passed between Fouché and Carnot at the period of the Restoration, when the former, as minister of police, was sending all the proscribed into exile. Carnot wrote, *Où veux-tu que j'aille, traître?*' Fouché replied, ' *Où tu voudras, imbécille.*'

I am still, after all I have heard in Majorca, astonished at the manner in which Madame de Coigny, a professed *dévote*, Alava, and the Prince Pierre d'Aremberg, talk before us heretics of their bishops, cardinals, legates, and even their popes. Alava was telling us of the legate in Spain during the reign of Charles III. He had some discussion with Aranda, then minister, and refused some boon requested for Spain, detailing with great pomp his fears lest the interests of their holy faith might suffer by such concessions. Aranda, provoked, at last said, ' How can you bring forward such arguments to me who know that you are an atheist as well as myself? ' The *pious* legate quietly replied, ' *È vero, ma questo non si dice.*'

Alava amused me in telling of the same man, the

---

uplifted sword, and was on the point of cutting him down, when Cambronne cried out to him to hold his hand, and surrendered. Just afterwards Halkett's horse fell, and Cambronne made an attempt to escape, but was overtaken by the General, who pulled him back by the *aiguillette*, and delivered him over to a guard of Osnabruckers. Cambronne himself always denied the historic *mot* attributed to him, which, according to M. Fournier (*L'Esprit dans l'Histoire*), was invented by M. Rougemont, the editor of the *Indépendant*, in which journal it originally appeared.

manner in which he received the often-repeated question of that fool Charles IV., who made all around him observe the striking resemblance between his son Don Francisco de Paula and the Prince of Peace. The sneer with which the legate first looked at the Queen, then at Manuel, and replied, '*È vero, Sire,*' was very well described.

They all speak of the present Pope (Leo XII.) as having been *fier libertin,* and are not shy of letting you see that they consider his present austerity as mere hypocrisy. Of the late Pope (Pius VII.) they speak with the veneration which his character seems to demand from all, but which is certainly not felt by the bigoted Catholics, who cannot endure his liberal ideas. They were speaking of the time that he passed in confinement at Fontainebleau. Napoleon wanted to force him to consent to measures which his conscience disapproved, and one day, tired out, said to one of his ministers (Fouché,[*] I believe), 'Why do not you try what ill-treatment can do, short of torture? I authorise you to employ every means.' The reply was, '*Mais, Sire, que voulez-vous que l'on fasse d'un homme qui laisse geler l'eau dans son bénitier sans se plaindre de n'avoir pas du feu dans sa chambre?*'

One evening we talked of that extraordinary per-

---

[*] In his apocryphal *Mémoires,* Fouché is made to say that Napoleon, knowing his repugnance to violent measures against the Pope, never trusted him with the conduct of them.

sonage the Prince de Ligne, who for fourscore years had lived with every person of distinction in Europe, and who, to the last moment, preserved not only every useful faculty, but wit and gaiety besides.   He preserved also to the last a singular facility of versification, and was particularly fond of writing epitaphs on himself. They say that he must have written above 500, generally impromptus, and of course worthless.*

Madame de Coigny told us an anecdote of that famous progress which Catherine la Grande made through the southern part of her empire, and which the Prince de Ligne has so well described.   She was attended by the ministers of the three great European Powers.   They arrived at Kiow.   She first asked the Austrian, Cobentzel, what he thought of the town.   He made a set speech on the ruins of the ancient town, contrasting them with the new buildings which she had made, and of course extracting from that part of the subject a long tirade of compliment, &c. &c   When this oration was ended Catherine turns to Ségur, the French minister, ' *Et vous, Monsieur, qu'en pensez-vous ?* ' ' *Madame, il me semble que Kiow offre le souvenir d'un grand empire et l'espoir d'un autre.*' †   Catherine then says, ' *A votre*

---

* He was always writing about himself in prose as well as in verse.   Amongst the heads of chapters in his *Mémoires et Mélanges,* we find, ' De Moi pendant le jour,' ' De Moi pendant la nuit,' ' De Moi encore,' ' Mémoire par mon cœur,' ' Mes Écarts, ou Ma Tête en Liberté.'

† Kiow was the capital of the ancient empire of Muscovy.

tour, Monsieur Fitzherbert (afterwards Lord St. Helens), *qu'en dites-vous ? '* ' *Ma foi, Madame, je trouve que c'est le plus vilain trou que nous ayons encore vu dans toute notre route.'* Madame de Coigny says she has laughed at Lord St. Helens about this speech ; he replied that everything that was pretty, everything flattering had been said, so that nothing remained for him but the plain truth. She added, ' *C'est si Anglais.'*

I did not know till I heard it from Alava the exact circumstances of the first arrival of the news of the battle of Waterloo in London. It seems that one morning a partner of the house of Rothschild came to Lord Liverpool, informed him that he had a few hours before received the glorious news, or at least the bare outline ; that, having made all the advantage which this exclusive knowledge could give him on the Stock Market, he now came to impart it to Government. He *would* not answer any enquiries as to the means by which he had acquired the intelligence, and *could* not give any particulars: he only repeated the assurances of truth of the information. Lord Liverpool thought it cruel on such vague foundations to raise hopes or fears.

---

* Ségur's version is: ' " Comment trouvez-vous la ville de Kioff ? " dit-elle au Comte de Cobentzel. " Madame," répliqua le Comte avec le ton de l'enthousiasme, " c'est la plus belle, la plus imposante et la plus magnifique ville que j'aie vue." M. Fitzherbert répondit à la même question : " En vérité, c'est un triste lieu ; on n'y voit que des ruines et des masures." Interrogé à mon tour, je lui dis, " Madame, Kioff vous offre le souvenir et l'espoir d'une grande ville." '

To one of his colleagues (Vansittart, I think), who happened to come in, he told the circumstance, and they agreed to conceal it from every other human being till more was known.   There was a cabinet dinner that day at Lord Harrowby's : not one word was said respecting the news; and Lord Liverpool was returning home full of anxiety.   In the street his carriage was stopped by an unknown, who, with some apology, said that he was just come from Downing Street; that a carriage with six horses, dressed with laurels, French Eagles and colours hanging out of the windows, had arrived : that the glorious news was instantly spread; and that the messenger was gone to Lord Harrowby's in pursuit of him, through another street from that in which he was met.   This, I think, I heard at the time, but certainly till now never heard the thing accounted for.

It seems that the Duke of Wellington, after writing his despatch home, said to Pozzo di Borgo, 'Will you write to Louis XVIII. at Ghent? tell him only that Napoleon is utterly defeated : that in less than a fortnight I shall be in possession of Paris, and hope very soon after to see him reinstated; say that excessive fatigue prevents me from writing.'*   A messenger was of course immediately sent off to Ghent : when he arrived, Louis and his little Court happened to be assembled at break-

---

* The Duke himself wrote to this effect to Louis XVIII. on the morning of the 19th, but it is highly probable that a brief announcement of the victory was despatched at once.

fast, in a room whose windows down to the ground were wide open. The embraces, the ejaculations, of course instantly apprised those under the windows of the arrival of good news. Among these was a spy from the house of Rothschild, who had many days been upon the watch: he no sooner heard the news than he rode post to Ostend: there, happening to find a small vessel just sailing, he embarked, and got one tide before the English messenger, who arrived shortly afterwards.*

DEATHS OF THE EMPERORS ALEXANDER AND PAUL.

Florence: Dec. 24th, 1825.—We are all here full of speculations upon the subject of the death of Alexander,

* The official intelligence of the victory of Sunday, the 18th, did not arrive in London till late in the evening of Wednesday, the 21st. The despatches were brought by the Honourable Major Percy, brother of the present Earl of Beverley, addressed to Earl Bathurst, and were first opened by Lord Liverpool, at Lord Harewood's house in Grosvenor Square. The result was first announced by the newspapers on the 22nd, but there is a passage in the *Times* of that day which partially confirms the Rothschild agent story: 'Those who attended to the operations of the Stock Exchange yesterday (21st) were persuaded that the news of the day before would be followed up by something still more brilliant and decisive. *Omnium* rose in the course of the day to six per cent. premium, and some houses, generally supposed to possess the best information, were among the purchasers.' The popular version of the story was that the agent did not stay to verify his conclusion, but started immediately after witnessing the signs of joy manifested by the royal party.

which this day's post has announced. Many are inclined
to believe that his death has been occasioned by the
hereditary complaint which proved fatal to his three
predecessors. We had much conversation on the subject,
and I heard for the first time that it is now universally
believed that Catherine was strangled. There is a
species of poetical justice in this, which makes one more
inclined to believe than one should otherwise be; it is
even added that Marcoff on his death-bed confessed
that he was the agent employed on this occasion. Lord
Dillon afterwards gave us the particulars of the death of
Paul, derived from a Mrs. Browne and a Miss Kennedy,
who were at that time in the nursery of the two younger
princes, Nicholas and Michael.

It seems that the day before some rumour of the
conspiracy reached the ears of Paul: he sent for
Count Pannin, who was at that time his minister,
and bitterly reproached him for his want of vigilance. Pannin, undismayed, professed his perfect
acquaintance with all the designs of the conspirators; acknowledged himself as one of them, alleging
as his motive that all other means of defeating their
purpose would have proved vain: and added that now
he had all the clue, and had the means of arresting the
conspirators as soon as any overt act could be proved
against them, which at present was not the case.

Paul burst into tears, embraced Pannin, called him
his saviour, the guardian of his country, &c. &c. The

Emperor continued oppressed and agitated all the evening, which he passed alone with the Empress; saw all
his children, kissed and blessed them, and unable to
shake off the agitation produced by the conversation
with Pannin, retired at an earlier hour than usual.
Soon after the conspirators rushed into the room:
they were Beningsen (the distinguished general); Ouwarow (the man whose tremendous black murderous
countenance made such an impression on me when
he was in London, as aide-de-camp to Alexander);
Subow, a Georgian prince: Pannin, who remained
behind a screen.* Paul resisted stoutly, attempted to
conceal himself, &c.; and they seem to have hacked
him most cruelly. At last Beningsen and Ouwarow
took the sash of one of the sentinels on duty and closed
the scene by strangling him, but not till he had received
some tremendous blows on the head, and not till one of
them (Beningsen, I think) had trampled upon him, and
had with his sharp spurs inflicted two wounds in his
stomach.

Miss Kennedy with her young charge slept in the
room immediately over that of the Emperor: she
heard the violent uproar ('row,' Lord Dillon called
it), trembled, quaked, got the infant out of its own bed

There were in all thirty conspirators, including (besides those
named above) two named Subow, Prince Jaschwill, Count Pahlen,
Tatischeff, &c. The circumstances are differently narrated in each
of the best authenticated accounts.

into hers, and with him in her arms lay expecting some horrible event. This dreadful interval lasted more than an hour, when Madame de Lieven (the mother of the Prince Lieven who was ambassador in England, and then *grande maîtresse* of the Empress) rushed half dressed into the room, and desired Miss Kennedy to bring the Grand Duke to his mother instantly, if she wished to save his life and her own.

By the time she reached the apartment of the Empress, all the children and their respective attendants were assembled there, half dressed and frightened out of their wits. Alexander and Constantine, who were both past twenty, were absent at Petersburg. The Empress, quite frantic, rushed out of the room, collecting her children round her; and followed by the troop of terrified, half-dressed women, went to the Emperor's room. The sentinels, gained over or terrified by the conspirators, at first refused her admittance; but she, partly by her commanding manner, beauty and dignity, and partly by literal strength of arm, overawed them, drove them back, and obtained admission for herself and her terrified train. She threw herself on the mangled body; would not for a long while believe that life was extinct; then poured forth the most bitter execrations against the murderers, and lamentations for her lost husband; who (strange to say) brute as he was to everybody else, was kind and still very dear to her. At length, wearied out, she sank half exhausted and half choking: one of the ladies got her a glass of water; the rough sentinel who had opposed her entrance, and who probably, at the orders of the conspirators, would have killed her, stopped her from drinking, and said to the attendant, 'Woman, what have you brought? I insist upon your drinking half the contents of that glass before the Empress touches it.'

The feelings of the Empress were naturally most excited by her fears for her children, whom she ex-pected to see murdered before her eyes. In vain the conspirators assured her that she and they were safe: then, with unparalleled brutality, in that chamber, in the presence of her murdered husband, told her all was over, and shouted in her ears, 'Long live Alexander.' That he was privy to the murder there seems but too much reason to fear; the apology made for him is that he was told by the conspirators that his father must be *deposed*; that all resistance was vain: that if he and Constantine wished to avoid sharing his fate, they would remain perfectly quiet, and appear ignorant of what was going on. I should have said before that this scene passed at the summer palace, out of Petersburg; and that the first object of the Empress, when she in any degree recovered her senses, was to get her children into the winter palace at Petersburg, where she felt that in the multitude she should find safety and pro-tection. This was at first refused, but with the spirit of a heroine she rushed amongst the Guards, saying,

'Who will dare to stop a mother protecting her infant children?' In short, she once more prevailed, and they allowed her to go: two carriages were brought forward, but she would not hear of being separated from her children, and therefore waited till some old lumbering vehicle was found in which they could all go together.

I had always understood that Constantine was a horrible brute, but had not an idea of the extent of his cruelty till this event brought his character so much into discussion. I am told that a servant of his said, 'This has been a quieter journey than usual: we have killed only two postillions;' and declared that in the last journey Constantine had shot three with his own hand from the carriage. With this ferocity he unites great cowardice. An Englishman now here, a Mr. Aubyn, who has served with him, told me that he has seen him betray great personal fear in action. It was said by somebody that his character was softened, and that since he had been in Poland, where he is Viceroy, you did not hear of such horrid acts of barbarity; which was allowed. And yet, said some one, the following fact took place latterly in Poland:

An officer married a young Jewess: he was punished for this crime, and Constantine sent for her to receive the punishment of the knout. Her beauty produced such an effect upon him that he doomed her to the severer penance of becoming his mistress. The husband was sent to Siberia: the wretched wife destroyed herself.*

' People do not seem to rate the characters of the other brothers higher. Nicholas, they say, is more dangerous, inasmuch as he has the art to conceal his vices; Michael seems to be considered as a mere brute. After all, horrible as all this is, it is impossible not to own that in the customs of that semi-barbarous nation, some little excuse is to be found. The person who from childhood has been accustomed to see, or at least *hear*, the knout administered for the most trivial faults, must in time become hardened in human suffering. I understand that the Russians resident in this town have been obliged to adopt some other means of punishment for their wretched servants. It was not unusual, on entering a house, to hear the most dreadful screams, and to be told by the lady of the house not to mind: it was *only* her maid who, having dressed her ill, was receiving so many strokes of the knout.† Complaints were made: the police interfered, and the knout was strictly prohibited. The extremes of splendour and of misery seem to be their habitual modes of life. Demidoff, who in a state of representation lives more magnificently than any person I ever saw, keeping a company

* Revolting as this reads, the famous Maréchal Saxe treated an actor and his wife much in the same fashion with the aid of a *lettre de cachet*.

† Most probably of the whip. The knout is reserved for more serious occasions, which, I believe, are defined by law.

of French actors at his own expense, filling his rooms with every magnificence which money can buy—from chairs and tables up to diamonds and pearls, which are exhibited in large cases lined with velvet, and covered with plate glass, exactly like those in Rundell's shop—is living himself in dirt and misery, greater than that of any English cottage.

Lord Dillon gave an extraordinary instance of this mixture in Madame Gerebstoff, who passed many years in England. He had some business with her, and went one morning to her house in Harley Street at an hour rather earlier than that of visiting. The servant hesitated about letting him in; he rather insisted on the plea of business, and was taken up to the drawing-room, where he found Madame de G. lying on the couch in a blue silk gown, her hair dishevelled, and a diamond tiara hanging down on one shoulder, the rouge on her cheeks streaked, her person and dress looking as dirty as possible. Seeing probably his amazement, she said: ' *Ah! mon cher, je suis rentrée si tard hier, que je me suis couché à la Russe. Je vais prendre un bain, et puis je m'habillerai.*' *

---

* 'La superficie en tout offrait l'image de la civilisation, mais sous cette écorce légère, l'observation retrouvait encore facilement cette vieille Muscovie.'—*Ségur.*

DUCHESSE D'ALBANY.

Florence: January 14*th,* 1826.—I have been dining with the Lawleys in the house formerly inhabited by the Duchesse d'Albany. The conversation turned much on the subject of the late possessor, who, if she be not much belied, must have been a very odious woman. The only cause I can find for doubting the truth of what has been told me, is that it appears scarcely possible that such a creature as she is represented could be to Alfieri an object of such strong, such constant affection. It is, I am told, quite certain that her marked predilection for Fabre excited in the poor poet a fit of such violent jealous passion as to have produced gout in the stomach, of which he died suddenly. Some are uncharitable enough to suspect Fabre of having poisoned him; but there is not the slightest evidence to warrant the suspicion of his having ever administered any poison but that of jealousy.

It seems this Fabre was a French picture-dealer, a thorough blackguard, who was introduced to the Duchesse as a secretary by Alfieri himself, during the lifetime of Charles Edward. It was not long before he aspired to the affection of his mistress, and supplanted Alfieri in the position of what is here called *il patito.* That there must have been something peculiarly shame-less in the woman who chose to record her own shame in marble is evident, and this is what the Duchesse has done by her monument to Alfieri.*

That she must always have been ugly is (as I hear) also proved by a portrait painted by Fabre in 1793, and placed in the French saloon at the Gallery, which I have not yet taken the trouble of seeing. Her table is said to have been the object of her strongest affection through life, and to have overcome her love of money. By a sort of poetical justice, not often seen in real life, the pangs which she had inflicted upon poor Alfieri were visited on her own head or heart. The latter years of her life were embittered by her excessive jealousy of the attentions paid by Fabre to the very handsome wife of a seal engraver, whose name I have forgotten.

An eye-witness told Sir Robert Lawley that her death-bed (in 1824) afforded the strongest instance of the ruling passions strong in death. She blessed God for a long and happy life, and instanced three peculiar causes of thankfulness: first, that she had always had the best of wines; secondly, that she had always had a good cook and an excellent dinner; thirdly and principally, that she had not outlived the seal engraver, and thus had

* The monument is the simplest record of an attachment which was not condemned by society: '*Victorio Alfierio Astensi Aloisia e Principibus Stolbergis Alboniæ Comitissa M.P.C. An. MDCCCX.*' There is no ground for the supposition that Alfieri's death was hastened by jealousy, and Fabre was a French painter of unimpeachable respectability.

been spared the misery of seeing Fabre married to her rival. Sir Robert says that the Florentines, who could not forgive her treatment of Alfieri, had ceased to visit her after his death;* and were very much astonished, when the peace of 1814 brought shoals of English, to see some of our first ladies at the feet of this odious woman, and suffering themselves to be treated as *subjects* by this mock sovereign. The dirt of her house, when he took it, he says was quite incredible: that and everything else belonging to her, with the exception of a very small legacy to some starving Stolberg relations, she bequeathed to Fabre. He told Sir Robert that, it was very singular, within a couple of months of her death, she had been furnishing herself with various articles, as if she had expected to live a hundred years. She had ordered a new carpet to be made at Tournay, for one of her rooms. She had bought a dozen pair of cotton stockings, and a dozen petticoats; the first article Sir Robert purchased, and was earnestly requested by Fabre to buy the others too.†

---

* So far was this from being the case that Napoleon sent for her in 1809, and began thus: ' I know your influence over the Society of Florence. I know also that you employ it in a sense adverse to my policy.'

† See *Die Gräfin von Albany*: Von Alfred von Reumont (2 vols.) Berlin, 1860; and the review of that book in the *Edinburgh Review* for July 1861. As I wrote that review, I may not be deemed wholly without predilections; but Miss Wynn's informants strike me to have been in every way unjust towards the Duchesse and Fabre, and to have made no allowance for Alfieri's treatment of her. At the same time, it must be admitted that

AN ARCHBISHOP ON FALSE PRETENCES.

Rome: March 25th, 1826.—I have been waiting to write the account of a singular impostor, hoping always to pick up more particulars, but I fear in the midst of the wonders that surround me I may lose the recollection of what I do know.

Some time ago an Egyptian arrived at Rome bearing a letter from the pacha, in which he stated to the pope that, having in his dominions a very large Catholic population, he wished to have a bishop to be at the head of this Church, and sent the bearer, hoping that he might be ordained.   The request was most willingly granted.   The Egyptian was clothed, fed, lodged, and taught: the teaching was rather a slow process, but the ignorance of an African was not likely to excite suspicion.   In short, the Egyptian was named Archbishop of Memphis, and with this title returned to his own country.   The pacha wrote an angry expostulation to the pope for interfering with his subjects, and it was not till then discovered that the first letter was a forgery and the Archbishop of Memphis a daring impostor.   He was sent here, and was sentenced to death, which has since been commuted to hard labour as a

---

much of her conduct and character sadly militate against romance. Another very high authority, Lord Broughton, has taken the unfavourable side.

galley slave for life. I have been told that all this while he is archbishop; for that dignity once conferred cannot, according to the Catholic canon, be taken away. Others tell me he is degraded, and I cannot get at the truth.

THE DUC DE BERRI.

Having heard and written down at the time all the accounts I heard of the assassination of the Duc de Berri, and of the birth of his posthumous son,—aware that my informants were ultra-royalists, I was not a little amused in hearing yesterday from the E.s, the story of the liberals. In the royalist history, the variations are unimportant; but our friends, I see, are very much inclined to believe that the Duc de Bordeaux is not the child of the Duchess, but the offspring of one of his mistresses, of the mother of *les petites anglaises* mentioned in the letter of Madame de Goutault.* True it is that, among the known and undisputed facts, there are many suspicious circumstances; the extraordinary privacy of the birth,—the unaccountable *délaissement* of the Duchess

---

* The Duke's English mistress, who attended his death-bed, as related by Madame de Goutault, in a letter (transcribed by Miss Wynn) narrating all the circumstances of the assassination and his death. The doubts relating to the birth of the Duc de Bordeaux were not more plausible than those thrown on the birth of the Chevalier St. Georges, which are now rejected as preposterous.

though all Paris knew that the *accouchement* was daily, nay hourly, expected—the wonderful strength of the Duchess, whom Henry saw at the window, within the first forty-eight hours, I think—her known partiality for Mademoiselle, and her indifference to the boy—the one, she says, '*est mon enfant, l'autre c'est l'enfant de la France*;' the fact of her having escaped a miscarriage after such a shock and such exertions. Another singular circumstance—the extravagant liberality and attention displayed not by the Duchess only but by all the royal family to *les petites anglaises* (now Comtesses d'Issoudun) and to their mother, would be thus accounted for.

The most suspicious part of the story is, that the *procès-verbal* giving the account of the birth of the child, which was proclaimed by authority, was altered: in the first copy, only half-an-hour was said to have elapsed between the time when the ladies took leave of the Duchess and that when they were not only safe in their nests but so fast asleep that they could not hear her bell. In a second, this was made an hour. Still the certainty that the fable (if fable it be) must have been fabricated within the first twenty-four hours after the assassination of the father, and the coincidence with the circumstances which had been brought forward to shake the legitimacy of the young Napoleon, are in my mind strong evidence against this story.

It is singular that, the day after, I heard a report which, admitting both stories to be true, would furnish a striking instance of poetical justice. This child, this pretender, is so little promising in body or mind, that Charles Dix considers himself under the necessity of marrying to provide another heir. It is impossible not to wish that the Duc de Chartres, who has a good, quiet, unprincely education, and is said to do great credit to it, is not left to take his chance.

They say that while the cannon were firing to announce the birth of the Duc de Bordeaux,—after the twenty-four (I think) which mark the birth of a female, while everybody was listening for the twenty-fifth which was to announce an heir, the Duc de Chartres said, 'Now we shall see whether I have a wife or a master.'

<hr>

CHRISTOPHE, KING OF HAYTI.

December, 1826.—In a MS. journal of Mr. Courtenay's, I find some curious particulars respecting the family and government of that extraordinary man, Christophe. He says* Henry Christophe was born a slave in the Island of St. Eustatia, the property of a Mr. Vittor. At a very early period he manifested a disposition impatient of control, accompanied with strong natural abilities, which, however, were not improved by cultivation. When he was about seventeen years old, a Frenchman of St. Domingo having, in a casual visit to

* Mr. Courtenay must be considered as speaking throughout.

Mr. Vittor, discovered the talents of Christophe, and purchased him from a master who was very glad to get rid of such a troublesome lad, Henri was removed to Cape Franç ois and apprenticed to a baker, with whom he remained till the French Revolution emancipated the slaves. Soon after he became general of a brigade in the Colonial service. In the attempt made by the French to re-establish slavery, he distinguished himself as a patriot, fighting under the banner of Toussaint and Dessalines; and upon the death of the latter (1811) became King of Hayti; and there he now (1818) reigns, probably the most despotic monarch on earth. At first he manifested a most sanguinary disposition; he has been often known to stab or shoot with his own hands persons in high situations about him, for imaginary offences. Since his authority has been more firmly established, he has relaxed in his severity, and has given his subjects a good code of laws.

Mr. Courtenay describes their arrival at Cape Henri, the capital of the Island of Saint Domingo and of the Haytian Empire, and speaks of the extreme civility with which Sir Home Popham (whom he accompanied) was received. A palace, a guard of honour, a stable of horses appropriated to his use, a splendid table, &c. &c. Cape Henri, when in possession of France, was considered the richest and most splendid city in the New World. The streets are formed by ranges of palaces, all of which, without exception, were burnt or destroyed during the fervour of revolution. The square, in the centre of which is an enormous iron crown, was the scene of many horrible massacres by both parties during the struggle for independence. The French made a practice of nailing the epaulettes to the shoulders of the black officers who were taken prisoners. In this state, so cruelly incapacitated for further service, they were sent back to deter others from following their example. The private soldiers were despatched in various ways; the most common was to sew them up, six or eight together, in sacks, and throw them into the sea, or to boil them over slow fires. After so many inhumanities, their present antipathy to the French cannot be wondered at; although at the conclusion of the Revolution the Haytians had it in their power to revenge themselves most amply, they acted with considerable moderation, and permitted the remains of the French colony to embark on board a British squadron.

Not a circumstance, let it be ever so trifling, escapes the knowledge of the King; his spies are everywhere, and are only known to himself; his memory is so good, that it is said he is acquainted with every person in his army, by character as well as by name and person. In the space of ten years this extraordinary man has corrected all the abuses he found existing, and has so completely organised his government that it might stand the test of comparison with any of those in Europe. Christophe has been very anxious to establish morality in his dominions; and for that reason, has taken the most severe measures to enforce matrimony.   In fact, he obliges every person to marry whom he discovers to be in a single state. All the young girls fly at his approach ; for whenever he meets one, he begins a string of interrogatories. If he finds her unmarried, he generally informs her he will send a husband next day.   He probably sends a black from his regiment of Guards: the lady being as probably, in all but name, a white person.   It is in vain to ex-postulate, even to plead a prior engagement, unless the marriage can be performed before the King's appointed time.   The punishment for adultery is death to both parties; but I understand there is not any instance known in which this law has been enforced to the letter.   On a recent occasion, the Countess Rossiere was sentenced to ride in a state of perfect nudity on the back of a donkey through the streets of San Souci at noonday, and her paramour suffered a punishment still more severe.

All persons have the right of appeal to the King from the courts of law, whenever they conceive themselves aggrieved.   In a recent case of this nature, three judges, who were strongly suspected of corruption, were sent to the citadel of Sans Souci to work as common labourers.   Christophe is absolute in all things; and

---

* He underwent the fate of Abelard.

although he has given his subjects a code of laws, he does not hesitate to break them himself, whenever it suits his convenience or his caprice to do so.   He is the sole proprietor of land, the produce of which is sold for the benefit of the state; no other person can be a free-holder; but tracts of land, at a nominal rent, are granted by lease as a reward for services.   Cattle and sheep are also a royal monopoly, and the revenue more than trebles the expenditure of the country.   The treasure collected in Sans Souci is said to amount to more than forty millions of dollars.

With respect to Christophe's private character, I was assured he is a most excellent husband and father, and has spared no pains in giving his children a finished education.   The princesses have had the advantage of English governesses, and the prince has been brought up by the Baron de Vastey, a clever gentlemanly white man, educated in France.†
I became acquainted with him and liked him much, though many of his countrymen assured me he was a perfect savage in disposition.   The Queen is a well-disposed and very good woman, quite free from the affectation and presumption which generally accompany a rise so very extraordinary as hers.   She

* He was a mulatto, and one of the most remarkable of the race.   He is the author of some creditable works; amongst others, of an *Essay on the Revolutions &c. of Hayti,* published in 1819.

was once, like her husband, a slave; she accompanied him during the whole progress of the revolution, with her children on her back, often without any other food but wild fruit, exposed to every change of weather, and often half-clothed.

At ten o'clock Sir Home Popham and all our party repaired to the palace by appointment: we were received with every demonstration of respect; a guard of honour in state uniforms, each man more than six feet high.

We were conducted through a hall, between two lines of officers, into a large and splendidly furnished room paved with marble and cooled by artificial means. In a few minutes the King and Prince Royal made their appearance; the ease and elegance of the King's deportment not a little surprised me. His dress was a plain green coat, with the Order of St. Henri (his own), white satin pantaloons, and crimson morocco boots. He took his hat off on entering the room, and desired us to sit down. His wool is perfectly grey, his countenance intelligent, and his whole person well proportioned; his manners are pleasing and rather prepossessing. He congratulated the Admiral on his arrival, regretted his distance from Cape Henri had prevented his arriving to welcome us sooner, &c. &c. He paid many compliments to Sir Home Popham, saying he was no stranger to his reputation, and conversing upon the code of signals invented by Sir Home and used by the British navy. He concluded with a pressing invitation to his Palace of Sans Souci, which I much regret the admiral could not accept, being obliged to return to Jamaica. .

The Prince Royal, only fifteen years old, is the fattest fellow I ever beheld, and I should not imagine him half as clever as his father. His dress was as splendid as gold, silver, and jewels could make it; in his hat he wore a large plum of feathers and a diamond star. In about half an hour we retired and left the Admiral tête-à-tête with the King. Their conference lasted about an hour. . . . . When they came back into the room where we were, the King began to quiz the Archbishop, and mentioned the stories constantly invented by the French about him; amongst others that of his having, in a fit of rage, thrown the Prince out of a corridor at Sans Souci. .The Archbishop laughingly observed that they gave him credit for more strength than he could boast, in supposing him capable of even lifting from the ground such a fat fellow. The King the same evening left Cape Henri, the heat of which disagrees with him : when he travels he goes at full gallop, and will keep it up the whole day to the great inconvenience of his attendants.

Not two years after this account was written, the singular and glorious career of Christophe closed in misfortune.* The widow and daughters came over to

---

* His troops mutinied, his deposition was proclaimed, and he shot himself with a pistol. One proximate cause of his fall was

England, having previously resided some time in America in the vain hope that a second revolution would
place the eldest daughter on the throne of the father.
I heard of them passing the winter of 1822-23 at
Hastings, and the following spring I saw the daughters
frequently.   They attended the lectures of Prati,
which I also attended.   From a Madame ———,
whom I often met, I heard a great deal about them;
they were living very quietly in a small house at
Islington, I think, but still preserving their *chambel-
lan* and some little semblance of royalty.   The eldest
daughter was described as a woman of superior talents,
who had taken great pains in cultivating her mind.
She was said to have been the confidante and counsellor
of her father during his latter years.   She spoke French
easily but not well, she had a good figure, and, as far
as I could judge from under a close black bonnet, an
intelligent eye.   The other sister was a heavy, stuffy,
short, fat person.   They were in deep mourning and
very plainly dressed.

---

his incapacity, from palsy, to make the requisite exertions for the
preservation of his authority. His sons were killed by the troops;
his wife and daughters were saved by British protection. The
wife was allowed to carry off her jewels, and a moderate income
was secured to her. See *The Present State of Hayti*, by James
Franklin, 1828; and *Brief Notices of Hayti*, &c., by John Candler,
1842. Christophe's authority only extended over half of the
Island of St. Domingo; and his subjects are computed at not more
than 200,000. His principal revenue was derived from plantations
cultivated by slaves or forced labour.

At one time I heard that Madame —— was thinking of writing a memoir of the life of Christophe, from the information she derived from his daughter.   One day I asked her about it ; she told me that she had quite given up the plan from finding their ideas so different; that many actions which the Haytian considered as *glorious,* she felt so *disgraceful* to the memory of Christophe, that she should have thought herself acting unfairly by his daughter in making them public on her authority; more especially as she could not consistently with her own character mention them without reprobation.   I proposed that the daughter should write the history herself, and only submit it to some person who would correct the language.   My proposal seemed to take; but very soon after that time the Haytians, only then beginning to give up hopes of restoration, left England.   In the summer of 1824 I heard of them travelling in Germany : at this period the King of Bavaria purchased a part of a set of the ex-Queen's jewels (rubies I believe) for a wedding present to his daughter, who married the Prince Royal of Prussia.   In 1826 I saw one of these Haytian Princesses walking in the street at Pisa.   My *laquais de place* called her a Principessa della Morea, spoke of them as living very retired, but knew nothing of the mother, who, I conclude, is dead.

LOUIS XVIII. AND THE FORTUNE-TELLER.

Wynnstay, 1827.—In the year 1791 Lady Malmesbury heard at Coblentz, from Monsieur (afterwards
Louis XVIII.), the following story. He was once tempted
to go in disguise to consult a famous fortune-teller at
Paris : after having heard his own fortune told, he asked
the woman whether it was true that she could prophesy of
those whom she could not see, merely by a view of their
portraits. She answered in the affirmative; and he
produced a picture of Louis XVI. in a masquerade dress,
without any of the insignia of royalty. She had scarcely
seen the picture when she returned it, exclaiming, ' *Ah
Dieu, le malheureux! il perira sur l'échafaud.*'
Monsieur left the woman, laughing in his sleeve at the
idea of having so completely deceived her and exposed
her ignorance; but when he told the story to Lady
Malmesbury, he said, ' *Depuis que tant d'évènemens
se sont passés en France, cela me donne beaucoup à
penser.*' At that period (1791) the King had just accepted the Constitution ; his popularity was at the greatest height,* and no event appeared less likely than his
execution. At the time when the prophecy was made,

---

* He accepted the Constitution (Sept. 18, 1791) three months
after the flight to Varennes, and he was under duress at the time.
A somewhat similar story is told of Bernini, the sculptor, who
was said to have prophesied the unhappy end of Charles I., on
seeing his bust.

several years before the Revolution, the event would certainly have been deemed *impossible*; and it is evident that nothing could have induced the fortune-teller to allude to it if she had known that the picture represented the monarch whose sway was then absolute.

[*From Lady Hart, who wrote down the story immediately after hearing it from Lady Malmesbury.*]

REVENGE.

January, 1828.—Mrs. Kemble told me that at the period of the first appearance of ' De Montfort,' * when everybody was decrying the possibility of the existence of hatred so diabolical, and were calling it quite beyond the bounds of nature, the subject was one day discussed at dinner at Lord Rosslyn's.† He replied that in real life he had known an instance of hatred still more inveterate, and related the following story :—

At a large school in the country a rebellion took place among the boys; the master, very anxious to know the name of the ringleader, at length, either by threats or bribes, or both, induced one of the boys to disclose the name of a boy named Davison. He was, of course, severely punished and expelled, carrying away with

---

* Miss Joanna Baillie's tragedy to illustrate the passion of Hate.

† The ex-Chancellor Lord Loughborough.

him sentiments of deadly hate instead of the affection he had formerly felt for his schoolfellow. Many years intervened, during which they never had the least intercourse. The young man who had peached went to the East Indies. He returned, and landed on the coast of Devonshire. Stopping to dine at a small inn, he enquired of the waiter what gentlemen lived in the neighbourhood, and hearing that the squire of the parish was a Mr. Davison, the name struck him ; he thought he recollected that his former schoolfellow used to talk of his home in Devonshire, and while his dinner was getting ready, he determined to go to the squire's house. A maidservant opened the door, and he sent in his name, saying that if Mr. Davison had been educated at such a school, he would recollect it. He was introduced, and most cordially received by his schoolfellow whom he found laid up with a fit of the gout, and was pressed to dine with many apologies for bad fare, &c. &c. ; Mr. Davison having unfortunately given permission to all his servants to go to a neighbouring place, and having kept only the woman who was his nurse.

Mr. Davison appeared so rejoiced in talking over old stories with his friend, and pressed him so strongly to be charitable enough to pass another day with him, that at last he consented. Next morning the unfortunate guest was found with his throat cut from ear to ear. Of course, the maidservant was taken up on suspicion ; indeed, as it seemed impossible from its nature that the wound should have been self-inflicted, and as she was the only creature in the house excepting her master who was unable to move, there did not seem a doubt. The trial came on: Mr. Davison appeared as prosecutor: Lord Rosslyn was his counsel. In spite of the poor girl's protestations of innocence, the case seemed nearly decided, when Mr. Davison sent a note to his counsel, desiring him to ask the girl whether she had heard any noise in the night. Lord Rosslyn objected; but his client insisted. This seems to have been one of those strange perversions of intellect by which guilt is ordained to betray itself when all the artifice which had accompanied it is lulled asleep. What could have been the object of this enquiry does not appear; its effect was fatal. The girl replied that she recollected hearing a noise along the passage, which had awakened her; but that, having been much fatigued during the day, she was too sleepy to get up to enquire the cause. More questions were asked, the noises and various other circumstances described; suspicions arose against Mr. Davison, and the business ended in his avowing himself the murderer.

He said that, from the moment in which he first beheld the face of his old schoolfellow, he had determined upon revenging his ancient quarrel by the death of the offender. He had crawled on hands and knees from his own room to that of his unfortunate guest, and unable to support himself without the use of his hands, had found great difficulty in opening the door; but helping himself by his teeth, had at last achieved it, reached the bed, and perpetrated the horrid deed; he had then crawled back, and had contrived to free himself from all blood-stains before he got into his bed. It was the extraordinary noise made by his crawling which had disturbed the maidservant, and at last led to his detection.

QUEEN CAROLINE.

We were talking one day of Queen Caroline; a doubt was expressed whether some of the blame which attaches to her character may not be removed by attributing some of her extraordinary actions to insanity, by which alone they can be accounted for. Mrs. Kemble told me she had known, at Lausanne, a man, now a landsman or magistrate, formerly an officer in the Duke of Brunswick's Guards, who told her that it was the general opinion that in early youth the Princess had shown strong symptoms of insanity, and he gave the following instance to prove his assertion:

A great ball was given, to which the Duchess would not allow her daughter, then aged sixteen, to go. The ball was just begun, when a messenger came to the Duke and Duchess to inform them that Princess Caroline was taken violently ill. Of course, they returned immediately to the palace, all the court following them; the

landsman, then on guard, being one among them.
When they reached the antechamber of the apartment
of the Princess, they found she was on a bed in the
next room, screaming with agony; they were told that
she was black in the face, &c. &c. The doors were all
open, when the Duke and Duchess went up to the bed
and tenderly enquired what was the matter. The
doctors were not yet arrived; the Princess said' any
attempt at dissimulation would be useless and impossible. 'I am in labour, and entreat you, madam,
to send for an accoucheur immediately.' These words
were spoken loud enough to be heard by all those who
were waiting in the next room; their astonishment
may be conceived. Soon after the accoucheur came:
as soon as the Princess saw him, she jumped out of bed,
wiped the livid colouring from her face, and with a loud
laugh said to the Duchess, 'Now, madam, will you keep
me another time from a ball?' At this period, whenever she did go into public, there were persons
appointed to watch that she did not give notes &c. &c.;
but it was supposed that she found means to elude their
vigilance.

The idea of the unsoundness of the mind of the
unfortunate Caroline is strongly confirmed by the fol
lowing circumstances, related to me by Lord Redesdale in May 1828. Having been invited to dine
with the Duchess of Brunswick at Blackheath, he
and Lady Redesdale, coming at the time specified,

found themselves long before the rest of the company. They passed half-an-hour *en tiers* with the Duchess, who, having known him from his earliest youth, began talking very confidentially and imprudently of the mis- conduct of her daughter, ending with saying, ' But her excuse is, that, poor thing, she is not right here.' She struck her forehead, and burst into a violent flood of tears.   By this time some guests were heard entering, and Lord and Lady Redesdale were obliged to support the poor infirm old woman to her room, and make the best story they could.

He told me also, and I forget how he knew it to be true, that when the Princess was at Baden and the Grand Duke made a *partie de chasse* for her, she appeared on horseback with a half-pumpkin on her head.   Upon the Grand Duke's expressing astonishment, and recom- mending a *coiffure* rather less extraordinary, she only replied that the weather was hot, and nothing kept the head so cool and comfortable as a pumpkin.   Surely nothing that was said by Brougham or Denman could plead so strongly in extenuation of the nudities of the Muse of History, &c. &c., as the pumpkin.

EXTRACTS FROM THE WORKS OF FRANCIS EGERTON, EARL OF BRIDGEWATER.

Birkenhead : January 23.—Mr. Nugent has just brought me a bundle of the publications on various subjects by Lord Bridgewater; all excepting one of *addenda* and *corrigenda* to an edition of Euripides; and a letter from the *Seigneurie de Florence au Pape Sixto* 4re, 1478—relate to himself, his family or inland navigation. A Life of the Chancellor Egerton seems interesting from the variety of documents, relating more to contemporary history than to his hero, which are thrown into notes; especially a letter from Essex to the Chancellor, who had tried to persuade him to return to the Court and sue for pardon to Elizabeth, after he had received the famous box on the ear. The most singular production is a single sheet beginning—

A report has been generally circulated that I have an intention of writing a life of F. E., third Duke of Bridgewater . . . consequently I am induced on my part to announce to the public that I will not write his life. It is true that for ten or eleven years before his death I and I only lived in the house with him   that I prepared materials with a view of writing his life.   When I reflected more and more continually every day upon what I saw, first I faltered, and lastly I became assured that I could bring neither the faculties of my mind or body on to the accomplishment of this task. How could I bring my mind to the task, were I impressed with the persuasion that the general system of navigable canals and inland navigation ought to be carried forward upon the enlarged, comprehensive, and elevated view of benefiting the public and the country? How could I bring my mind to the task, should I have seen such an object neglected or overlooked by one of the first and greatest subjects in Great Britain (most certainly in Europe), and all things appertaining to the navigation considered as in a merchant's counting-house, exclusively upon the strictest calculations of profit and loss and individual interest ?   How could I bring my mind to the task ? how portray a domestic tyrant, selfish in all things, living for himself alone, regardless of those duties which attach to one who inherits immense estates from a long line of ancestry, unacquainted with even the persons of most of his own family, his own name, his own blood, giving nothing in charity, with no service at home and yet never attending any public worship ? . . . Under all these considerations, and many more, I confess I faltered; I cannot bring myself to the task.   Briefly, therefore, &c. &c.   [Here follows an account like that for the peerage.]

London, 1809.   F. II. E.

Another singular paper is his petition to Louis XVIII. to be exempted from the *Droit d'aubain* on the Hôtel de Noailles, which he had purchased.   The grounds on which he requests this exemption are singular :

Que je suis resté plusieurs années en France, et que pendant tout ce temps je n'ai pas voulu acheter aucune propriété quelconque.   Qu'au commencement de 1815 j'ai changé d'avis. . . . Que je n'ai pas voulu profiter des délais que la loi et l'usage m'accorderaient pour payer les droits d'enregistrement, mais que les circonstances critiques où V. M. se trouvait alors m'ont déterminé à solder les droits le lendemain, 18 mars 1815, la somme de 30,743 francs.   Qu'il est impossible de ne pas reconnaître dans ces paymens onéreux faits par anticipation le vif intérêt que m'inspirait alors la situation de V. M.   Que je n'ai plus tardé à voir de quel œil on regardait ma conduite ; car Buonaparte, sous prétexte d'utilité publique qui exigeait que les bureaux du Secrétariat du Gouvernement passent dans mon hôtel, a mis sous le sequestre mon hôtel, mon mobilier, et m'a ordonné de sortir de mon hôtel, sous peine d'expulsion forcée. Que j'ai défendu mon droit contre Buonaparte, à mon risque personnel et à mes frais personnels. J'ai défendu aussi les droits de tous les propriétaires français. J'ai barricadé les portes et mis mon hôtel en état de siége. Je me suis vu forcé, pour la première fois de ma vie que j'ai su un procès, d'entamer un procès . enfin je me suis vu forcé de passer par mille tracasseries de toute espèce que je crois devoir désigner au Gouvernement réparateur de V. M. . Que les circonstances suivantes sont pleinement suffisantes pour empêcher que la concession en question ne devienne un exemple général. Que je suis allié à la famille royale d'Angleterre. [Here follows a long descent from Henry VII. and from Robert Comte d'Artois, frère de St. Louis.]

In the first instance I put away the addenda and corrigenda to his translation of Euripides, saying to myself, that must be totally uninteresting to me; but one word caught my eye which made me look for others, and in the notes I found a mass of heterogeneous knowledge; some unintelligible to me, being *hérissé de Grec*; some uninteresting; a long and severe criticism on the 'Phèdre' of Racine, much on Jewish customs, some music, some philosophy, some piety, an extract from his own will, &c. &c. In this confused mass I find a note on the original invention of arithmetical numerals in large characters, full of ideas which are quite new to me, and certainly very interesting. He surmises that this mode of numeration was taken from the hand and same system of doubling; he then produced this figure fingers, and resulted naturally from the necessity under which the most ancient proprietors lay of counting the herds and flocks in which their wealth consisted.

Holding up the palm of one of his hands before his eyes, the four fingers furnished him with a ready mark for each of four units; he coarsely imitated them thus, IIII; at five, the mark which naturally suggested itself was that which was made by the forefinger and thumb, thus, V; by adding his units to this he could count to ten; at ten it naturally suggested itself to double the mark already made for five, and thus make twice five; to his first vertical V he added another that was inverted ∧; thus he was enabled to count as far as fifty: at fifty he had to seek another mark for the method by which he obtained the mode of numeration required, and enabled him to procure a new mark at each five; which number, when doubled, makes a decimal, and resulted out of the lines which gave him the figure of his body. He rested the palm of one hand upon one side of the body on the lower ribs, and looking down to the figure presented by his arm, it formed a right angle and presented this figure L; thus he was enabled to count on to one hundred. To obtain a new mark he observed the same method: he doubled the I— which represented fifty; leaving the first mark vertical, he inverted the next, the second accessory figure, the upright, serving for both; the result is ⊏: at five hundred he wanted another figure, and still proceeding on the same system of doubling; he then produced this figure by adding another ☐. He had now obtained his unit, now softened in I; his five, now V; his ten, now X; his fifty, L; his hundred now softened into C; his five hundred now softened and rounded into D: he then doubled the square for a thousand thus, ☐☐; which is now softened into M, or into the letters CIƆ; by which last letters are denoted one hundred minus five hundred, or four hundred, and one hundred plus five hundred, giving ten hundred or a thousand.

It remains to be observed that by this series of operations is obtained the designation of positive and negative quantity; for, upon whatever side shall be begun to be marked the units, whether right or left, the figures placed on the same side denote they are *minus* that figure, as V minus I is IV; five minus two, III, &c.; five minus O is V positive. Again, the figures marked on the other side of the V, or the decimal, denote that they are *plus* that figure; five plus one is VI, &c. &c.*

LETTERS FROM BISHOP HEBER.

The first letter, and extract from second letter, from Reginald Heber to a female relative who had recently lost her husband at Hyères.

Jan. 2nd, 1821.—My dear Charlotte,—I have been for some time back desirous of writing to you, but have

---

* This seems to be now the received origin of numerals.—*Encyclopædia Britannica, Art. Arithmetic.*

been deterred by the fear of intruding too soon on a grief which I was well aware must have its course, and which is necessarily proportionate to the love, strong as death and stronger than the most trying worldly misfortunes, which you have uniformly shown to your husband, and which, as was to be expected and as I have always seen reason to believe, was mutual.   I could not help feeling, too, that your loss was too severe to admit of the ordinary topics of consolation: that the possession of the love and confidence of a man like our poor William, could not in the natural course of things be surrendered without a very bitter pang, and that his abilities and his amiable temper and manners must be recollected by you with regret now that for a time you are separated from him.

You have already been long tried in the furnace of affliction, and God has enabled you during many years to endure the bitterness of separation from loved objects, and in sickness and in banishment to find comfort in that divine religion which it is necessary to be a mourner to know the full value of. I trust and believe that He has not forsaken you now, and that from the same source of resignation to His will and confidence in His mercy, you have been supported and strengthened under this last and severest trial. I need not remind you you have still much to live for; that you are favoured beyond most mothers in the disposition and promising talents of your children,

and that if, as I trust will be the case, your health admits of your return to England, you will have more
opportunity of watching over their education and pro-
moting their best interests than, but for this heavy
visitation, you were likely to have possessed.

There are other considerations, too, which must have
their force in encouraging and enabling you to bear
your affliction. That affliction was sooner or later to
one or other of you inevitable. You must have mourned
for *him* or he for *you*; and if this last had been the
case, recollect how lonely and forlorn his exile must have
been, and that *your* death would have had the effect in
a great measure of depriving your children of *both* their
parents. Even in the circumstances of the fatal accident,
there is much to alleviate its heaviness. An instan-
taneous death without pain, and while engaged in
innocent amusement, is what poor William himself
would perhaps have chosen above most others. It would
have been far more afflicting both to himself and to you
if you had had to watch over a long and painful illness,
to witness suffering which you could not relieve, and
to long for advice and assistance of a better kind
than your place of residence could supply; above all,
it may be a comfort to reflect that, before he was thus
summoned to another state of existence, he had been
purified, and that the chastisements of Heaven have
thus been not only tempered but directed in mercy.

There is one source of consolation more, which I

cannot help mentioning, though from the difficulty and
perplexed nature of the disputes to which it has given
rise, and the abuses which have been grounded on it,
I mention it with great diffidence even to you, and
have never ventured to recommend it generally. Few
persons, I believe, have lost a beloved object, more
particularly by *sudden* death, without feeling an
earnest desire to recommend them in their prayers to
God's mercy, and a sort of instinctive impression
that such devotions might still be serviceable to them
in that intermediate state which we are taught by
Scripture precedes the final judgment. The Roman
Catholics, by their interested doctrines of hired masses
for the dead, and by their unwarranted and melancholy
notion of a purgatory to which even the good are
liable, have prejudiced the greater number of Protestants against this opinion; and it is, I confess, one
which is not so clearly revealed or countenanced in
Scripture, as to make the practice of praying for the
dead obligatory on any Christian. Yet, having been
led attentively to consider the question, my own
opinion is on the whole favourable to the practice,
which indeed is so natural and so comfortable, that
this alone is a presumption that it is neither unpleas-
ing to the Almighty nor unavailing with Him.

The Jews, so far back as their opinions and practices
can be traced since the time of our Saviour, have uniformly recommended their deceased friends to mercy;

and from a passage in the Second Book of Maccabees, it appears that (from whatever source they derived it) they had the same custom before His time. But if this were the case the practice can hardly be unlawful, or either Christ or His Apostles would, one should think, have in some of their writings or discourses condemned it. On the same side it may be observed, that the Greek Church and all the Eastern Churches, though they do not believe in purgatory, pray for the dead; and that we know the practice to have been universal, or nearly so, among the Christians little more than 150 years after our Saviour. It is spoken of as the usual custom by Tertullian and Epiphanius. Augustine, in his Confessions, has given a beautiful prayer which he himself used for his deceased mother, Monica; and among Protestants, Luther and Dr. Johnson are eminent instances of the same conduct. I have accordingly been myself in the habit for some years of recommending on some occasions, as after receiving the Sacrament, &c. &c., my lost friends by name to God's goodness and compassion through His Son, as what can do them no harm, and *may*, and I hope *will*, be of service to them. Only this caution I always endeavour to observe—that I beg His forgiveness at the same time for myself if unknowingly I am too presumptuous, and His grace lest I, who am thus solicitous for *others*, should neglect the appointed means of my own salvation.

But I intended to write a letter of consolation and am got into theological controversy, and I fear I may already have written too much in my small handwriting for your eyes. God bless, God comfort you, my dearest Charlotte! God make your children through their future lives a source of comfort to you in this world, and bring you and them to be with your William in one family in Heaven, through Jesus Christ our Lord.

. . . . I have long owed you my thanks for your letter, and the kindness with which you received my attempts at consolation under a loss which, alas! admits of little effectual comfort, except from the secret support and blessing of the same divine Being who only afflicts us for our good, and who, if we place our hopes in Him, will never lay more on us than He at the same time enables us to bear. But I felt myself at the same time bound to answer the very interesting and very difficult question which you had suggested to me concerning the state of the dead, and their acquaintance with what passes on earth, and I have really had no leisure to give to such a subject the attention which it deserves and requires, nor even to satisfy myself, much more another, with the conjectures (for they deserve no other name) which I have formed. That the inter-mediate state between death and judgment is not one of insensibility, or (as the Socinians fancy) a perfect suspension and interruption of existence, is plain I think from very many passages of Scripture. Thus, when Christ uses the argument taken from the Almighty calling himself the God of Abraham &c., to prove the life after death, he uses it in a manner which implies that the life of which he speaks is uninterrupted, since to make it answer his purpose, Abraham must have been *alive* when God thus spoke, not merely destined to live again at the general resurrection. In like manner, St. Paul speaks of his desire to depart from the world, to be *immediately* with Christ, which he could not have been if after death he were to sleep perhaps 3,000 years till the day of judgment. But, above all, the penitent thief was promised by our Saviour, that he should *that very day* be with Him in Paradise, a passage which will not bear any other meaning than that generally assigned to it, and which in that meaning is conclusive.

As to the condition of the dead, it has been always believed by the Christian world that the souls of men are in situations of happiness or misery—the one not so perfect, the other not so intense, as will be their doom at the day of judgment; and it has been even supposed, and seems likely from all which we know of our spiritual nature, that till that time their happiness or misery must rather consist in hope or fear and the approval or disapproval of conscience, than in any actual enjoyment or punishment; and the early Christians most of them believed that, by the prayer

of surviving friends, the condition of such persons
might be made better, and a milder sentence obtained
for their errors and infirmities from their Almighty
Judge, when the doom of all creatures shall be finally
settled.

This is, as you well know, a disputed point, but it is
one which the wisest and most learned divines have
always spoken of with doubt, without venturing to
blame those who, with becoming humility, recommend
the souls of those they have loved to mercy. But the
notion of a purgatory fire which all, or almost all,
Christians were to pass through as a necessary preparation for heaven, was never dreamt of in the Church till
the ninth or tenth centuries; and the Eastern Churches
to this day have never received it. It is, in fact, a
strange and dismal detraction from the efficacy of
Christ's blood, since the Church of Rome does not
admit those who die impenitent to any share in its
advantages, but sends them to hell immediately; so that
it only throws a fresh obstacle in the way to heaven, in
the case of those whose sins all sides suppose to be
already washed out by the work of redemption.

A more difficult question remains—Whether the
dead know anything of what is passing among men.
On this point I can arrive at no satisfactory conclusion,
any further than that there are some passages in
Scripture which seem very like it. As where St. Paul
encourages us, in Heb. xii. 1, *to run with patience*

our race, from the consideration that we are eucompassed with so *great a cloud of witnesses,* which *witnesses,* you will see in the former chapter, are the good and great men of former times. But I must defer these deep discussions till I have the pleasure of seeing you. In the meantime accept of my best wishes, my sincere affection, and permit me to add, my prayers.

THE RICKETTS GHOST STORY.

November 15th, 1830.—Mrs. Hughes told me the other day that she was writing the particulars of the Ricketts ghost story, as she had heard it related in her infancy by Mrs. Gwyn,* who had been an *eye,* or rather *ear,* witness. The story was alluded to; her aunt stopped the speaker, and begged she would wait till the child was gone to bed. She was not to be so put off, and when the orders for bed were issued she contrived to conceal herself behind the curtain: there she remained undiscovered till the tale had advanced to the hoarse voice, when her terror was so highly excited that it totally overcame her dread of punishment, and she rushed from her place of concealment, falling flat on her face. These circumstances of course strongly impressed

* One of the beautiful Misses Horneck, Goldsmith's friends. She married Colonel Gwyn, and died at a very advanced age in 1840. She was a strong-minded and clear-headed woman.

every circumstance on her ardent mind, and thus she related them to Sir Walter Scott,* premising that Mr. Strong, who was chaplain to Shipley, Bishop of Saint Asaph, had, when at Twyford and in its neighbourhood, frequently heard the legend told in the same manner. She likewise says she has heard the story, exactly the same, from the Duchess of Buckingham. The house alluded to is situated between Alton and Alresford.

My story says † that Mr. L., related to Lord S., was a very atrocious libertine. He was aided and abetted in all his evil practices by an old butler named Robin, who was distinguished by a remarkably deep-toned hoarse voice. Mrs. L. was known to be very unhappy and very ill-used, and was seldom seen by the neighbourhood, who were deterred from visiting at that house by the character of its master; but it became known that a younger sister of Mrs. L. came to visit her, and in process of time a criminal intercourse was suspected between her and her brother-in-law; a child was said to have been born and destroyed by the agency of the butler.‡

So far I am correct in my remembrances, but I am not clear as to the death and dispersion of the guilty trio. I think, however, that old Robin came to

---

* The story is slightingly mentioned as wanting evidence in *Letters on Demonology and Witchcraft*, p. 348.

† The speaker is Mrs. Hughes throughout.

‡ This imputation is not confirmed by the family annals. The lady apparently pointed at died in 1763.

an untimely end, and that Mr. L. grew disgusted with
the house and left it. Be that as it may, the house was to
be let, and was hired by Captain Ricketts for the reception of his family during his long absence from England,
either on the East or West India Station. When he
sailed, Mrs. Ricketts, with three young children and a
very small establishment, removed to her new residence.
I do not precisely remember how long it was before her
quiet was disturbed; but I think it was only a few days
after her arrival that, sitting alone in the evening about
nine o'clock, she was startled by the singular terror
expressed by her cat; the animal started from her
slumbers on the hearth, made a piteous cry, and after
running about the room as if wishing to escape, darted
to its mistress, and rolling itself up in the train of her
gown, lay there panting and exhausted.

Mrs. Ricketts was rising to summon a servant when
her ear was struck by a tremendous noise in the room
overhead; it had the sound of tearing up the boards of
the floor with the utmost violence, and throwing them
about. In a moment the servants, alarmed, rushed into
the room. Mrs. Ricketts, who was a woman of a resolute
spirit, headed the party to explore the room from which
the sound appeared to proceed, but on entering nothing
was seen, and the operations seemed to have been shifted
to another apartment. The whole house was searched
without effect, and the noise continued a considerable
time, varying its apparent station as it was approached.

The next night the annoyance was renewed, and after the floor-breaking ceased, three voices were heard distinctly—that of a female and two males; one of these so remarkably hoarse and dissonant, that one of the servants, who was from the neighbourhood, exclaimed, ' That is like the voice of wicked old Robin.' The female seemed to plead in agony for some boon; one of the men seemed to answer in a mournful grave tone, and the deep hoarse voice sounded angrily and positively. No distinct words could be made out, but now and then the voices seemed so close that, as old Mrs. Gwyn described it, ' you would have thought that by putting out your hand you would have touched the speakers;' to this succeeded a strain of soft aerial music, and the whole ended by a series of dreadful piercing shrieks, altogether not occupying less than half an hour.

Next day the whole establishment gave warning, and were reluctantly dismissed by Mrs. Ricketts, who took the precaution of making them sign their names as witnesses to a short account which she noted in a book, in which she afterwards kept a regular journal of the transactions of each night, continuing the practice of making every servant she dismissed (and she seldom prevailed on one to remain long with her), as well as the few guests whom compassion for her forlorn state induced to come to her, sign their names for a testimony of what they *heard*—for nothing was ever *seen*.

I am not sure whether these horrors were repeated

every night, but certainly so frequently as to leave Mrs. Ricketts neither peace nor quiet, and to produce agitation which affected her health. She had been in this state more than a twelvemonth when Mrs. Gwyn came to pay her a visit. She was much shocked at the altered appearance of Mrs. Ricketts. She had flattered herself that the accounts which she had received from her friend were exaggerated. However, when the usual period arrived, the whole routine went on, and Mrs. Gywn was terrified to a degree which left her only in astonishment that Mrs. Ricketts could have endured so much and so long. I remember her saying that the first burst of noise was as loud as if three or four carpenters had been employed: the whispering conversation often seemed to be close to her ear: and the soft music she compared to the tones produced by a then celebrated player on the musical glasses (Cartwright); the shrieks which closed the whole so sharp as to rend the ear. I remember the comparison the more distinctly, because I had been taken a few days before to hear the performance of Cartwright on the musical glasses. Indeed every particular of Mrs. Gwyn's narration is as vividly present to my imagination as if I had only heard it an hour ago; and the frequent repetitions I have since heard of it from my two aunts, who were also her auditors, have engraved every iota on my mind.

Mrs. Gwyn, though very sufficiently scared, would

have remained with her friend the few days she had promised, if her maid, a valuable faithful servant, had not been made so ill by terror that she could not in common charity oblige her to remain after the second night, when a repetition ensued. She therefore pursued her journey, after having added her signature to the book, which she described as then containing many pages. I remember that my aunt asked her whether Mrs. Ricketts would publish this book, and she replied that, should her friend survive Sir John Jervis (afterwards Lord St. Vincent) and Colonel Luttrell (afterwards Lord Carhampton), she believed it was her intention to do so. Mrs. Ricketts died some years ago at a very advanced age.

Mrs. Gwyn then went on to relate the substance of a correspondence which she kept up with Mrs. Ricketts, recording a circumstance which took place not long after she left her. The bedroom which Mrs. Ricketts occupied was separated from the nursery by a wide passage, the doors of the two rooms being exactly opposite. Mrs. Ricketts slept alone, and had a light burning on the hearth. One night, soon after she was in bed, she heard a heavy foot leap (as it seemed to her) from the window seat and walk slowly to the side of her bed, where it stopped. The curtain was drawn on that side, and she instantly threw herself out of the opposite side next the door, and standing in the doorway to prevent anyone from escaping, called for the nurse. The

alarm was instantly given. While the nurse remained
with her mistress upon guard, the nursery-maid summoned the rest of the servants ; a strict search was then
made, but nothing could be found to account for the
sound which had roused Mrs. Ricketts.

Next day an old carpenter of the neighbourhood desired to speak to her, and to mention a circumstance
which had occurred during the residence of Mrs. L.
He said he had been employed and well paid by old
Robin, the butler, for a job which was done in his
presence and after every other person in the house was
asleep. It was to take up a plank in one of the bed-
rooms, and saw away a joist so as to give room for a
small deal box about two feet long, which the old butler
deposited under the floor, and then the carpenter restored the plank and joined it as well as he could.
He said he had been sworn to secrecy, but as the
parties were dead and gone, he thought he might safely
mention a circumstance which he could not help believing might have some concern with the disturbances.
Mrs. Ricketts made him lead the way, and he went to
her apartment, and lifting up the carpet at the very
spot where it appeared to her the heavy step paused, he
showed her the joining of the plank : by her desire it
was taken up, and the joist, according to his account,
was found removed, and an empty space remained sufficient to contain such a box as he had described. If
it had been there, it had been removed ; no trace of

it remained. You may suppose what the box was suspected to contain.

The only other event I recollect was the return of
Sir J. Jervis to England, his visit to his sister Mrs.
Ricketts, his grief at finding her in such a state of
health and nerves, and his determination to remove her
from a place where he was convinced there was some
foul play. He took upon himself the risk of the displeasure of Captain Ricketts, who had expended a large
sum in settling his family, and whose apprehended
censure had deterred his wife from quitting the residence where he had placed her. Sir John would not
even suffer his sister to sleep another night under
the roof, but removed her and her children to a
farm-house in the neighbourhood, with every servant
belonging to them. He determined, with his friend
Colonel Luttrell, to watch through the night, and detect the imposture which he was convinced had been
carried on.

The ground-floor consisted of a large hall and two
parlours, one on either side: in these parlours the
friends, well armed and lighted, established themselves,
and at the usual hour the noises began. They both
rushed into the hall, each angrily accusing the other of
an attempt to play a foolish trick; but as soon as they
met they were aware the noise proceeded from other
quarters; the plank-tearing, the whispering, the soft
music, the shrieks went on in the usual succession, and

after an active search all over the house they were obliged to acknowledge themselves baffled.

Mrs. Ricketts never returned to the house except for a few mornings, which were devoted to packing, &c. &c. One of these mornings she sat down to rest in the housekeeper's room; her brother sat with her, leaning against a large press which had just been emptied of its contents. They were both startled by a noise close to their ears, which she compared to that of dry bones rattling in a box. Sir John threw open the door of the press, exclaiming, 'The Devil is here, and we shall have him:' however, nothing appeared, and this forms the last link of my chain.

A young friend, who saw much of Lord St. Vincent in his latter days, told me he was extremely angry whenever the subject was alluded to; and Mrs. Gwyn said Mrs. Ricketts was ever averse to the discussion, though she never refused to answer any question that was put to her. And now having told my tale, I must protest my utter disbelief of any supernatural agency. Had I written this during the first fifteen, nay, perhaps twenty, years of my life, I could not have made any such declaration; for this story was the nightmare of my existence, from the age of eleven to that of discretion—if I ever have attained that happy period. I consider it as one of the best planned and executed deceptions I ever heard of, for whatever purpose it might have been wrought. I do not believe the plot

P

has ever been discovered, though the general idea is, I think, that it was to further the purposes of a gang of smugglers.

INSANITY OF GEORGE III.—SIR HENRY HALFORD AND GEORGE IV.

May 1832.—Sir Henry Halford gave us the other day some interesting particulars respecting the malady of George III. He says it is one of the characteristics of that species of insanity, that, about three months after the seizure, there is a great change for the better, which sometimes ends in recovery; in other cases, in a more violent return of malady. He says we shall probably hear of that change in poor Lord Dudley in about two months; whether it will be permanent or not, is more than any mortal can tell. In the case of the King, this change took place in the month of February; it was not only that *hopes* were entertained, but many of the Council were of opinion that he *was* in full possession of his faculties. On one particular day they came out saying that he had spoken so collectedly—1st, on the necessity of sending troops to America, of the persons to command, of the points to which the troops were to be sent; 2ndly, of the expediency of the appointment of a Vice-Chancellor, of the persons best fitted for the office,* &c. &c.— that they

* This fixes the date. The first vice-chancellor was appointed early in 1813.

believed him quite restored and able to resume his power.   Lord Ellenborough used the words of Pilate : 'I find no fault at all in that just person.'

Sir Henry said, this not being his own opinion, he felt his situation an extremely unpleasant one: well knowing the cunning of all mad persons, he was aware that nothing but extreme vigilance would enable them to detect the delusions if they still existed.   One day when the King fancied himself surrounded by servants only, and when a medical attendant was watching unseen, he took a glass of wine and water and drank it to the health *conjugis meæ dilectissimæ Elizabethæ*, meaning Lady Pembroke.   Here was a delusion clearly established and noted down immediately : the use of Latin, which was not to be understood by those whom he supposed *only* to hear him, affording a singular proof of the odd cunning of insanity.

A few days after, Sir Henry was walking with him on the terrace; he began talking of the Lutheran religion, of its superiority to that of the Church of England, and ended with growing so vehement, that he really ranted forth its praises without mentioning that which Sir Henry believes to have been the real motive of this preference—the left-handed marriages allowed.   He was very anxious to see whether traces of this delusion would appear again, and went to the Duke of York to ask for information as to the tenets, practices, &c. &c., of the Lutheran faith.   The

Duke said, 'Watch him in Passion-week ; if he fancies himself a Lutheran, you will see an extraordinary degree of mortification and mourning,' &c. &c. When Sir Henry returned to the assembled physicians he wrote down the substance of this conversation, and without communicating it to anybody, requested those present to seal the paper and keep it in a chest where their notes and other papers of importance are kept, under locks of which each had a separate key. When the Monday in Passion-week arrived, and Sir Henry had nearly forgotten this conversation, he went into the King's dressing-room while he was at his toilet, and found the attendants in amazement at his having called for and put on black stockings, black waistcoat and breeches, and a grey coat with black buttons.

It was curious to hear that his delusions assumed, like those of other madmen, the character of pride, and that a sovereign even fancied himself in a station more elevated than his own. He would sometimes fancy himself possessed of supernatural power, and when angry with any of the keepers stamp his foot, and say he would send them down into hell.

It is always evident to me, that among all these royalties, among the three kings whom he has attended, Sir Henry's partiality is to the one who seems to me to deserve it least, to George IV. He gave us the following account of his first introduction to his intimacy.

He had never attended the Prince, and barely knew him when the last malady of George III. declared itself. Sir Henry was aware that he was surrounded by spies from the Prince; that one whom ' we well knew and would little suspect,' was living at the Christopher, &c. &c.   Anxious to stop this, Sir Henry went to the Prince and gave him the most detailed and most accurate statement of the situation of the King. The Prince expressed his gratitude, not unmixed with surprise at his candour.   Sir Henry promised that henceforth he might depend upon always having from him the most accurate information, if he would only promise not to seek it from any other source.   The Prince gave the promise and (wonderful to say) kept it. Sir Henry then went to the Queen, and told her what he had done. She, with a tremendous frown, expressed great astonishment. Sir Henry stated the obvious reasons for the step he had taken; she paused, her brow cleared : ' You are quite right, Sir ; it is proper that the Prince of Wales should be informed.'   From that moment, as he says, confidence and intimacy were renewed between mother and son.

At the period before mentioned, during the lucid intervals, Sir Henry describes himself as having had a very awkward subject to discuss with the King. The death of Princess Amelia was known to him.*   Every

---

* She died on November 3, 1810. Her illness was the proxi-mate cause of the return of the king's malady.

day the attendants expected and dreaded questions as
to her property, her will, &c.; the bequest of everything
to General Fitzroy was a subject so very delicate to
touch upon. The Queen dared not: Perceval and
the Chancellor successively undertook the disclosure
and shrunk from it, imposing it on Sir Henry. Never,
he says, can he forget the feelings with which, having
requested some private conversation with the King
after the other physicians were gone, he was called
into a window with the light falling so full on his
countenance that even the poor nearly blind King
could see it. He asked whether it would be agreeable
to him to hear now how Princess Amelia had disposed
of her little property. ' Certainly, certainly, I want to
know,' with great eagerness. Sir Henry reminded him
at the beginning of his illness *he* had appointed Fitzroy
to ride with her; how he had left him with her at
Weymouth; how it was natural and proper that she
should leave him some token for these services; that
excepting jewels she had nothing to leave, and had
bequeathed them all to him ; that the Prince of Wales,
thinking jewels a very inappropriate bequest for a man,
had given Fitzroy a pecuniary compensation for them
(his family, by-the-bye, always said it was very inade-
quate), and had distributed slight tokens to all the
attendants and friends of the Princess, giving the bulk
of the jewels to Princess Mary, her most constant and
kindest of nurses. Upon this the poor King exclaimed,

'Quite right, just like the Prince of Wales;' and no more was said.

Sir Henry is apt to be the hero of his own stories, and to boast a degree of intimacy and confidence which I am sometimes inclined to doubt. The history of the change on the subject of the Catholic question is very curious, but I own I feel it rather difficult to believe that Sir Henry was admitted into a secret so closely kept. Be that as it may, his story is that, at the close of the session, the Duke of Wellington wrote to the King a letter which he showed to Sir Henry, stating that he felt the time to be now arrived when the boon of emancipation could no longer be refused to Ireland; telling him that, if his objections remained insurmountable, he must abandon the stronghold of his faith. The Coronation Oath, which had been proved not to hold water as an argument, must not be brought forward again. This letter, Sir Henry says, produced much and very painful cogitation, and agitation enough to have roused the King from his state of indolence to very deep thought. A second letter Sir Henry saw when the King was more inclined to concession, in which the Duke requested leave to impart his intentions to two cabinet ministers and to one or two of the bishops.*

---

* It appears that letters substantially to this effect were written by the Duke of Wellington to George IV. (*Memoirs* by the Right Honourable Sir Robert Peel, Bart., M.P. &c., published by the trustees of his papers, Lord Mahon, now Earl Stanhope, and the Right Honourable Edward Cardwell, M.P., Part 1, pp. 180, 201.)

COUNTESS MACNAMARA. THE BOURBONS.

Richmond: August 1832. — We have just had
Countess Macnamara here : she is as usual full of her
Bourbons, very literally 'plus Catholique que le Pape,
plus Royaliste que le Roi;' for she complains of the
relaxation of discipline in the former, and says that all
the evils of France are to be ascribed to the republican
spirit of its late sovereigns.   Monsieur Dixhuit, she
said to me with the peculiar emphasis which I thought
reserved for Philippe—as Satan is not Monsieur—
Monsieur Dixhuit was at heart a more thorough republican than any man in his dominions.   All his measures
tended that way, and when Charles X. came, poor good
man, who never meant anything but what was right,
he was too indolent to change the ministry or the
measures of his brother.   It would have almost exceeded my belief to have been told that any English-
woman could take up the cudgels for Miguel, but I
heard her pitying him as an illused and calumniated
man, maintaining to my brother Charles, who might
have rather better means of information, that he was
not privy to the murder, not cruel, &c. &c.   All this
is only curious as furnishing a singular page in the
history of human nature, showing how entirely the
wise ultra-Bourbon party, whose echo she is, can over-
look even the radical sin of illegitimate authority when

redeemed by despotism and bigotry. In the midst of all this absurdity, she gave me a singular instance of devotion to her beloved Bourbons, which, being asserted on her personal knowledge, is I suppose in the main true.

A Miss W., who some fifty years ago was an admired singer on the English stage, made a conquest of a Mr. A., a man of large property, who married her. Whether the lady's character was not immaculate, or whether, the march of intellect not having begun, actresses of the best character were not yet reckoned fit society for ladies, does not appear; certain it is that, finding she could not get any society in England, the A.'s went to establish themselves at Versailles, where they took a fine house, gave fêtes, &c. &c. His wealth gave splendour; her beauty, her singing, her dancing, gave charm. The Polignacs came to her fêtes, and afterwards introduced her to the little society, to the intimate réunions, of which Marie Antoinette was a constant member. When adversity befell this object of admiration, of almost idolatry, Mrs. A. devoted herself, her talents and (better than all) her purse to her service.

It was chiefly during the Queen's melancholy abode in the Temple that Mrs. A. most exerted herself. In bribes, in various means employed for the relief of the poor Queen, she expended between 30,000*l.* and 40,000*l.* sterling. This of course was taken under the name of a loan, and soon after the restoration Mrs. A. made a demand upon Louis XVIII.: every item of her account was discussed and most allowed, till they came to a very large bribe given to the minister of police, one to the gaoler, and bribes to various persons, to manage the escape of the Dauphin and the substitution of a dying child in his place. Louis XVIII. would not agree to this article, and insisted upon its being erased from the account as the condition upon which he would order the gradual liquidation of the rest of the debt. To this condition Mrs. A. would not accede: Louis XVIII. died: the accounts were again brought forward. Charles X. was just going to give the order for paying the debt by instalments when the revolution came, and Mrs. A. seems now further than ever from obtaining any part of her money.

It is to me very odd that Mac does not seem to feel that, admitting all her premises, her story tells very much against her beloved Bourbons. She always speaks of the reign of Charles as if it had lasted as many months as it did years, as if he had not had time to execute any of the good purposes that were in his heart. She concludes the history I have just written by saying, 'I had a message for Mrs. A. from *Holy*rood, which I was desired to deliver in person. I had great difficulty in tracing her; at last I found her a week ago,' (she told me where, but I have forgotten). She represents her as preserving remains of beauty at about seventy, *coiffée en cheveux*, with a mask of paint. I gravely asked whether she was still an enthusiast in the cause; to which she replied, ' No,' in what I fancied a hurried embarrassed manner, which impressed me with the idea that Mrs. A. is naturally enough rather exasperated at their conduct towards her. It seems that they are all convinced, and this Mrs. A. is ready to make any oath, that the Dauphin did not die as was supposed in the Temple. The Duchesse d'Angoulême has always said, ' I have no evidence of his death, and know that it did not take place in the Temple, but I have no evidence of his being alive at any subsequent period.'

The rancour of Mac against Louis-Philippe sounds particularly ill *here*: she believes him capable of every crime. In this neighbourhood where he lived so many years, not only there is nothing alleged against him, but every body mentions him with respect. I hear he is now paying small pensions to some of the poor, whom he was in the habit of relieving. Miss Dundas spoke with tears in her eyes of his invariable kindness to her father, who attended his family as physician, and of the attention shown to her brother and her for his sake, when they were at Paris some years ago.

THE OLD WOMAN OF DELAMERE FOREST.

Vale Royal :* November 1832.—Since I have been here I have been collecting all the particulars respecting 'The old Woman of the Forest.' Giving her credit for an inventive imagination, there is enough in the facts to interest one. In July 1815 a report had reached this house that a strange woman was come to live in the forest; many fables, reporting her a heroine in disguise, were already afloat among the servants, when, on the 17th of July, the woman came to this house bringing the following letter :—

'Most honorable and highborn Lady,

My Lady Thumley,

'As I have heard that I am at the present at your property, namely the Oakmere; we are latly comen out of Germany ware I lost my husband; as I cam into England I vind rents so high that I do not know to do for myself without charity, as the same way as most of the people live abroad, so I am gone about to seek some waste ground, for there I can live and provide for myself, for I have a little to make a small beginning, but halas I find that all the commons are forbid now I am at hand this place I am able to live if I may be there but I do not mean to make myself a Paris, for I never intend to submit to Paris ceping, for I belong to

---

* The seat of Lord Delamere in Cheshire.

a foring chappel in London, but I may yet do for myself if I am permitted, therefore I humbly beg my noble Lady you would not deny my this favour to stop here for a few weeks till I write up to London, for I cannot pay for lorging.   I humbly beg that your honor may send some of your trusty servants to enquire and to see ware. We can we shall not trouble anybody for anything nor hurt nor destroy anything, rather protect the remanes of the Trees.

' Most Noble Lady, I humbly beg deny my not a little rest at this peaceable place.

' I your most obliging and humble stranger,

' MARIA HOLLINGSWORTH.

' Oakmere, July 17, 1815.'

The poor woman stated that she was the daughter of a Lutheran clergyman, born at Leuwardin, in West Friesland, in 1765; her appearance bespoke great poverty; but her rags did not conceal the faded remains of beauty, and her manners and language appeared very superior to her situation. She told her little tale with intelligence and simplicity. She said that she had married a British soldier : that she had followed his fate and shared his hardships through many campaigns, till he was killed at Bergen-op-zoom, leaving her with two infant children, a son and a daughter. She came over to England, and through some Hanoverian friends obtained a small pension from Queen Charlotte, and some inferior situation for her son in the Royal kitchen at St.

James's. The motives to which she alludes in her letter were more fully developed to account for her wild scheme of settling on the forest.

She told us how she had procured a small cart, which afforded shelter to herself and her daughter; a donkey to draw it, and two goats, from whose milk they derived a chief part of their nourishment. In many places they had attempted to make some stay, but had always been driven away as vagabonds by parish officers. Beginning to despair of obtaining in England the object of her desire, a solitary abode rent free, she had determined to go to Liverpool, and get a passage to America. Delamere Forest lay on her road; it was at that time quite unenclosed; a dreary waste without any habitation for miles. Here her hopes revived: she found a sheltered spot near the large pool called Oakmere, where she determined to stop to wash her clothes. Making some enquiries, she found the land adjoining to be extra-parochial, the property of Lord Delamere. Here the dreaded parish officer, dressed up in brief authority, could have no power if she once obtained the sanction of the proprietor. Lord Delamere allowed her to live there, and she soon set to work to make for herself a permanent abode. Upon a rising bank above the mere, sheltered by a few Scotch firs, stood two ribs of whales, which had been placed there by Philip Egerton, Esq., of Oulton, who had rented the land from the Cholmondeley

family.   Between these ribs Mrs. H. formed a rude
kind of dwelling, by turning up her cart and making a
wall of sods and a roof of boughs. Thus barely sheltered
from the storm, in a hut about eight feet by ten and
little more than five feet high, did this poor woman and
her daughter live many years.

She became an object of great curiosity in the
neighbourhood.   The most absurd fables were told : it
was even said that Napoleon was living in this strange
disguise.   Visitors began to be attracted by curiosity,
and charity induced them all to contribute in some
shape or other towards relieving the wants of the
poor recluse. As her means increased, she gradually
improved her little dwelling.   She added to her walls,
put in a door and a small casement; and to make her
roof a little more weather-proof, she extended over
it the skin of her donkey, who had died, probably
from starvation.   She hired a labourer for a few days,
made a fence, which enclosed her dwelling and a little
bit of ground, in which she made a potato ground and
a little garden, and a small shed to shelter her goats.
From the produce of that bit of garden, cultivated by
herself, and from that of a few fowls, which in course
of time she procured, she and her daughter contrived to
live; the latter going occasionally to Tarporley market
to sell eggs and vegetables.   She added to her live-
stock a dog, and provided further for her protection by
the purchase of a pair of pistols.

One of her professed objects in wishing for a solitary abode was the leisure it would afford her to devote herself to the education of her daughter, without the dread of bad society and example to counteract her precepts. The girl was taught to read and write English, French, and German. Thus passed some eventless years, during which the numbers of her visitors increased, and her means gradually improved ; occasional supplies came from those who had formerly known her. The first winter was cheered by a welcome present of warm clothing from Lady Bulkeley. In process of time, Delamere Forest was enclosed ; some two or three small cottages sprung up in the neighbourhood of Oakmere, at a distance from any town or village. Mrs. Hollingsworth finding that the children of these cottagers had neither the means or the opportunity of learning anything, offered to teach them to read gratuitously. Unfortunately differences arose, and at the end of three or four years she had quarrelled with all her neighbours.

In the year 18— she received a letter from her son, who had been bound as apprentice to a cabinet-maker at Hanover, informing her that he was on the point of embarking for Buenos Ayres. He added, that as the vessel by which he was going was to touch at Liverpool, he hoped to be able to see his mother before he left Europe. The mother was of course delighted with the thoughts of seeing her long-absent son, and continually watched from a neighbouring eminence every person who strayed towards her lonely dwelling. After many disappointments, one summer evening she saw a man with a satchel of carpenter's tools on his back coming across the forest, evidently seeking some dwelling, and as he drew nearer both mother and daughter felt convinced that they saw him whose arrival they had so anxiously expected. They saw the man stop at a neighbouring cottage, apparently to enquire the way, and dared not go there to meet him. The owner of the cottage into which the traveller had entered was unfortunately one with whom Mrs. Hollingsworth was at variance, one of whom she had a very bad opinion; she had, therefore, the misery of thinking that her son was in the house of one who was her enemy, of one capable of any atrocious action.

Night came on, the traveller did not appear again, and the poor woman returned to her hut, hoping she had been disappointed, and had again mistaken a stranger for her son. Anxiety prevented her from sleeping : in the dead of the night her watchful ear caught the sound of distant footsteps, which induced her to get up. Creeping along, concealed by the low fence of her little garden, she saw her neighbour and his son coming towards the mere, bearing between them a heavy sack; the moon was shining bright. She saw them walk into the water, which was very shallow in this part: she heard a heavy splash. Still the men did not return : they seemed to consult, and fearing that there was not depth of water sufficient to conceal their dreadful burthen, they took it up again, and returned with it to their house. The mother, still more wretched, continued to watch; she saw the two men bearing the sack as before, and having provided themselves with spades, come out and walk across the forest. She followed them at a distance, but her strength would not allow her to keep up with them, and she soon lost sight of them. Still she watched, and in about half an hour saw the father and son return to their cottage, carrying the sack empty.

Now, firmly convinced that her murdered son had been buried, she returned to her hut to brood in silence over her misery; she felt that her suspicions rested solely on what she alone had seen, and dreaded to make them known to anyone. However, she very soon saw that a cart was added to the stock of her neighbour, that he appeared in a good new suit of clothes, and thought these evident signs of wealth, which were not in any way accounted for, a strong confirmation of her suspicions. She went by night and dug about that part of the forest where she had lost sight of the supposed murderers, but was always interrupted and prevented by other neighbours. She then went to Mr. Wilbraham,* who had before relieved her wants, and implored his assistance, as a magistrate, in her search for the body.

---

* George Wilbraham Esq., of Delamere House.

Thus far the tale of the old woman, frequently repeated to my sister, goes. What follows is Mr. Wilbraham's account:

The old woman said she had had a violent fever; and had, in a vision, seen all that to my sister she afterwards described as an actual occurrence. Mr. Wilbraham, willing to humour her fancy, sent the overseer with a labourer to dig wherever she directed. This search proved wholly fruitless; but soon after, Mrs. Hollingsworth having heard that the body of a man had been found in a pond at Marbury, near Whitchurch, she went there immediately, and asserted that she knew the corpse to be that of her son, which after having been buried in the forest had been removed and carried for greater security to this distant pond. She afterwards went to Liverpool, where she said she discovered that a young German exactly answering the description of her son had landed from a Hamburgh ship, and had enquired his way to Delamere Forest, on the very day on which she saw the traveller in conversation with the supposed murderer.

Mr. Wilbraham, hearing this, thought further investigation necessary : he wrote to the chief of the police at Liverpool, stating the facts of the case, and requesting him to make every enquiry. In answer to this application, he heard that a young German had certainly landed on the day specified, but that all the rest of the tale was a fabrication. Soon after, Mr.

Wilbraham being in London called upon Mr. Gollermann, who had been employed as an Almoner to Queen Charlotte, to distribute her bounty to the distressed Germans in England. After having told the whole story, Mr. Wilbraham requested him to make some enquiry in Hanover about the young Hollingsworth. The result was, he was reported to be alive and well. Mr. Wilbraham, determined to leave nothing undone that would satisfy the mind of the mother and establish the innocence of him whom she had accused, wrote to the young man, strongly urging him to come over to tranquillise his mother. Some weeks afterwards, he and his sister came to Delamere House. She fully recognised him, so did the mother, but she did not seem happy; she evidently could not bear that her story, which had made much noise, should be so totally disproved. Hollingsworth went to Manchester, and got employed in his trade of carpenter.

This is the substance of what Mr. Wilbraham wrote down for me. Strange to say, after all this, the old woman always persisted in saying to my sister and me, that, though appearances were so much against her that she could not maintain it, her own conviction must ever be that the young man was an impostor and no son of hers. The daughter more than joined in these assurances, and even went so far one day as to declare to us that the young man had made love to her and wanted to marry her. I understand the supposed murderer (whose name I have never heard) is now living at Tarporley respectably. In the strange tale of the old woman, I cannot help believing there was much of self-delusion, and that, when that was removed, she had recourse to falsehood to bolster up her fallen credit: but it seems to me quite impossible to say exactly where delusion ended and deception began. I see that my sister and I should not fix the boundary at the same place: she has more faith in the old liar than I can have.

It was not till some time after this strange occurrence that I happened to see the woman for the first time: we went to her hut; she was then (1827-8) living quite alone: her daughter's education being finished, she sent her to London to be confirmed and to seek a service. The mother's pride seemed highly gratified in reading to us a letter which she had received from her daughter. It was written partly in German, and partly in English; the former was translated to us, and very much was I astonished at the language, sentiments, and intelligence of the writer. She began by describing her wonder in first seeing London: a great deal of very proper feeling not unmixed with cant (as I thought), was expressed as, with respect to her confirmation, she spoke of the kindness with which she had been received by their friends, and of a play at Covent Garden, to which they had taken her, which she seemed to bewail as a sin, and assured her mother it should never be repeated.

She then spoke of the family in whose service she had been placed by the clergyman of the Lutheran chapel.

Mrs. Hollingsworth gave me the idea of a very shrewd woman, who in good language, though her pronunciation was decidedly German, expressed strong religious feelings, mingled with such uncharitable opinions of all mankind, that I could not but term her religion cant. It was at this time that she gave my sister an MS. of about twenty folio sheets, containing a history of her life. I read it aloud, and can only recollect that it did not even reach the period of her marriage; that, with much cant and more long-windedness, it afforded rather an interesting picture of primæval manners and a long list of suitors whom she had refused. I felt that, with much curtailment, this might have made an interesting beginning to her strange story. I lament now that I did not write this at the time. At a subsequent visit she told us that she began to find her absolute solitude very dreary, and that as age and infirmities increased she felt it not safe. She added that by the interest of the Lutheran clergyman and of other friends, she had obtained an admission to the Dutch Almshouses in London. She had just been giving a leave-taking tea drink to two gossips, her neighbours, and had a letter from her daughter; and it was then that, speaking of the *man calling himself her son,* and some of the evidence against her statement being brought forward, she said, 'I know that very well. I know what everybody says and believes, but if the whole world were to tell me that this piece of paper was black, I could not contradict them, but I never could be persuaded that it is not white.' Before she went away she gave my sister a German Prayer-book, for the use of the Lutheran chapel at St. James's. In the first page is ' *A. M. Hollingsworth ein geschenck van der Gravien van Munster, door middel van de goede vrow Goltermann.* This book was given me by the Countess of Munster through the virtues of Mrs. Goltermann. I desire me Lady Delamere to take it in rememberance of me, Anna Maria Hollingsworth, July 11, 1829.' At the same time she sent to Vale Royal as a tribute of her gratitude, the last of her family of goats, with the following rude lines:—

THE PERTITION OF A KIDD.

A lonesome stranger creves a boon,
  To rove within the shade,
In your spacious park allone,
  An hopes your frindly ade.

My friendly dame is going to leve,
  The place ware I did dwell,
I humbly begg do me resieve
  An use a stranger well.

Then I will in return agien,
  Cheer your lonesome walk;
In all my nature still remane,
  In innocence with you talk.

In June 1832 we went to Bishopsgate Street, in search of the Dutch Almshouses, which are in a court near there. A low arch with a gate opened into a paved passage or alley. At a little shop next door we enquired whether Mrs. Hollingsworth was still in the Almshouses, and whether she could come and speak to us at the carriage door; a young woman told us that she was her daughter just come (from Pimlico, I think) to see her, and she would go in and fetch her if she was well enough. The poor soul came coughing and so weak she could hardly reach the carriage, but she seemed quite delighted when she saw my sister, whom her daughter had not recognised. We got out, found at the end of the alley seven or eight steps, down which we went to a court, round which were built about a dozen small houses. Our old woman had a room about twelve feet square, neat and tidy, full of old rude knick-knacks; amongst others a sort of model of the hut in Delamere Forest. As far as one could judge during the short time we remained, the woman seemed contented, but sinking fast. The daughter, a decent-mannered person, with language very superior to her appearance, told us she was in service, and could seldom get leave to come and visit her mother. We enquired about the MS. we had seen, and asked whether she had ever concluded it, which we found she had not, and that she had given what we had seen to a bookseller at Manchester. Both mother and daughter vehemently repeated their assertions that the traveller was not their relative; and at last the daughter asked how she could acknowledge or consider as a brother a man who had attempted to seduce her and wanted to marry her.

MADAME D'ARBLAY.

March 1833.—I have been reading the life of Dr. Burney by his daughter, and am more disappointed than I can express. We were well aware that her style, always affected, grew more so in each successive work; but that the authoress (the unaided authoress, I firmly believe her) of 'Evelina' could write such stuff as I have just read, I should hardly have thought possible. Her overweening admiration for that very insignificant personage, her father, I can forgive. I can believe it was quite equalled by Miss Edgeworth, so very much the superior of Madame d'Arblay in talent. But I cannot endure her excessive personal vanity, her nauseous repetition of all the compliments made to her under the shallow pretence of telling the world how much pleasure the paternal heart of Dr. Burney derived from them. Then all this absurdity and arrogance is made more disgusting by her frequent allusions to her extreme modesty! Look at the genuine modesty of great talent in Miss Edgeworth's memoirs of *her* father; admire the good taste with which *she* speaks of her works, the anxiety with which she allots a share in their production far larger than any reader is inclined to allow to her father.   How I wish she would fulfil her promise, and let us see in her long-talked-of work what she can do without him.   From what I heard last year from her nephew, I fear that a distrust of her own powers may chill their energy.   He told me that she has not to anyone imparted the title, or even the subject, of the work in which she is engaged; that the dread of producing something inferior to the fame which she has acquired seems to act as a bugbear upon her imagination, and he fears may prove a decided check to it.

After all, Miss Burney's book has been valuable to me, it has proved a hook by which I have caught some very interesting stories; among others, one which strongly exemplifies the ignorance in which Napoleon kept France of everything which he did not wish to publish. Madame d'Arblay had been with her husband in France for some years, when the events of 1814 restored, with the Bourbons, the communication between England and France.   Madame d'Arblay hastened over to see her family.   Dr. C. Burney told my uncle that his sister was dining with him a day or two after her arrival. The china or earthenware which he used happened, with the word *Trafalgar*, to be ornamented with various emblems of that victory.   Madame d'Arblay, pointing to her plate, said, 'What can this mean, brother?' 'I think if you look at the word, Trafalgar, you will not need any other explanation,' was the natural answer.   'But what can that mean?' rejoined she; and in short it turned out

that it was the first time she had heard of the battle
with which all Europe had seemed to us to ring.

Madame d'Arblay in her book speaks of some verses
by Canning, which were read to the Princess of Wales
by Mrs. A. Hayman ; who tells me this is not true :
they were promised, but Canning said he had burnt
them upon reading 'De Montfort,' dismayed by the
example of the Quizzer destroyed.*

SIR WALTER SCOTT.

My uncle gave me a curious account of the introduction of Mr. Scott to the Princess. Mrs. Hayman, in sending the invitation to my uncle (Lord Grenville), added a
personal request that he would come early to protect the
poet (for as such only was he known), who she believed
would not know any one other guest. Scott arrived late,
was only presented to the Princess just before she went
to dinner ; at table, his place was of course far removed
from hers, and little if any conversation took place
between them. Very soon after the gentlemen came
up from dinner, the Princess said, ' Mr. Scott, I hear you
have a great collection of stories which you tell remarkably well : pray let us hear one.' Without any dis-
claiming speeches, without hesitation, almost without

---

* De Montfort's hate had been exasperated by the ridicule and
irony of his victim.

delay, Scott began, 'Madam, there was once,' &c. &c. The story was much applauded : another was called for and followed with equal facility.

My uncle mentioned this as an extraordinary feat of self-possession and ready wit. I am certainly not inclined to doubt the extraordinary talents of Scott, but in this instance many circumstances appear to me to diminish the wonder. The trade of Scott in his character of London and Edinburgh lion was as decidedly at that period that of a teller of stories as it has since been that of a writer of novels. The tales had probably been told a hundred times, and on this occasion his friend Mrs. Hayman, I doubt not, gave him a previous hint of what would be asked from him.*

To this I cannot help adding a story of the embarkation of poor Sir Walter Scott at Portsmouth, which I heard from Dr. Somerville last June. He was touring

---

* Scott mentions this dinner in a letter to Mr. George Ellis, describing his visit to London, dated April 7th, 1806 :—'I had also the honour of dining with a fair friend of yours at Blackheath, an honour which I shall long remember. She is an enchanting princess, who dwells in an enchanted palace, and I cannot help thinking her prince must lie under some malignant spell when he denies himself her society.' His popularity dates from the publication of the *Lay of the Last Minstrel*, in 1805. At a later period and after a longer practice in being lionised, in 1809, he made extremely light of his own social accomplishments. 'All this is very flattering,' he would say to Mr. Morritt, 'and very civil. If people are amused with hearing me tell a parcel of old stories, or recite a pack of ballads to lovely young girls and gaping matrons, they are easily pleased, and a man would be very ill-natured who would not give pleasure so cheaply conferred.'

with his family in 1831, and learnt at his arrival at the hotel at Portsmouth, that Sir Walter was there waiting the pleasure of the wind for embarkation. They went into his room, and with an exclamation of pleasure made the usual enquiries after his health. Sir Walter rose, and in advancing to meet them tottered, and would have fallen on his face if the strong arm of Dr. Somerville had not supported and borne him back to his chair. When he was a little recovered, he said, 'After what has just passed, it is quite needless to answer your question; you *see* how I am. It is all here,' added he, striking his forehead. 'Take warning from me, Mr. Somerville, and spare your head. I have brought this on myself by taking too much out of me.' Sir Walter sailed October 27th, 1831.*

PARTY FEELING IN FRANCE.

July 1833.—I have just heard from Dr. Somerville a strange instance of the virulence of party feeling now raging in France. He had shown some civilities to a Monsieur and Madame de ———: they vowed eternal friendship in a few days. Some time after this, the Somervilles went to Paris: their dear friends, the de ———'s, were absent, and did not

---

* Besides other reminiscences of Sir Walter Scott by Dr. Somerville, these diaries contain a complete copy of Sir William Gell's; but they have all been incorporated into the *Life* by Lockhart.

return till the Somervilles had been some time settled, indeed not till the Doctor had returned to England. Great was the joy of meeting, and that of the de ————'s did not evaporate in professions. Parties were immediately made to show those sights to which favour alone could gain admission, a dinner proposed, &c. &c. The day after their first meeting, Madame ———— being in the carriage with Mrs. Somerville, asked her whether she had been to some party or sight past. 'No,' answered Mrs. Somerville, 'it was unfortunately at the time when I was at La Grange,' (the country seat of La Fayette). The genuine Frenchwoman expressed her surprise by a start, a bound from her seat which made Mrs. Somerville tremble for the springs of her carriage: then followed a string of '*Mon Dieu! est il possible*!' &c. &c., 'that *you*, such a woman as you, should visit such a man? There is not a person belonging to the *bonne société* who would speak to you if you were known to have been in such company.'

Mrs. Somerville repeated that she had not only passed a week at La Grange, but considered it as one of the most agreeable she had spent in the whole course of her life, and that she hoped to repeat the visit. Her friend said that she felt under great obligations to Mrs. Somerville, had conceived for her an affection which nothing could shake, 'but I own to you,' she added, 'had this been our first interview, after what has just passed, it should have been our *last*. However, I have one favour to ask of your friendship, *et je vous la de mande à genoux.* You are to dine with me on such a day: *au nom de Dieu,* I entreat, do not mention the name of La Fayette, or in any way allude to this visit. Of the party invited to meet you there is not one individual who would not, after such an avowal, avoid you as if you came from a plague-house, or would ever speak to you.' Mrs. Somerville replied, that she would never wittingly speak on a topic unpleasant to the master of any house where she found herself a guest: at the same time, as she never did anything she was ashamed of, she would not shrink from her friendship for La Fayette, if, in the course of conversation, she was questioned on the subject.

Dr. Somerville tells me that, even under Napoleon, the police never was so active, nor so expensively organised, as under the Citizen King. When the Duchesse de Berry was wandering about, the strictness about passports was most absurd. Dr. Somerville went with Mr. Hankey to the Passport Office, where every individual was then expected to appear, and all, even children and maids, were obliged to have their separate passports, describing person, age, &c. Dr. Somerville, having seen this ceremony performed on the four elder children, at last said to the official, 'I see you are a gentleman, and I am convinced that a secret entrusted to your honour will, in spite of everything, be in safe keeping. I will, therefore, in strict confidence, tell you an important secret : you see there the Duchesse de Berry in disguise,' and he pointed to the youngest child, a girl of four years old, who, upon being looked at, hid herself under the table. The officer, laughing, said: ' *Que voulez-vous, monsieur? Je sens comme vous tout le ridicule de ce que je fais ; mais les ordres nous viennent d'en haut ; nous devons obéir à la lettre.*'

A few days after this, Dr. Somerville departed by the *Malle Poste* : being within a few miles of Montreuil, he missed his passport, and consulted the *conducteur* as to what he was to do ; he fully expected to have been lodged in a prison till he could in some way have been identified, and asked whether he had not better tell his tale and surrender himself at once. The *conducteur*, hearing that he was known to Quilliac, at Calais, promised, if he would only lean back in the cabriolet, he would pass him through the gates without any enquiry. However, he had not an opportunity of proving the total uselessness of the tiresome passport, for a few minutes afterwards it was found in the straw at the bottom of the carriage.

MANUSCRIPTS OF TASSO.

Rome: December 1833.—I have just picked up a very interesting account of some late discovered books and manuscripts belonging to Tasso. I copy the memorandum written for me by Mr. Horner, to whom these papers were shown by the Conte Alberti:

'When Tasso was imprisoned, his manuscripts were all seized and put into the hands of Guarini, the author of the "Pastor Fido," and then minister of state of Alfonso, Duke of Ferrara. He was shortly afterwards sent on an embassy from Alfonso to the Court of Florence, and failing in the object of his mission, was subsequently dismissed. Still, either designedly or by accident, he retained the manuscripts which the death of Tasso had rendered comparatively unimportant to Alfonso, and on the death of Guarini they were inherited by his son Alessandro Guarini, from whom they passed into the hands of Carlo Tomaso Strozzi. They were purchased from him by a person of the name of Foppi or Foppo, and finally came into the possession of the Falconieri family at Rome. With their descendants the MSS. remained till the Conte Alberti, hearing that these books existed and were but lightly appreciated by their owner, became the purchaser of them, at a very small price. The Conte Alberti being in reduced circumstances, and finding the inconvenience under a despotic government of being the possessor of manuscripts, by which he had been already led into very unpleasant situations, he has offered these for sale to the Grand Duke of Tuscany. After having subjected them to the most rigid scrutiny, which has satisfied him as to the authenticity of these papers, Leopold has made the liberal offer of 1,000l.;

R

the bargain, however, has not yet been closed, and I imagine that, were a larger sum offered from any other quarter, Conte Alberti is at liberty to take it.

'I myself saw only three of the books; one of them was a compilation of sonnets all written upon scraps of paper, backs of letters &c. &c. incorrect, but abounding in beauties, and interesting as portraying the progress of the poet's passion for Leonora, and also clearly establishing the fact of his only feigning madness in obedience to the commands of Alfonso, who wished thus to screen the reputation of his sister. There may be about 100 sonnets. I also saw the " Laborinto d'Amore " given to the poet by Leonora, in a cover embroidered by her own hand in allegorical devices. It is in very good preservation, and in the first leaf is a sonnet written by Tasso, which alludes to this circumstance. The third was a Virgil, full of marginal notes written by him. I believe there are many other books rendered interesting by the annotations of Tasso, which are to be sold with the rest; among them, I know, is a treatise by Aristotle on the " Art of War," from which the poet has evidently derived as much knowledge of military tactics as was necessary for the composition of his " Gerusalemme." There is also either a part or the whole of that poem in the author's handwriting as it was originally composed, not as he afterwards gave it to the public.'

Thus far Mr. Horner wrote for me to send to England, in hopes of procuring a better bargain, not only for

Conte Alberti, but for the *world*. He told me that
Leopold is supposed to be so jealous of the reputation
of his predecessors, or more probably so deeply im-
bued with the Austrian fear of giving publicity to
invectives against princes, even when so many centuries
have covered their ashes, that he has absolutely prohibited the publication of any of these books. Conte
Alberti says he should be sorry that they should go out
of Italy; but he fears they may be as effectually buried
in the *private* library of the Grand Duke as they have
been in that of the Falconieri. If he could but be
assured that they will be deposited in the Lawrentian
Library, where the public might have access to them,
he would be satisfied.*

DUCHESSE DE BERRY.

Rome, Jan. 3rd, 1834.—I have picked up here
some more strange particulars about the extraordinary
history of the ci-devant Duchesse de Berry. I had

---

* Alberti's collection eventually turned out to be composed of
some of the most curious literary forgeries on record. Only a part
of the first volume which he brought out was genuine. All
the rest have been declared by competent authority to be spurious.
His pretended miniature of the Princess Leonora was discovered
to be a copy of a miniature of a lady of the noble family of Trotti.
The complete detection took place in 1843, in the course of an
action brought by a bookseller of Ancona to whom part of the
MS. had been sold.

been astonished, with many others, at the manner in which she was received here.   I had heard that the Pope had deputed Cardinals to welcome her, had assigned her a guard, and had given a sanction to the sort of Court which she attempted to keep up.   Yesterday, Mr. ——, the brother-in-law of Cardinal W——, cleared up this mystery.   It seems that the present Pope, then a Cardinal, was really the person who first introduced Deutz to her notice.   He therefore consi-dered himself as the innocent cause of her ruin, and as bound in conscience to reach out a strong hand to save her from utterly sinking.   It seems now the universally received opinion that Deutz is the father of the child which is just dead.   Whether Lucchesi Palli has any right to that which is to be born, seems very doubtful.

The infatuation of the unhappy woman seems perfectly incredible; she might in so many ways have averted the open disgrace of the catastrophe.   There can be no doubt that the French Government would have been too happy to allow her to escape quietly.   One of her own near friends told Miss A—— (from whom I heard it) that the Queen of the French wrote to her frequently in the kindest manner and strongly urged her to escape.   In one of the Queen's letters was the following striking expression—'*Dans tous vos malheurs, rappelez-vous que vous n'avez pas à porter cette couronne*

---

* Gregory XVI.

d'épines qui me pèse.' Any one of those ladies, so fondly, so firmly devoted to her cause, would have taken upon herself the child of disgrace: it was not the first nor the second even, and all had been quietly managed before. It seems perfectly clear that, if Deutz was not the father, it must have been a married man, or one who could not be passed off as her husband. Then when they were to buy one, one should think they might have found a better than Lucchesi Palli, who was known never to have left the Hague for twenty-four hours during the fourteen months which preceded the birth of the child.

LOUIS PHILIPPE.

Rome: Jan. 20*th.*—I dined yesterday with Sir Coutts Trotter: so happening to talk of Louis Philippe, he told me an anecdote strongly illustrating the more amiable parts of his character. Sir Coutts said he had never lived in intimacy with the Duke of Orleans, but the Duke had had many transactions of business with their house. He then went on to relate, that, passing through Paris a few months ago, he left his name at the Tuileries: the next day, to his great astonishment, he received a message to say that the King was very anxious to see him, and that he must dine with him in private that day. Sir Coutts of course obeyed, and found himself sitting at table with the King, Queen, Duke of Orleans and one of his brothers, and some of the Maréchaux, without more form or ceremony than 'we have at this table,' said he. He was ordered to take the Queen into dinner, and of course to sit next to her. The conversation turned chiefly on England, on those whom they had known there. The Queen spoke of the wonderful change in her situation since they had met in England, and added, ' *Mais j'étais bien mieux, je me trouvais bien plus heureuse quand j'étais de l'autre côté,*'—meaning in the Palais Royal. Here the King, who was sitting exactly opposite on the other side of the table, interrupted the conversation with ' *Mais, Sir Coutts, je vous assure ce n'est pas de ma faute si nous nous trouvons ici.*' He went on to say how often he had remonstrated with Charles X. on his measures : how he had foretold exactly that which did happen afterwards ; and all this was said in the presence of five or six other persons.

I found that Sir Coutts, like myself, believed what they said to be true,—that Louis Philippe had not sought the painful pre-eminence in which he finds himself. There is one thing which must be allowed : of the very many English who were formerly thrown into contact with him, almost all speak highly of him. I have never heard of any one person who found that the Duke of Orleans at the Palais Royal, or Louis Philippe at the Tuileries, had forgotten the kindness or hospitality shown to the exiled son of Égalité. This is much more than can be said for those of the *Branche ainée,* who one and all *ont tout oublié* in this sense as well as in that in which it was originally said.*

LÉONTINE FAY.

Jan. 6th, 1835.—I have seen Léontine Fay, and think her nearer Mars than any actress I have ever seen. She is so quiet, so ladylike, in her manner; her coquetry seems so *genuine*. Her husband Volnys is perhaps even superior to her. In *Le Quaker et la Danseuse* he was perfect in everything but his dress. Is it not strange that, on the French stage, where accuracy of costume is in general so strictly studied, a Quaker should appear (and that in England) in a blue coat and white waistcoat? Then it is an abuse *du privilege qu'ont tous les français d'être ignorans* to call solemnly upon Ben Jonson as the founder of the sect to look down upon every breach of the strictest rule of morality: '*Ah, Ben Jonson, qu'aurais tu dit?*' and this not once but several times repeated; and the performers seemed quite unconscious of the cause of the laughter of the audience, evidently wondering that this part of Volnys' acting should prove so entertaining.

* Miss Wynn was probably alluding to the *mot* attributed to Talleyrand, but really written of the emigrants by Le Chevalier de Panat to Mallet du Pan, from London, 1796: *Personne n'est corrigé : personne n'a su ni rien oublier ni rien apprendre.*

CHARLES KEMBLE.

June 11*th*, 1835.—Saw last night C. Kemble as Hamlet: he is wondrous stiff and old. I had been reading in the morning his daughter's memoirs, in which there are occasionally passages of genius, of great discrimination, and good sense. I was struck with an observation on the disadvantage of representing tragedy in a small theatre which would be admirably fitted for comedy. It is not only the foil and tinsel which lose on nearer inspection: the expression of the stronger passions becomes coarse &c. &c. How I felt the truth of this last night, when I looked at Kemble's wrinkled face, at the coarser Mrs. Glover (the Gertrude): perhaps, too, the quality of Ophelia's voice might have been refined by distance; her tone was harsh, but her acting not bad enough to shock one, which is more than I can say for most of the performers.

The great error of Kemble seems to me, that he substitutes sneering scorn for dignity, and, truth to say, gives great force to some passages of the part, the ' little more than kin and little less than kind,' for instance; the scene with Rosencrantz and Guilderstein ; the play scene ; but he made a very awkward job of lying at Ophelia's feet; he sate in the midst of the little stage very stiff, and evidently rising with difficulty. The scene of the King at his devotions and Hamlet's speech are omitted, and I for one do not regret these expressions of diabolical revenge. I was surprised at the scene with the Queen; it was so much better, quieter, more son-like than I expected; there was also more of regret for Polonius than seemed to belong to the cold Kemble school. I never was so much aware of the fault of the bungling catastrophe, especially of the absurdity of Hamlet's stabbing the king in the midst of his court, without one hand lifted to prevent the outrage.

MR. COESVELT'S PICTURES.

June 18*th*.—Went to see Mr. Coesvelt's pictures, and return convinced that, for my own pleasure, I should prefer that to any collection I know in London; perhaps one reason is that it is so entirely Italian; another is that, among the pictures, there is not one of which the subject is disagreeable; no disgusting nudity, no painful martyrdom, &c. &c. He has both increased and diminished the collection since I saw it in Brook Street, four or five years ago. He has two or three very fine Raphael's; one that I am inclined to place higher than any one I know in England; that is from the Alva collection. There is an Infant St. John, whose look of pure intense adoration towards the Infant Christ is finer than almost anything I know. I should say that Parmegiano is here on his throne; that here I have learnt to value him more highly than I have ever done before. Still I do not like his large pictures as well as the smaller ones; there is one large one recently added to the collection which Mr. Coesvelt values very highly, but which I think a rather French and *manieré* Parmegiano.

A few days afterwards I went to see the King's pictures, and felt that they lost much by comparison with Mr. Coesvelt's. Perhaps their inferiority in my eyes would be expressed in a very few words—*their* boast is Flemish, Mr. Coesvelt's pictures are all Italian.

BALLOONS.

July 7th.—Went yesterday to see the aerial ship as they call the new balloon. It is very interesting, though I cannot believe that it will actually perform the voyage from London to Paris, in about six weeks from the present time (if the wind is perfectly fair), in five hours. The form of a cylinder with conical ends, and the various contrivances for admitting or excluding the atmospheric air, seem to place it a little less at the mercy of the wind than former balloons. Still the directing power, or rather the stemming power, is quite wanting. They have the power of raising themselves into the higher regions of the atmosphere, where they may expect another current, or may go almost upon the sea, as the buoyancy of the whole machine would prevent it from sinking. Still it is owned, that if there is a wind against them, even such as would only carry them five miles an hour, they cannot go. Therefore it seems to me utterly impossible that the machine should ever be brought into use as a conveyance; but I suppose that for scientific purposes it might be useful in investigation, and perhaps were navigation still dependent on winds and tides and the power of steam undiscovered, it might have been of real use. The gallery in which the passengers are to go, seems to me perilously slight, and obviously unequal to the encounter with any severe weather. The ribs or joists of the floor are covered only with basket-work, which seems very insufficient for a number of persons (the crew alone is seventeen) to tread with safety.*

MR. DAVIDSON'S EASTERN STORIES.

July 14th.—How I wish I could fix here one quarter of the amusement and information which I have derived from the conversation of Mr. Davidson, the eastern traveller; he seems to me like a man walked out of the 'Arabian Nights' bodily. When, just after dinner, he began a story in which Oriental salutation formed a feature, he to our great surprise jumped from his chair, repeated a few Arabic words, which he translated,

---

* It would seem from this description, compared with that of the French monster balloon, that the art of aerial navigation has made little progress in the last thirty years.

'I devote myself to you in thought' (he struck his forehead); 'in love' (striking his heart); 'in deed' (showing his hands); 'from the crown of my head to the sole of my foot'—so saying, he prostrated his length (full six feet) on the floor at Charlotte's feet. Then, from under his neckcloth, he pulled a beard full twelve inches long, told us of a Frenchman very recently dead, whose beard showed the ointment flowing from Aaron's beard 'even to the hem of his garment' to be no figure. This man's was so long as to sweep the ground when he sate down, coal black and very fine: it was regularly anointed and incensed, the fumigation passing between the throat and beard held out.

'Little facts (he said) curiously illustrate the unchangeableness of the grandiloquent Eastern character. A very few years ago, a troop of Mamelukes, riding near Constantinople, stopped some shepherds, from whom one of the Mamelukes requested a draught of milk they had just drawn. Having drunk it, he refused the wretched remuneration required, telling the shepherd it was but too much honour for him to furnish milk to a Mameluke, and utterly despising the threats of the outraged shepherd, who declared he would have justice, if he applied to the Sultan himself. He actually made his complaint within the hour, and brought his adversary before the distributor of justice. The Mameluke utterly denied the whole transaction, declaring he had not drunk a drop of milk. The modern Solomon settled the difference between the conflicting testimonies by ordering the defendant to be opened, that it might be ascertained whether his stomach contained milk. Of course the milk was found, and the poor shepherd received some fraction of a farthing, being the lawful price of his commodity.

'Strong murmurs began to rise among the troop of Mamelukes, who thought death rather a severe punishment for such an offence, and seemed a little inclined to avenge their companion. Upon this, the judge (I am not sure whether it was not the Sultan) assured them he should never have thought of putting to death a Mameluke for taking a little milk from a shepherd, who was, in fact, too highly honoured in furnishing him refreshment; but that the soldier had been proved guilty of telling a lie, had disgraced the name of Mameluke and deserved death for that offence. This explanation, of course, delighted the whole corps.'*

I was asking one day about Lady Hester Stanhope. He did not see her, having arrived just after the death of her only English companion, who having begun as maid, ended as secretary, friend, &c. &c. He describes her, as others have done, turning night into day, and sleeping through the daylight, with very weak eyes and without any decided pursuit but astrology. He says

---

* This story, so far as relates to opening the stomach of the soldier, is told by Gibbon of one of the barbarian monarchs who overran the Empire.

she has lost much of her power, or rather, of her widely
extended influence; still possessing the most arbitrary
authority over her own small district. This diminution
of power may be ascribed partly to her increase of
years, which prevents her from riding and showing
herself among them, partly to the want of that novelty
which dazzles, but chiefly from the want of money,
from the weight of debt, which prevents her from
spending among them the annual income which she
derives from England. Upon this subject he gave us
a story curiously illustrative of Oriental character.

About two years ago, Lady Hester went into Persia,
with a view of obtaining assistance and protection from
the Shah. She provided a present of English goods,
which was really very handsome. This was (according
to etiquette) offered to the Shah by means of the inter-
preter, through whom were also sent the thanks with
all the grandiloquence of the East; his sense of the
magnificence of the present: sun, moon, and stars were
all eclipsed: gratitude was described in the same terms:
their admiration for the spirit, liberality, greatness of
mind, of the English aristocracy: of which he felt,
the influence so strongly, as to be aware that to the
English the true way of showing the sense of favours
received was to gratify their noble nature by asking
more. Aware not only of this, but that his poor empire
did not contain anything worthy of being offered to the
great English lady, he would ask of her the favour of

a loan. Her project (which the Shah had discovered) was to borrow money from him which she never could have returned.

July, 1835.—Another visit to Mr. Davidson, to me far more interesting than the last; when the chief topic of discourse and object of investigation were his arms, though curious, beautiful, and even awful, when you come to arrows, of which the slightest scratch will infuse a poison producing inflammation and extensive discoloration, and to a lance which he does not remove from a scabbard, fearing the accidental ill-effects that might arise from handling a point which has been three years in the poison of the Upas-tree. Still all this was not in my way. Yesterday he showed us the model of the Pyramids, and instead of giving us a lecture upon the subject, entered into a sort of discussion with Mr. (Sir Gardner) Wilkinson, the traveller, and author of a very celebrated work on Thebes. Davidson has a theory of his own on the subject of the Pyramids. He considers them as signs or monuments in commemoration of the Deluge, deriving the present name from Py (the) Aram (ancient). The most startling fact which he told us was, that in Mexico and on the coast of Coromandel there exist to this day pyramids of still greater magnitude than the Egyptian, but not as high. One of those in India is said to be a mile between each angle, but not as high as the Egyptian. All are of antiquity far beyond any tradition; all face the cardinal points; all have the entrance to the north; and this entrance is never in the centre of the side on which it is placed.

These points of coincidence in buildings so very remote, in three different quarters of the globe, are certainly very curious; but I should find it very difficult to believe that, if these edifices had the distinction which Mr. Davidson assigns to them, they would never be mentioned in the Bible. By Mr. Wilkinson's book, I find their existence is proved by hieroglyphic inscriptions to have been as remote as the time of the Pharaoh of Joseph. The cause of the various measurements of the base of the great pyramid of Cheops is that, sand having accumulated round it, it is not easy to ascertain the height from which to measure; of course the least difference makes a very great one in the circumference. The base is called 728 feet, the perpendicular height 500 feet: it occupies eleven acres, and is equal in extent to the whole of Lincoln's Inn Fields, from house to house. Humboldt's measurement of the great pyramid of Chobula in Mexico: height 172 feet, base 1,355 feet square.*

EASTERN MAGIC.

Heard from Mr. Wilkinson the other day a curious account of the juggler, fortune-teller, or more properly, seer (Qy. is this the origin of the name?) who has long

* In Ward's *Mexico*, the height is stated as 177 feet; base, 1,778 feet square.

been established at Cairo. I heard the same report from Mr. Davidson of this trial; and that given by Mr. Yorke (now Lord Hardwicke) of another to Miss Walpole coincides in every material particular. A boy under ten years of age is taken out of the street, selected by the enquirers; he is placed in a circle, magic characters described, magic words repeated, a drop of ink is put into the palm of his hand; he is asked what he sees there, and after a short time he says that he sees a monarch on his throne, attendants, &c., and seven standard-bearers, with flags of different colours. He is then, by permission obtained from the monarch (supposed to be the Devil), empowered to see any person who may be required.

When this English party went, they got an English boy, speaking Arabic; he was kept many days in their house, to prevent communication; all the forms were gone through; the boy was excessively frightened: Lord Prudhoe was called for by his English name, quite unknown by any person at Cairo; the boy, puzzled, said, 'I see a Frank, but he is in a Turkish dress,' describing that always worn by Lord Prudhoe—his sandy whiskers and beard, a dagger or sword, with a silver scabbard; known to all the party, &c. &c. They tried experiments, too, with Cairo boys; all began with exactly the same rigmarole about the sultan, the standard-bearers (Mr. Davidson lamented that he had not observed whether the seven colours

S

named were the primitive), and proceeded in the same
way. One person evoked was Shakespeare, whose name,
they say, could not have been known; the boy described
the pointed beard and ruff; in six trials, four descriptions were exact, the others absurdly the reverse. Mr.
Wilkinson spoke very coolly; said, 'Nobody could be
more incredulous than I was; indeed, I regret that I expressed so much incredulity, because they were more
cautious, and I had no opportunity of investigating the
matter; but I could not discover any trick.' Lord
Prudhoe has certainly received some disagreeable
impression, and desires his friends not to question him
on this subject; he said this to Miss Walpole. Lord
H—— told her he feared that the English boy had
never been in his right mind since the scene.

Charlotte * writes (Dec. 1835): 'The only thing in
which we have been disappointed is in the Cairo magician. After some trouble we got the right man (Lord
Prudhoe's), and picked out our own boy, who was to see
the figures in his hand. We had three, who all at first
saw the same things in their hands on the ink; it
enlarged; figures with different coloured flags appeared,
and then a man with a crown; but to none of the boys
did the figures we called for come up. How the first
part was contrived, we cannot make out; we had the
man in our own room, and the boys certainly did not
know anything about the matter; one of them, an

* Mrs. Rowley, then travelling in the East with her husband
and brother.

Italian, was so frightened by the sight of the flag-bearers, that he burst into tears and would not go on. The magician really seemed astonished at his failure, and of course said that it was the first time,' &c. &c.

Scott, in his ' Egypt and Candia,' gives a more particular and more satisfactory account. He begins by providing his boy. The magician commenced his operations by writing some characters on a long slip of paper, &c. &c.; then, after wiping the boy's forehead (from which fear already made the perspiration start), he stuck another piece of paper, covered like the former with hieroglyphics, under his skull-cap, so as to throw a shadow upon his eyes, and prevent his looking up. Taking the boy's hand in his, the magician then described with ink a square figure in the palm, drawing divers figures in a very mysterious manner. Finally pouring a quantity of ink (quite a pool) into the boy's hand, he was desired to keep his eyes steadfastly fixed upon it, and his head was forced down to within a few inches of his hand. The magician began muttering some unintelligible jargon with great rapidity till he was nearly breathless. He sprinkled incense, coriander seeds, &c. into a charcoal fire, then consumed one of the sentences written on the long slip of paper, then asked the boy repeatedly if he saw anything; upon receiving a negative, observed, he feared the lad was very stupid. The boy, half frightened, was spurred into intelligence; with some more efforts he saw a little boy.

' Has he not something in his hand ? ' ' Is it not a flag ? '
' Yes, yes ; he has a flag.'   In this way the boy was persuaded that he saw seven flags, seven tents, the Sultan,
and a large army—then comes the jugglery of the naming
a person who is to appear to the boy, who is to describe
him ; he failed most completely in every instance but one.

' A lady of the party afterwards took the lad's part,
and though fully convinced of the absurdity of the
juggle, fancied she saw a flag and two stars.   We
tried to persuade her that it was the reflection of her
own eyes, and of the slip of paper dangling from her
forehead ; but she became so much excited, that her
friends would not allow her to remain longer under the
magic influence.   The conjurer refused to try his art
upon grown-up males.   The delusion is evidently
produced by gradually working upon feelings already
predisposed by superstition or other causes to the
necessary state of excitement ; as the diseased system
of a dreamer makes the victim believe that he sees
anything brought to his imagination.   The fumes of the
incense, the unearthly sounds, were enough to cause a
wandering in the boy's ideas, and the constrained posture
of the head, and the fixedness of his eyes upon the
shining pool of ink which reflected *ad infinitum* his
own black face and bright eyes, may easily be supposed
to have completed his mystification.' *

* Eöthen's trial of the Chief of the Magicians at Cairo is one
of the most characteristic passages in the book.

JEROME, KING OF WESTPHALIA.

Wynnstay, Sept. 1834.— We were talking of the characters of several members of the Buonaparte family. Mrs. Bowles * told us a curious anecdote of Jerome. At the period when he was King of Westphalia, Hyde de Neuville—who, I think, was *ostensibly* French minister, and *certainly* French spy over him—represented to Napoleon that, in various instances, he was doing wrong; for instance, that his army was ill-disciplined and ill-managed in every respect. Napoleon promised the minister that his representation should be attended to; and that, by the next messenger, a strong remonstrance should be sent to Jerome. It so happened that the despatches were delivered to him at the table where Hyde de Neuville was dining with him. Of course he, anticipating their contents, watched their effect on the king; he saw a frown gathering on his countenance but very speedily dispersed, and at the same time marked a tall grenadier, who had brought in the despatches, standing behind the chair of the king, and evidently reading over his shoulder. Hyde de Neuville could bear silence no longer. He hoped his Majesty had received good news from the Emperor, of his health, &c. &c. 'Excellent!' was the reply, 'and towards me his expressions are peculiarly kind and flattering.'

He then read the letter. Compliments on the state

---

* The Honourable Mrs. Bowles, sister of Lord Palmerston.

of the army, expressions of high approbation, of
every point of conduct upon which he anticipated
blame, struck Hyde de Neuville dumb with astonishment. He soon after contrived to have a conversation
with the tall grenadier on the subject of the Emperor's
letter, cautiously expressing surprise at its gracious
tenour. In reply, he owned to the having read the
letter (this Neuville well knew); and said he never had
been so astonished as at the readiness with which, in
reading it aloud, the king turned all the strong censure
which it contained into approbation. This story was
told some years after by Hyde de Neuville to Lord
Palmerston, from whom Mrs. Bowles had it.

DR. PLAYFAIR'S PATIENT.

Dec. 30th, 1835.—H. C———* told me that Dr.
Playfair, the shrewd, plain, very straightforward Scotch
physician who attended him at Florence, was talking to
him of a consumptive patient (he was so diplomatic,
he would not even tell the sex), who for some months
had been as well aware as his physician that his
state was quite desperate. The patient, who was inclined to scepticism, had held many conversations
and disputes with Dr. Playfair on the subject of a
future state. The last hour was evidently come,
but he did not seem aware that he was worse than

---

* Hugh Cholmondeley, now Lord Delamere.

usual. Dr. Playfair sate by him (for I can feel no doubt of the sex), watching the ebbing breath, the voice becoming from debility hardly audible, when in a tone as strong, as clear as that of health, the dying man said, '*I know.*' Dr. Playfair thought he alluded to some trifling thing respecting his medicines; 'Oh no, you don't: I know a great deal better than you.' His patient said, 'You are mistaken; you do not understand me; you *do* not know; I *did* not know; now *I do know*;' and so saying expired.* C—— was so struck with these singular words, that he asked Dr. Playfair's leave to write them down in his presence.

BARON OSTEN'S ACCOUNT OF HIS ESCAPE FROM THE JAWS OF THE LION IN 1827.

(*Transcribed from his own MS. extract from his Journal.*)

May 20*th*, 1827.—We heard again of some bullocks having been killed in the same jungle where we had killed three lions on the 14th. On the strength of this information we set out immediately, and found a whole family of lions. We killed five, but I had a very narrow escape of being killed by one of them. After

---

* 'They who watch by him see not, but he sees—
Sees and exults. Were ever dreams like these?
Those who watch by him hear not, but he hears;
And earth recedes, and heaven itself appears.'
Rogers—Human Life.

having killed four, I had wounded a fifth, and Grant, with five pad-elephants, was beating towards me, when he roused the wounded lion, who immediately attacked and wounded one of the elephants. He then came straight at me. I bent a little forwards over the howdah to take a steady aim at him, when unfortunately the forepart of the howdah gave way, and I fell, with all my guns, right on the top of the lion, who immediately seized hold of me. I broke my left arm in the fall, and got a severe blow from the lion on the head, which considerably stunned me. I felt and recollect, however, that he was tearing at my right arm, and I never can forget the horrible gnarling noise he made. Grant's and all the other elephants turned tail and ran away, so that I was left alone helpless in the jaws of the lion.

How I got out of them alive is to me a miracle, and I cannot otherwise account for it than by giving credit to my mahout's statement. He says that his elephant backed about fifty yards, but that he succeeded after some time in driving her up close to the lion, when she took hold of a young tree and bent it with great force over the lion's back, when he relinquished his prey, and was soon after killed by one of the chikarees (chasseurs on foot). When I came to my senses, I found my left arm broken, a severe contusion on my head, and eleven wounds from teeth and claws in my right arm.

Another similar catastrophe occurred this day. A lioness was actually tearing one of the chikarees to pieces, when a fortunate shot of Grant's killed her, and saved the poor man's life; but he was desperately wounded, his blade quite laid bare, the blood streaming from his head and face. I underwent three times the painful operation of having my broken arm set, twice by natives in the jungle and a third time at Kurnmaal, where I was removed in the evening, and laid up for three weeks, when I was well enough to be carried to Meerut. Poor Grant accompanied me to his house at Kurnmaal, but after ten days he sallied forth again, as he said, to revenge my fate. He left me in the greatest spirits, and in better health than he had enjoyed for years. Four days after, he was brought back a corpse, having fallen a sacrifice to cholera-morbus. A more liberal, kind-hearted man, and a better or keener sportsman, I never met with.

MEXICAN MORALS AND MANNERS.

Nov. 1836.—Read yesterday a very entertaining letter from Mrs. Ashburnham, the wife of the newly appointed consul to Mexico. Her account of the manners, of the ignorance, profligacy, and devotion of the natives, strongly reminded me of Majorca; the (so-called) ladies living in their bed-rooms, or in their kitchens—every wife with one lover at least, who passes the life-long evening puffing his cigar at her feet—a lady receiving company with six dragoons sitting *on* the bed *in* which she was talking of nothing but house-hold affairs—every woman, even those of seventy, *coiffée en cheveux,* with one flower stuck perhaps in the grey locks, which do not hide the redness of the head; children from their birth for some years with an *edifice* of satin, gold, &c. &c., erected on their wretched little heads. She says that they have an opera, much better than could have been expected in such a society; that there the ladies are always dressed with a species of fire-fly in their hair: these fire-flies are certainly more brilliant than any diamonds, but they must be not only living, but lively and kept in a state of agitation to emit this light; then they protrude their six ugly legs. What a horrid tickling, crawling sensation they must give!

The houses are described as built round a court like all Spanish houses. Cages filled with the beauti-ful birds of that climate are suspended as lamps are in our rooms; the court and galleries full of flowers, the galleries especially of one plant which the hum-ming-birds particularly affect; but they are described as so shy that they do not perch even for a minute. Mrs. Ashburnham speaks of her astonishment at receiv-ing from a lady she hardly knew, a message to say, that ' she kissed my hands and begged to inform me that she had another devoted servant at my disposal, whom I was in all things to command and on all occasions.'

This simply meant that she was brought to bed, and was as well as could be expected. These notices are sent every nine or ten months from every well-regulated family all over the town.

AUTHORSHIP OF JUNIUS.

Jan. 1837.—I have had a great deal of conversation with Lord Braybrooke on the old subject of Junius. I see he puts little faith in the promised revelation of the mystery by the Duke of Buckingham,* and I may as well, before I proceed, write all I remember of what the Duke told me some five or six years ago. He said that, examining some papers of our grandfather (George Grenville), he found a letter which entirely cleared the matter; that he had immediately written this to Lord Grenville, and had offered to exchange his secret information for that which he had always understood was in my uncle's possession. No answer was returned, and the Duke said that, as it was evident that Lord Grenville did not wish for any communication on the subject, he thought it more delicate towards him not to make it to anyone as long as he lived. Four years

---

* The first Duke. The chiefs of the Grenville family succeed each other thus : 1. Earl Temple, son of the Countess Temple ; 2. Earl Temple, son of George Grenville, died 1779; 3. Earl Temple, created Marquis of Buckingham, died 1813 ; 4. Marquis of Buckingham, created Duke in 1822, died 1839; 5. Second Duke, died 1861; 6. Third Duke, now living.

have now elapsed since the death of Lord Grenville, and nothing is made known on the subject of Junius.

Whether the Duke is still restrained by delicacy towards my dear surviving uncle,* whether subsequent discoveries have cast a doubt upon that which he considered so positive, I of course know not. At the time when he told the above to Lady Delamere and me, he was in a very communicative humour, allowed us to question, and promised to refuse to answer unless he could reply truly. He said that Junius was not any one of the persons to whom the Letters have been ascribed; that, from the situation in which he found the paper in question, he had every reason to believe that his father had never read it. I know that very soon after my uncle's (Earl Temple's) death he told Charles that he had found a private letter from Junius to my grandfather. Nugent, I understand, was with him when the paper was found; indeed, I believe was the first to open it, and of course, partakes in the secret.

The impression left upon the mind of my sister by this conversation was, that Lord Temple was the man. If so, he must have had an amanuensis in the secret, for the hand of a Secretary of State must have been too well-known in all its manner not to have been discovered.

The same objection has been made to the supposition

---

* The Right Honourable T. Grenville.

of Lord Chatham, and has been removed by a conjecture that the letters were transcribed by Lady Chatham.

From all that I have been used to hear of *little* Lady Temple—thought so *very little* by all the younger members of his family—I am inclined to think that the same conjecture could not apply to her; that hers was not the pen of a ready writer, that in her orthography even, she was (according to the fashion of that day) very deficient.*

Lord Braybrooke conceives the pretensions of Sir P. Francis as being better supported than those of any other of the candidates for the authorship. In support of this assertion, he told me a singular story. Giles, whom we all remember so well, told him that when his sister, Mrs. King, was a young Bath belle, she received

---

* The facsimiles given by Mr. W. J. Smith, in the third volume of his edition of *The Grenville Papers* are in a good clear hand, betokening a ready penwoman. In that volume he has printed three private letters to Mr. George Grenville, supposed to be from Junius, prior to his adoption of that signature. These three throw little or no light on the disputed question of the authorship. I have heard the late (the second) Duke of Buckingham make a statement similar to his father's, and leading to a conclusion that he, too, was in the secret. The strongest argument against Francis is, his obvious wish to enjoy at least the posthumous reputation of the authorship, and his inability to leave any proof better than the copy of 'Junius Identified,' bequeathed to his wife. When that work was published, he saw and had some conversation with the publisher, whom he impressed with the conviction that he was by no means offended at the imputed identity. Mere similarity of style in compositions *subsequent* to the publication of the Letters proves little or nothing.

anonymously a copy of love verses; that some years after Sir Philip Francis owned himself to be the author of these. It happened that the mystery long attached to these verses had induced her to preserve the original paper, and upon comparison with the autographs in Woodfall's edition, it proves that the handwriting is the same as that which Junius *feigned*, and not his natural hand. Mr. Giles, to establish this curious fact, had Sir Philip's verses exactly copied in lithograph, and gave one of the copies to Lord Braybrooke. He has inserted it in his 'Junius,' and promised, but afterwards forgot, to show it me.

Lord Braybrooke told me that there was a moment when he expected some very interesting information on this subject. The present king, William IV., gave him a message of apology to Lord Grenville for having driven, by a mistake of the coachman, close to the house at Dropmore, began talking about my uncle's supposed knowledge of the secret of Junius, and added, 'I will tell you what my father said one day to me upon this subject. He was, after every attempt to discover the secret, quite as much in the dark as any of his subjects; but he added: 'I will tell you, my son, now that you are grown up and can understand them, what are my conjectures upon the subject.' One can imagine the anxious curiosity of Lord Braybrooke at this preface, and his extreme disappointment at the conclusion, 'I am convinced that it cannot be the work of any *one* person, and that several were concerned.' * Now, setting aside the evidence of unity of style and purpose, which is strong against this supposition, it would make the mystery even more wonderful than it has appeared—indeed, one may say, impossible.

Lord Braybrooke told the King an anecdote connected with this, though perhaps not much to the purpose. Lady Holland, in one of her imperious moods, made Rogers go to Sir P. Francis to pump him upon the question of authorship. Her unwilling angry ambassador returned, and was of course very closely questioned ; he was sulky, and to the leading, ' Come, tell me what you have discovered ? ' replied, ' I have found out that Francis is Junius—*Brutus.*' Lord Braybrooke said it was quite evident to him that the merit (such as it was) of the reply was quite lost upon King William, whose acquaintance with Junius Brutus, if it ever existed, was quite lost.†

---

* This is hardly reconcilable with a statement attributed to George III., soon after the cessation of the letters, that ' Junius had been provided for and would write no more.'

† The evidence touching the Junius Brutus story is curiously conflicting. Lady Francis, in her letter to Lord Campbell, says : ' He (Sir Philip) affronted poor Sam Rogers, whom he liked so much, to avoid an ensnaring question.' Mr. Prescott writes from London : ' Perhaps you have heard of a good thing of Rogers, which Lord Lansdowne told me the other day he heard him say. It was at Lord Holland's table, when Rogers asked Sir Philip Francis (the talk had some allusion to Junius) if he, Sir Philip, would allow him to ask a certain question. ' Do so at your peril,' was the amiable

This forgetfulness, strange as it is, is perhaps less so than that of Lord Euston. A few days after the publication of Woodfall's 'Junius,' Nugent, seeing it on the table of the Duke of Grafton, turned to Lord Euston and said, 'It is an odd coincidence to see this book for the first time in this house.' Lord Euston stared and asked, 'Why should it not be here?'

GOOD SLEEPERS : MR. PITT—THE DUKE OF WELLINGTON.

At the same time I heard an interesting story upon the authority of Mr. Grenville. He told Lord Braybrooke that at the time of the mutiny at the Nore, when, of course, the anxiety was intense upon the subject of the fidelity of the troops, a messenger arrived at a late hour of the night to Dundas with a letter from

reply. If he is Junius, said Rogers in an undertone to his neighbour, then he must be Junius *Brutus'* (*Ticknor's Life of Prescott*, p. 314). Moore relates the story with the addition that Lord Brougham was by (*Memoirs*, vol. vi. p. 66). But Rogers' own version (given in the *Table Talk*) is : 'I was conversing with Lady Holland in her dressing-room, when Sir Philip Francis was announced. "Now," she said, "I *will* ask him if he is Junius." I was about to withdraw, but she insisted on my staying. Sir Philip entered, and soon after he was seated, she put the question to him. His answer was, "Madam, do you mean to insult me?" and he went on to say, that when he was a younger man people would not have ventured to charge him with being the author of these letters.'

General ——, who had the command at Sheerness, containing the melancholy tidings of the apostacy of the marines. It was stated that, to a man, they had joined the mutineers, and that there was every reason to apprehend that the next day they would march upon London. Dundas went immediately to Lord Grenville with the news, and together they went to Mr. Pitt. He was in bed and asleep. Of course they roused him, talked over this misfortune, consulted as to the precautionary measures to be taken, few and unavailing as they seemed. After a short time, Mr. Pitt said, 'I think we cannot do anything at this hour of night, and as far as possible, we have arranged everything for the morning. I am anxious to get some sleep to recruit before the arduous day which awaits us, and shall wish you good night.'

The two others were far too anxious for sleep. I believe they remained together till, in the course of less than one hour, another messenger appeared bearing another letter from Sheerness. This was from the officer second in command, who, after many apologies for assuming an office that did not belong to him, said that, having heard that the commanding officer had just sent off a messenger with despatches, he felt it his painful duty to inform the Government that the fatigue, the excitation of that eventful day had proved too much for the General, and had produced a sort of delirium; that probably, therefore, he might not have stated very accurately the state of affairs. He had the satisfaction of being able to say that they wore a much better aspect: that the marines were all staunch; so were the officers to a man; and the evil spirit which had existed seemed to be in a great measure quelled, &c. &c. Lord Grenville and Dundas went once more to Pitt to communicate a change even more unexpected than it was favourable. He was, as they anticipated, in bed; but great was their surprise when they found that, during the short anxious hour that had elapsed since their last visit, he had been fast asleep.*

This is called a proof of greatness of mind. I am more inclined to believe that youth, health, and fatigue produce a sort of absolute necessity for sleep, which no mental excitation can remove, and I am confirmed in this opinion by hearing that, in his after days and especially in his last illness, poor Pitt never

---

* Earl Stanhope (*Life of Pitt*) tells the story thus: 'A strange instance of Pitt's calmness at a time when all around him shook, was wont to be related by the First Lord of the Admiralty at that period. On a subsequent night, there had come from the fleet tidings of especial urgency. Lord Spencer thought it requisite to go at once to Downing Street and consult the Prime Minister. Pitt being roused from his slumber, sat up in bed, heard the case, and gave instructions. Lord Spencer took leave and withdrew. But no sooner had he reached the end of the street than he remembered one more point which he had omitted to state. Accordingly he returned to Pitt's house, and desired to be shown up a second time to Pitt's chamber. There, after so brief an interval, he found Pitt, as before, buried in profound repose.' (Vol. iii. p. 39.)

could sleep. The Duke of Wellington is always brought forward as the most extraordinary instance of a person who, under the most violent excitations of his eventful career, could always and at all hours of the day or night, get sleep during any repose, however short it might be, that circumstances allowed. Perhaps great bodily fatigue enabled him to find tired Nature's sweet restorer. I wonder whether he is a good sleeper *now*.*

I hear, that not long ago, one of the many officers who have written memoirs of his campaigns

---

* There is much good sense in this observation, but what enabled the Duke to sleep was his power of fixing on a course of conduct, doing or ordering to be done all that was necessary, and then dismissing the subject from his mind till the time for action came. This is the point of Alava's remark (ante, p. 153). It is impossible to be a great commander, or even a truly great man in any line, without this power ; for without it both mind and body will prove unequal to a strain. There are two instances of its display by the Duke not generally known, and resting on the best authority. On arriving personally before St. Sebastian, he was informed that the breaching batteries would not open for two hours. 'Then,' said he, turning to his aide-de-camp, 'the best thing we can do, Burghersh, is to go to sleep.' He got off his horse, slipped into a trench, sate down with his back against one side, and was fast asleep in a moment. Lord Burghersh (the late Earl of Westmoreland) did the same.

The other occasion was, when having endured great fatigue, the Duke had gone to sleep in his tent, after giving strict orders not to be disturbed. An officer came in from the rear-guard—the army was in retreat—to say that the enemy were close at hand. The aide-de-camp on duty thought the contemplated emergency had arrived, and woke the Duke. 'Send the man in.' He entered. 'You have been hotly pursued the whole day.' 'Yes, my lord.' 'Are the troops much tired?' 'Dead beat, my Lord.' 'Then the French must be dead beat, too—they won't attack to-night. That will do.'

wrote to beg permission to dedicate his book to the Duke. He declined the dedication in a civil kind manner, alleging as his reason the extreme difficulty of ascertaining the real facts in the midst of scenes of such confusion as great battles, and his reluctance to giving the sanction of his name to any inaccurate statement. He gave as an instance of his assertion, the story so frequently told, so universally believed as to have acquired the character of indisputable fact, that he met and conferred with Blücher at *La Belle Alliance*; the fact being, that they did not meet till some hours after, and at another place, the name of which I have forgotten, if I ever heard.*

Before the officer and aide-de-camp were well out of the tent, he was fast asleep again.

On the morning of one of his greatest battles, Napoleon had to be awakened by his staff.

Lord Macaulay describes Frederick the Great as bearing up against a world in arms, with an ounce of poison in one pocket and a quire of bad verses in the other. Thus provided, he could sleep.

The superhuman energy and activity of Lord Brougham are only explicable on this principle. He can abstract his thoughts from an exciting topic, and he can sleep. During the Queen's trial, he had dined and slept at Holland House. The next morning before breakfast his host found him writing in the library. 'Are you polishing off your peroration?' 'No, I am drawing a clause of my Education Bill.' One day at Paris, he read a paper on Optics at the Institute, was busily occupied the whole forenoon with his colleagues of that distinguished body, and at seven was the chief and best talker at a dinner-party, comprising D'Orsay and Dumas. He told the acquaintance who was with him most of the time, that he had slept soundly for an hour after leaving the Institute, and could do so at will during any interval of rest at any time.

* The question, which was the real place of meeting, is one of

Lord Braybrooke's stories do not abound in names or dates; the following was quite without, but seems little to want that recommendation. The Duke finding himself near some garrison town in England, received a visit from the commanding officer, who made a speech from the regiment on the subject of their anxiety to show him any possible respect, ending with their regret thattheir mess dinner could not produce anything worthy of being offered to him, and that it would be ridiculous to invite him to it. 'Why?' said he. The day was fixed

---

interest and importance, artistically and historically; for on it depends, first, whether Mr. Maclise's celebrated fresco is a true record of a memorable event; and secondly, whether the English army had pushed on far enough to take that share in completing the victory which the Duke claimed for it. The seventh volume of M. de Bernardi's *Staatengeschichte* contains a chapter on the battles of the 16th, 17th, and 18th, composed with admirable skill from Prussian authorities and the Prussian point of view. The main object is to prove that the flank attack of the Prussians decided the day; that the final advance of the English line was a superfluous movement dictated by political considerations; and that, unless the English had halted at La Belle Alliance, they would have got mixed up with the Prussians. There, consequently, he fixes the place of meeting, and there (he insists) it was that the Duke gave up the pursuit to the Prussians, on the ground that the English were too exhausted to follow it up.

On the other hand, the Duke says, 'I continued the pursuit *till long after dark*, and then discontinued it only on account of the fatigue of our troops, who had been engaged during twelve hours, and because I found myself on the same road with Marshal Blücher, who assured me of his intention to follow the enemy throughout the night.' In a subsequent letter (1816) to Mr. Mudford, he says: 'It happens that the meeting took place after ten at night in the village of Genappe, and anybody who attempts to describe with truth the operations of the two armies, will see that it could not

by him; some of his old friends and companions were
got to meet him. He came in high spirits and good-
humour, and began talking over his campaigns and old
stories with his comrades. Growing pleased with the
deep attention with which the younger officers listened
to him, he became more communicative, and at last
said that, as nothing gratified him so much as a spirit
of enquiry in young soldiers as to every subject connected with their profession, he begged that any one
present would question him as to any point of his
military history on which they wished for information,
promising that, unless he felt it inconsistent with his
duty, he would answer fully and fairly. Upon this, an
officer present ventured to ask whether it was true that
Napoleon had surprised him at Waterloo? He said he
was as far surprised as a man can be who knows he is
to expect attack; he knew that Napoleon would march
towards Brussels; that Blücher was coming to his

---

be otherwise.' But the French did not leave Genappe till after
eleven, and the Prussians did not arrive there till after midnight,
and there Blücher and his staff halted for the night. It is clear,
therefore, that the Duke was mistaken in fixing the place of meeting at Genappe; and Mr. Gleig is probably right in fixing it at *Maison
Rouge*, or *Maison du Roi*, in which he is followed by the author
of Mr. Murray's *Handbook for Belgium and the Rhine.* But M.
de Bernardi will surely admit that the Duke and the British army
cannot be mistaken in believing that they continued the pursuit
long after passing *La Belle Alliance*; whilst the supposition that
our great Commander, in the crisis of a great battle, was thinking
of anything but the best way of winning it, is one which in England
will simply excite a smile. M. de Bernardi's own statement, that
the English generals near the Duke objected to the advance as
hazardous, is in itself a refutation of his theory.

relief; he had a frontier of many hundred miles to defend; he could not possibly foresee on what point the attack would be first made; and certainly the speed of the advance of Napoleon exceeded what he could have expected or believed possible.*

DEATH OF WILLIAM IV.—ACCESSION OF QUEEN VICTORIA.

June, 1837.—The reign is not yet quite a week old, and yet how many strange occurrences and stranger feelings one wishes to reçall, that all have passed before the eyes or in the mind in this short space. First, how strange it is that, in thinking of a departed sovereign, one can from the bottom of the heart pray, '*May my latter end be like his.*' Who that can look back some years—say to the period when we saw the Duke of Clarence at Stowe, where he was certainly endured only as an appendage of the Prince of Wales—who would have thought that he would have died more loved, more lamented, than either of his predecessors on the throne? least of all, who could have thought he would have died the death of a good Christian, deriving comfort and hope from religion, and every allevia-

---

* The question of the young officer has been frequently repeated; and perhaps as good an answer, or rather retort, as any was that of the late Professor Wilson on some one asking whether the French did not surprise Wellington at Waterloo. 'Yes; and didn't he *astonish* them?'

tion which the most devoted conjugal affection could shed over him. Even his sins seem to have poured from their foul source pure streams of comfort in the attentions and affection of his children. The Queen is said to have complained that in the last days, after he well knew his situation, she never was left alone with him. The public, edified by every detail which comes to light, can feel but one regret, which is, that the Princess Victoria was not summoned to receive his blessing.

It is very interesting to compare the appearance of the town now, with that which it wore after the death of George IV.; *then* few, very few, thought it necessary to assume the mask of grief; *now* one feeling seems to actuate the nation; party is forgotten and all mourn, if not so deeply, quite as unanimously, as they did for Princess Charlotte. After a few days of short unsatisfactory bulletins, a prayer for the King was ordered, and sent with pitiful economy by the two-penny post, so that, though the prayer appeared in every newspaper of Saturday evening, it was received by hardly any of the London clergy in time for morning service on Sunday. In our chapel, prayers were desired for *Our Sovereign Lord the King, lying dangerously ill*; and these introduced in the Litany just as they would have been for the poorest of his subjects! To me this simple ancient form was far more impressive than the *fancy* prayer, though it was a good one of its sort.

On Monday we were listening all day for the tolling of the bells, watching whether the guests were going to the Waterloo dinner at Apsley House. On Tuesday, at $2\frac{1}{2}$ A.M., the scene closed, and in a very short time the Archbishop of Canterbury and Lord Conyngham, the Chamberlain, set out to announce the event to their young sovereign. They reached Kensington palace at about five : they knocked, they rang, they thumped for a considerable time before they could rouse the porter at the gates; they were again kept waiting in the court-yard, then turned into one of the lower rooms, where they seemed forgotten by everybody. They rang the bell, desired that the attendant of the Princess Victoria might be sent to inform H.R.H. that they requested an audience on business of importance; after another delay, and another ringing to enquire the cause, the attendant was summoned, who stated that the *Princess* was in such a sweet sleep she could not venture to disturb her. Then they said, ' We are come to the *Queen* on business of state, and even her sleep must give way to that.' It did; and to prove that *she* did not keep them waiting, in a few minutes she came into the room in a loose white night-gown and shawl, her night-cap thrown off, and her hair falling upon her shoulders, her feet in slippers, tears in her eyes, but perfectly collected and dignified.

The first act of the reign was of course the sum-moning the Council, and most of the summonses were not received till after the early hour fixed for its meeting. The Queen was, upon the opening of the doors, found sitting at the head of the table. She received first the homage of the Duke of Cumberland, who, I suppose, was not King of Hanover when he knelt to her : * the Duke of Sussex rose to perform the same ceremony, but the Queen, with admirable grace, stood up, and preventing him from kneeling, kissed him on the forehead. The crowd was so great, the arrangements were so ill made, that my brothers told me the scene of swearing allegiance to their young sovereign was more like that of the bidding at an auction than anything else.

MACREADY'S LEAR.

Feb. 10*th,* 1838.—I saw last night Macready in King Lear, and little expected, in the present degraded state of the stage, to see any performance that would give me such pleasure. First of all, it is Shakespeare's Lear : not a word is added to the text; the painfully fine catastrophe is acted ; and the play, in the regular theatre phrase, *well got up,* excepting in the female parts, which were almost as ill dressed as they were acted. I cannot

* He became King of Hanover by the same event which made her Queen of England.

conceive a better model for a painter of Lear than Macready exhibited in face, figure, dress, and apparent age. The latter seems to me the leading point of his representation of the character, in which he substitutes the imbecility of age for insanity, which I have hitherto considered as the leading feature of Lear. The more I think, the more I am inclined to believe that this was the intention of the poet; at the same time, I must own that it has, as far as dramatic effect is concerned, some objections. The curse, the appeal to the elements, which one has been used to dislike as a rant,* appeared tame and ineffective, partly, I believe, because so early in the play I had not entered fully into the conception of the actor; but I still think upon retrospect, that both, especially the curse, might have been made to tell with singular effect if repeated in a tremulous and very solemn manner. I hope to judge of this ere long upon a second view.

I felt almost as if I had never read, certainly never seen, that finest of all scenes, that on the Heath, so much was I delighted with the effect produced by the Fool (now reinstated for the first time for many years). The artless affection, shrewdness, archness displayed by Miss Horton, the sweetness of the snatches of song,

---

* 'I tax not you, ye elements, with unkindness.
   I never gave you kingdoms, call'd you children.'
These lines have been cited as one of the most splendid efforts of Shakespeare's imagination.

seemed like the drop of comfort infused into the bitter cup of the poor old King.   They made me feel that the commentators who assert that, when in the last sad scene he says, '*And my poor fool hanged!*' he cannot mean to allude to the boy, had never seen it so acted. Much as I admire the strict adherence to the text, I must say that one omission quite new to me pleased me very much.   When poor blind Gloster, fancying himself on the edge of the cliff, says, 'Now, fellow, fare thee well,' instead of falling down, he is interrupted by the arrival of Lear, and you are spared the absurdity of persuading a man whom you have seen falling from his own height, that he tumbled down a precipice.

In the battle there was one novelty which I think from a greater distance than the box in which we were, might have a great effect.   The scene was a distant view of a battle, or rather of heaps of slain; when the challenge is given, a *champ clôs* is immediately formed by a palisade of spears and battle-axes.   The last scene is *almost* too painful; I felt it would have been *quite,* if Cordelia had not been such a detestable snub-nosed creature.   I suppose it would be high treason against Shakespeare to alter the catastrophe, and to give to it what might be called a melodramatic German charac- ter; but I could not help wishing the representation to conclude when Lear says—

> 'She lives! if it be so,
> It is a chance that does redeem all sorrows
> That ever I have felt.'

CHANTREY'S STUDIO.

This morning I have been to Chantrey's to see the equestrian statue of Sir Thomas Munro, which is to be packed up for Madras in a few days. I am much pleased with it, but cannot agree with those (my uncle is one) who call it the finest equestrian statue in the world. Without going so far as Rome to the unrivalled horse which Michael Angelo bade go on, I am not sure that, in my private opinion, a better may not be found at Charing Cross. I was at first struck with the thickness of the jowl and set-on of the head; this I was told was modelled from a beautiful Arab which had been sent as a present to George IV. The man added that other parts had been copied from other horses, and then I found out what it was that was not pleasing to my eye. These separate beauties do not accord to form a beautiful whole; the legs seem to me those of a powerful English hunter, quite out of keeping with the small Arab head and tail. Probably this effect is increased by the nearness of the legs to the eye of the spectator, and may, to a certain degree, be removed when the statue gets on its proper pedestal, which is to be very much higher than that on which it is *pro tempore* fixed.

I was much interested in hearing from an intelligent workman some of the details of the foundry, and in seeing the wonderful effects produced by English

machinery. After having seen at Munich every part
of comparatively small statues cast separately, so that
I suppose they are in about fifty pieces which are afterwards to be riveted together, it did seem very extraordinary that this immense mass was cast in four pieces
only. I wanted to see more of the furnace, but there were
so many people about that one could not question the
workman comfortably; but he told me that he frequently went into it to see that all was right when the
thermometer is at 370°. This seems almost incredible
when one considers that this is much more than half as
hot again as boiling water; and into this they go without any of the previous preparation of increasing temperature, which in the Eastern baths enables a person
to endure heat very far inferior to this, but which
would not otherwise be endurable. Here the workman
goes from the atmosphere of a cold room into this, or
rather first into a sort of chamber: and there, as he
told us, is the great suffering, the first shutting the
outward door. In this furnace the metal remains many
months, and I fancy always at the same temperature.

Chantrey's Horse was, it seems, originally modelled for
a statue of George IV., and he is to ride it. Flatter him
as highly as possible, still the difference between his
pasty-pudding features and the fine bold line of those
of Sir Thomas Munro will be severely felt. Quiet
seems to be the characteristic of Chantrey's sculpture,
exactly the reverse of Canova, who always offends

by a sort of flutter. I am not sure whether Chantrey
is not in the contrary extreme: in looking down his
gallery a want of action struck me; perhaps the eternal
monumental sculpture does in some degree lead to this,
and I should have thought that he would have been
glad to *gallop* away from it. Instead of that his
horse stands still. I understand he piques himself
upon having executed the first equestrian statue with a
horse in repose, and his admirers tell you, 'You see he
is just going to move.' I am perfectly aware of the
absurdities that have been committed in the attempt
to give motion and action to sculpture, but I own it
seems to me that Chantrey has cut the Gordian knot
which he was perhaps capable of untying.

MACREADY'S CORIOLANUS.

April 20th.—I went last night to see Macready in
Coriolanus, feeling that I should not like him: that in
this one part, and in no other, the greatness of Kemble
was unapproachable. I am quite sure I was extremely
interested to feel that I had gained a new view of the
character, but cannot quite decide whether I like it
better than the old one. I should say that Kemble was
more Roman, more dignified, and Macready more true
to universal nature. The first seemed to be impelled
by a feeling of withering contempt, bordering on mis-
anthropy, to scorn the tribunes and the people as

creatures of an inferior nature; Macready seemed a man of quick, irritable feelings, whose pride was rather galled than wounded, and I suspect this is the Coriolanus of Shakespeare and of nature.

It hardly seemed in nature that Kemble's Coriolanus, so proud, so unbending, should have been led astray, should yield to the solicitations of his mother, though that mother was Mrs. Siddons.* In Macready it seemed impossible he should resist, though Volumnia was odiously vulgar, and gave me more the idea of a *poissarde* than of a Roman matron. Nothing could be finer than his acting in this scene; never did I feel so strongly the tenderness and beauty of his affection for Virgilia. She has so little to say or do, that, being rather handsome and very well dressed, the actress (whose name I forgot) could not offend.

I never saw a play so beautifully, so correctly got up. It was not only the costume, the scenery, the numberless accessories that were carefully attended to, but the far more difficult task of regulating the by-play of the inferior actors was also accomplished. The effect given by the number of the mob, by the variety of action which seemed to give Shakespearian individuality to every member of it, is indescribable. The

---

* The late Sir G. C. Lewis (in his *Credibility of the Early Roman History*) treats the alleged compliance of Coriolanus with his mother's intercession as an incredible absurdity. How could he, with Tullus Aufidius by his side, have led back the Volscians?

cowed, degraded appearance of the Volscians in the Triumph was very striking; Coriolanus sitting at the hearth of Aufidius as fine a picture as can be imagined. Still I was too near the stage to judge of the full effect, or even to see the whole of the fine scenes.

FROM THE ORDERS OF CHARLES II. FOR THE HOUSEHOLD.

(Transcribed from the Stowe MSS.)

Chapel.—When wee are present, no man shall presume to putt on his hatt at Sermon, but those in the stalls on the left hand, which are noblemen or counsellers, or the Deane of the Chapell, when wee are absent. As our expresse pleasure is that our Chappell be all the yeare through kept both morning and evening with solemne musick like a Collegiate Church, unlesse it be at such times in the summer, or other times when we are pleased to spare it, so wee will have all decent honour and order kept, and therefore when any of the Lords of the Councill be below, our pleasure is so much respect be given to our Councill (being our representative body) as that no man presume to be covered untill they shall require them, and then only the sonnes of noblemen or such as serve us, or our dearest consort the Queene in eminent places. In all those places, both noblemen and others shall observe great distance.

U

and respect to our person, and also civility one towards another. And those that are younge shall not offer to fill up the seates from those which are either elder or more infirme or counsellors, though perhaps below them in rank.

<hr />

THE PRETENDER AT THE CORONATION.

Pölnitz in his 'Memoirs' (vol. iii. p. 254) gives a contemporary account of the incident at the coronation of George I., which Sir W. Scott has in 'Red Gauntlet' introduced as taking place at that of George III.; and I remember to have read it also in some of the publications of the former period thus :

Immediately after the champion's challenge, a lady's glove was thrown from the gallery containing a written defiance, and an invitation to the ring in Hyde Park for the following day. At the appointed time a considerable crowd was assembled. No champion appeared, but there was an old woman observed moving round different parts of the circle, supposed to be a noted swordsman in disguise. The following note is by my brother Charles.

'My grandmother often repeated to me the account which she had herself received from Lady Primrose of Charles Edward's visit to London in 1750 (a letter from the historian Hume to Sir J. Pringle, published in " Gentleman's Magazine," May 1788, relating the

same incident, assigns to this visit the date 1753).*
She described her consternation when Mr. Browne (the
name under which he was to go) was announced to
her in the midst of a card party, among whom were
many who she felt might have seen him abroad and
would very probably recognise him. Her cards almost
dropped from her hands, but she recovered herself, and
got him out of the room as quickly as she could. He
slept at her house that night only, and afterwards went
to that of a merchant in the city. The impression he
left on the mind of Lady Primrose, a warm and attached
partisan, was by no means favourable. I have read
myself among the Stuart papers a minute of the heads
of a manifesto in Charles Edward's own handwriting,
among which appeared, " *My having in the year* 1750
*conformed to the Church of England in St. James's
Church.*" Some idea may be formed of the extent of
the panic felt at the time of his advance to Derby from

* Hume speaks of a second visit on the authority of Lord
Holderness, and adds, ' You see this story is so near traced
from the fountain-head as to wear a great trace of probability.
Query, what if the Pretender had taken up Dymock's gauntlet?'
Miss Strickland, in her *Life of Mary II.*, says, ' This incident has
been told as a gossip's tale pertaining to every coronation of the
last century which took place while an heir of James II. existed.
If it ever took place, it must have been at the coronation of
William and Mary. That there was a pause at this part of the
ceremony of above two hours, and that when the champion
appeared the gauntlet was heard to be thrown, but nothing that
was done could be seen on account of the darkness of the evening,
all this rests upon the authority of Lamberty, the historian and
diplomatist.'

the account given by an old workman at Wotton, of his having at that period assisted in burying by night all the family plate in the garden.—C. W. W. W.'

The recantation here mentioned is a circumstance quite new to me, and seems to remove the only one redeeming point among the many base ones which marked the character of Charles Edward. I always thought he had, like the rest of his unfortunate race, been a sincere bigot. His weakness and cowardice seemed to be proved beyond a doubt. In the letter above quoted in the 'Gentleman's Magazine,' Hume says that Helvetius assured him that, when Charles Edward embarked at Nantes for the Scotch expedition (1745), he took fright, and would not go on board; and his attendants, 'thinking the matter had gone too far, &c. &c., '*literally* carried him into the ship by night *pieds et poings liés.*'

It is a singular proof of the forbearance of the reigning family, and also of the fidelity of the adherents of the fallen race, that even now the real character of Charles Edward is so little generally known. The veil thrown over the drunken dissolute close of his career seems never to have been fully withdrawn by any English writer; and even Alfieri attached, probably married, to the woman who had certainly been unhappy and much illused by Charles while she was his wife, is unwilling to speak of him or his brother, *laudare non li potendo, ni li volendo biasimare,* but

tells enough to prove him an odious and brutal monster.
I do not understand how, among the many Italian tour-
ists who have indulged us with so many histories of
bad fare, hard beds thickly inhabited, there has not
been one who has enriched his pages with some of the
many traditions still extant, still easily authenticated,
at Florence and Rome, referring to the two last Stuarts.
They were the *last*: therefore there could not now be any
objection; and though the records could not be very
interesting, they would probably *sell*.*

QUEEN ANNE.

Wynnstay: Dec. 1838.—I have been dipping into the
'*Political State of England*' of the year 1714, at the
account of the death of Queen Anne, in which several
things have astonished me; but none so much as the
statement that, from the suddenness of her seizure, her
state during the short time that she survived it &c.
&c., she died without 'being able to receive the *holy
Viaticum*!' In this publication, which seems evidently
the parent of our 'Annual Register,' I am surprised to
see how little appearance of regret was shown for a
sovereign who, weak and foolish as she was, had a most

---

* Since this was written, the most complete exposure has been
made in a thin quarto, printed in 1843 for the Roxburgh Club by
Earl Stanhope, entitled *The Decline of the Last Stuarts: Extracts
from the Despatches of British Envoys to the Secretary of State.*

prosperous and even glorious reign—for a woman to whom all parties, I believe, have given the credit of good intentions. However, certain it is that the sure thermometer of British public feeling, the Funds, rose upon her first apoplectic seizure, fell the day when there seemed to be a rally and an expectation of prolonged existence, and rose again the following day when she died. A few months before she had written a very harsh letter to the Electress Sophia, which is said to have hastened the death of that princess, who died of apoplexy just three months before Queen Anne.

The orders for the mourning are curious: for six months the order is for the *deepest* mourning (long cloaks excepted; query, were the women to wear the close cap of widows?)—'*that no person* whatsoever, for the first six months, use any escutcheons of armes or armes painted on their coaches, nor use any varnished or bullion nails to be seen on their coaches or chairs.' The anniversary of the landing of King William was of course then, as now, kept; but much more is said of that (the 17th Nov.) of the happy inauguration of Queen Elizabeth's glorious memory; houses illuminated, bonfires in the streets, &c.; which, by the bye, three months after the death of Queen Anne, when everybody was in this deepest mourning, must have had a queer effect. Queen Anne had a larger and more noble household than Queen Victoria. Groom of the Stole and Lady of the Robes, Duchess of Somerset; Lady Privy Purse,

Mrs. (Lady) Masham. Ten Ladies of the Bed-chamber —three of whom were ducheses, and five countesses.*

OLD-FASHIONED MANNERS.

Sir William Williams, my great-grandfather, seems to have been addressed by his children and dependants with much more respect than we have lately seen evinced in writing to the Queen. The tutor of his sons always writes from Oxford of my grandfather as *My Master*, of his brother as Mr. Robert, and addresses Sir William as 'Your Honour.' In 1714 my grandfather writes for Sir J. Wynn, 'He has desired me to acquaint you that, if you approve of it, he would be highly glad if you could meet us at St. Albans to conduct us into town, for he is the most apprehensive of danger betwixt that place and London of any; he is by no means for my staying in London any longer than the Mellins are delivered, and if possible, to return to Barnet or Highgate that night, but hope, sir, you will send him word that it is not practicable for me to return sooner than the Monday following, suppose we come in Friday or Saturday night. The noise of our going is spread all about the country, and somebody has told him that Prichard the Highwayman is gone abroad, which makes

---

* It appears from Lady Cowper's *Diary*, that the situation of Lady of the Bedchamber to Caroline, Princess of Wales, was a prize eagerly contested by duchesses.

him under ye greater concern, so would gladly have returns for some parte.

'Dear Sir

'Your ever dutiful son

'WAT. WILLIAMS.'

In a letter dated 'Duke Street, January 30, 1729,' he says—

'Nothing spoken of but ye great acconomy at St. James's, there are so many astonishing instances that it would be too tedious and something dangerous to mention them—the great man is in ye judgement of mankind in a very uneasy situation. Stocks fell very much upon ye publishing ye treaty of peace. Her Majesty is very uneasy at ye English ladies for going so fine; she says they rivall even majesty itself. And, forsooth, if waiting women in this country go as fine as German princesses, she would therefore have none but noblemen's ladies wear silk, and none jewells, nor laces—stuffs full good enough for country gentlemen's wives, and every servant maid to wear a badge of her profession on her shoulder. The Queen wears calf-skin shoes, and the eldest princess scour'd cloaths, and ye youngest patched coats.

TOUCHING FOR THE KING'S EVIL.

Feb. 1839.—Found at Bodryddan * in the sermons

---

* The seat of William Shipley Conway, Esq. (her nephew), near St. Asaph.

of Bishop Bull, who died 1710, one on St Paul's *Thorn in the flesh*; and the following passage :—

'The gift of miracles, and particularly the gift of curing diseases without natural medicine, was so given by Christ to His Apostles as not to be at their absolute disposal, but to be dispensed by them as the Giver should think fit. St. Paul, though as great a worker of miracles as any of the Apostles—though he even raised the dead to life, yet could not cure himself of that thorn in the flesh, that painful disease which Satan, by God's permission, had inflicted on him. Hereby it appears, that this gift of God was so bestowed on the Apostles that they could not exercise it arbitrarily and at their own pleasure, but only when, where, how, and on whom God pleased to direct them to use that power, that so the glory of all the wonderful cures wrought by them might at last redound to God the author, and not to man the instrument. And perhaps this is the best account that can be given of the relique and remnant of the primitive gift of healing for some hundreds of years past, visible in our nation, and annexed to the succession of our Christian kings. I mean the cure of that *otherwise* incurable disease, the King's Evil. That divers persons desperately labouring under it have been cured by the touch of the royal hand, assisted by the prayers of the priests of our Church attending, is unquestionable, unless the faith of all ancient writers and the consentient reports of hundreds

of the most credible persons in our own age, attesting
the same, be questioned. And yet, they say, some of
the persons return from that sovereign remedy *re
infecta*. How comes that to pass? God hath not
given this gift of healing so absolutely to our royal
line, but that He still keeps the reins of it in His own
hands, to let them loose or restrain them *as He pleaseth*.'

In Brady's *Clavis Calendaria*, I find :—

' Edward the Confessor was the first monarch of this
country who possessed the privilege, alleged to have
been continued to his successors, and to have been
practised by them till the accession of the House of
Brunswick, of curing that dreadful malady the King's
Evil.'

In another part of the same work, from the ' Mercurius
Politicus ' of June 28, 1660, is quoted the account of the
ceremony, concluding in this manner: ' His Majesty
(Charles I.) stroked above 600 ; and such was his princely
patience and tenderness to the poor afflicted creatures,
that though it took up a very long time, His Majesty,
who is never wearied with well-doing, was pleased to
enquire whether there were any more who had not yet
been touched.'

My brother Charles supposes that in those times it
was of great importance to keep up every ceremony which
could tend to establish the divine right of the reigning
family. Thus he explains the unaccountable credulity of
Bishop Bull, asserting the existence of the miracle instead

of adopting the line of conduct now so universally practised by the more enlightened of the Roman clergy, who walk in processions, send their mules to be blessed, nay, even crawl up the Scala Santa, professing that they do not believe in the efficacy of any of these mummeries, but are afraid of shocking the weak consciences of the ignorant by omitting them. Upon the same principle Charles supposes that George I. was unwilling to subject his disputed title to the crown to a test so likely to fail. At the same time, I am inclined to believe that the angel of gold which the King tied round the neck of the patient must in many instances have proved a very efficacious remedy.

THE EMPEROR NICHOLAS.

Extract from a letter to Miss Williams Wynn, dated
' St. Petersburg, Feb. 2, 1826.'

We are here in the midst of most interesting events. The accounts given in the newspapers respecting the Empress mother heading the troops, or taking any steps to cover the ' pusillanimous ' Nicholas, are totally destitute of foundation. He showed himself worthy of his situation by the courage and presence of mind he displayed. At one moment, he was alone conversing with and explaining to the peasants the reasons for their being called on to take a new path, when his aide-de-camp said in his ear, ' Come away, you might be surrounded by assassins; some of the troops marching up belong to the mutineers.' The Emperor immediately mounted his horse, and in a loud voice called to his aide-de-camp in Russian, to lead those troops (pointing to the mutineers) to the *place du sénat* (the place to which he saw them marching); to place the Paulofsky here, the 2nd regiment there, the Dragoons here, &c. &c., and added in a low voice in French, 'Ne faites rien; je ne sais pas encore sur lequel des régimens je dois compter.' It was a trying moment, and had the attack been made two hours later, we should probably not have seen the end of it so soon.

CATHERINE OF MEDICIS.

Eserick: Dec. 1839.—Reading an odd book entitled *Vita di Caterina de' Medici,* di Eugenio Alberi, the object of which is to prove her the most innocent, the most virtuous of women, from MS. communications from the ambassadors, and from others in the archives of the Medici at Florence, I must confess that this piece of special pleading does not produce any effect upon my mind. It is evident that even if the ambassadors had been allowed to peep behind the black mask of treachery, which to me seems very doubtful, it is not in their communications, it is not in any part of the papers preserved in the house of Medici, that you are to expect that any fact inculpating a member of their family will be preserved, or at least allowed to be published. I cannot forget the jealousy supposed to exist in 1833 of the publication of those remains of Tasso which exposed the cold-hearted cruelty of the House of Este, though they were above 300 years old. Yet it is upon the silence of these narrators that the innocence of Catherine is rested, or rather inferred from their not alleging her privity to these dark deeds. The author evinces a degree of bigotry which I should scarcely have believed possible in 1838, the date of the publication. From such publications as the 'Grande Estoile apparue en 1572, le merveilleux desbordement du Rhône en 1570,' he quotes the descriptions of the fears and misery of the people, &c. &c., as proofs of the divine wrath!

Charles IX. is exculpated from the guilt of having fired upon the people by the following passage from Capefigue: 'Le fameux balcon du Louvre que l'on montre encore aujourd'hui comme étant celui d'où Charles a tiré sur le peuple, n'existait pas. Je m'en suis assuré,' &c. &c. Granting this, I should like to ask the historian whether he would doubt any part in the Roman history because it is proved from any evidence that it could not have taken place in the spot to which the traditions of antiquaries have assigned it. For instance, is the captivity of St. Paul doubted, or even the existence of the Mammertine prison, because many do not believe that the latter was the scene of the former, or that the spot now indicated was that of the prison? *

As to the St. Bartholomew, a letter from the Medicean Archives is quoted by this writer even as a ' *Testimonianza dell' incredibil gioja* cagionata ai Cattolici da quel fatto. Che si desidera ora da questo Carlo veramente magno e della *gloriossissima sua Madre*,' &c. &c. 'Sia laudato l'omnipotente Dio, che mi porge occasione di scrivervi sopra così celesti nuove, e sia benedetto il trionfante san Bartolomio, che nel giorno di sua festa si è degnato di prestare alli suoi divoti il suo *taglientissimo coltello* in così *salutifero sagrifizio*.' He mentions the commemorating picture still extant at the Vatican, but not the inscription which a few years ago made it so offensive; the solemn thanksgiving in the church of San Luigi du Framesi by Gregory XIII. in person, the medal struck, the gift of 1000 scudi from the Cardinal of Lorraine to the bearer of the news. He never seems to advert to the contradiction which these facts oppose to his hypothesis of popular disturbance without the knowledge of the sovereign. Perhaps it is but charitable to suppose that, having given the impetus, the ball rolled and increased much beyond their expectations or intentions.

---

* Capefigue may be right in saying that the balcony in the Louvre from which Charles was traditionally said to have fired on the Huguenots never existed; but another tradition, better accredited, marked out the *Petit Bourbon*, destroyed in 1758, as the scene of the exploit. The question is fully discussed in *L'Esprit dans l'Histoire.*

Among other offences to my feelings, Alberi adds that of throwing doubts on the authenticity of a fact reconciling one to human nature so disgraced by these events; I mean the celebrated letter of the Vicomte d'Orthez, Governor of Bayonne, who found in that garrison ' des bons citoyens et braves soldats et pas un bourreau.' The invention of this letter has been ascribed to Voltaire, but it seems that it was published by Aubigné in 1618. The arguments against the authenticity are, 1st, its style, said to be much more modern than that of the sixteenth century; 2ndly, the silence of contemporary writers, and the circumstance of the descendants of Orthez not having brought forth this claim upon the favour of Henri, &c.; but I do not believe that he would have been anxious to encourage resistance to royal authority.*

IMPRESSIONS OF IRELAND IN 1840.

1841.—I regret that I did not in last December, immediately after my return from Ireland, record the impressions made by that entertaining trip. We embarked at Talacre in the afternoon of November 16, and in two hours reached Liverpool, but either from the want of skill in the captain or of strength in the vessel,

---

M. Fournier (*L'Esprit dans l'Histoire*) comes to the conclusion that the letter was the invention of d'Aubigné.

which made him fear getting foul of the pier, we were kept beating about for two hours more, till the little packet from Birkenhead came alongside and landed the passengers. In the night the wind was so high that it would have been madness to embark early in the morning as we had intended. The wind abated towards midday, and in the evening we embarked; and after a passage of twelve hours, made disagreeable by the swell, landed early on the morning of the 18th.

Before we reached the handsome hotel in a street nearly as fine as any I know in any capital, the jaunting cars in which we were conveyed, and the beggars, seemed to give one a foretaste of Ireland. In the afternoon we drove through very dirty suburbs, the habitations and the population seeming every mile to get more and more poor and ugly ; the former never in one instance possessing unbroken casements, the absence of glass being supplied by some dirty rags, or by a wisp of hay. This, I was afterwards told, was owing to their practice of rearing fowls for the Dublin market in their kitchens, to the warmth of which the fowls return with such eagerness that they break the glass to get in.* The inhabitants do not seem to have left off the practice of wearing the old clothes of the London beggars. Most of the women were smoking their pipes.

I never went into any of their huts, and am quite

---

* As an Irishman never thinks of timely repairs of any sort, the state of his casements is susceptible of a more obvious explanation.

at a loss how needlework so perfectly neat, so clean, can come out of such habitations, and from such hands.

Mr. Evans tells me that one cause of the miserable appearance of the villages is, that when a new house is built, they never give themselves the trouble of pulling down the old one which it is to replace; that is left to fall when it can no longer stand. Nothing could be less pretty, or seem longer, than our road to Portrane, and it was quite dark when we got there. Next morning my eyes opened to the fine sea view bounded by such bold rocks, and separated from us by a profusion of evergreens which at that time of year were delightful to behold, and gave to the scene a false air of summer very refreshing to one's eyes. On the 27th we returned to Dublin, and passed one day there. I ceased to wonder at the eagerness of the people for Repeal when I saw the magnificent houses unoccupied by the nobles of the land, converted into hotels, warehouses, public offices, &c. &c.; the fine streets looking deserted, grass growing in many of them. I felt it not unnatural that the common people should imagine that, if their peers and commoners had a parliament of their own to attend instead of coming to London, their houses would be once more inhabited, streets would be filled, trade flourish, &c. &c.

Now whether there, or almost anywhere else, the present generation would have the means of living with the profusion of their ancestors, I doubt; but I feel quite sure that, unless steam and some other modern improvements of minor importance could be forgotten, the Irish would still leave *their* capital to seek *ours*. Having felt this, I was much amused with the sort of confirmation given to this idea by the account which Mr. Conolly gave me of the manner in which his uncle, the late possessor of his property, used to travel to London some four score years ago. He and his neighbour the Duke of Leinster, who had married two sisters, the daughters of the second Duke of Richmond, used to contrive generally to travel together. Sending their servants, carriages, luggage, &c., by the Parkgate Packet, which in those days was often four or five nights out, and wishing to avoid this tedious passage, they used to embark for Holyhead. Between that port and Chester there was not at that time any carriage road, indeed nothing but a mountain path. These grandees used to bring over their saddle horses; each lady got upon a pillion behind her husband; a groom carried in saddle-bags the necessary changes of attire; and thus they travelled to Chester, sleeping two or three nights on the road, and one of the sleeping-places was the Black Inn at Rhyddlan. Lord Mostyn told me that (at a period somewhat subsequent, I suppose) the innkeeper of Chester contrived to have relays of horses at some points of the road, and thus forwarded travellers.

I expected much contrast between the two houses to which we were invited, but not so much as I found;

not such a striking difference in the country within a
circle of ten miles from Dublin. Mr. Conolly's is called
the finest house in Ireland; it possesses the nearly
unique advantage of having some fine timber in its
park; but here, as in everything else, appears the odd
want of keeping, of neatness, which is evident in every
thing Irish. Many of the fine old trees which were
blown down in the fatal storm of January 1839, were
still cumbering the ground and rotting.

Returning, we took another road by the banks of the
Liffey, where we drove for two or three miles on a sort
of terrace between an overhanging bank of strawberries
and one underhanging to the river. The whole scene
struck me as a comically well-proportioned miniature
of some part of the road on the banks of the Rhine; the
strawberry plants bearing about the same proportion to
the vine that the Liffey does to the Rhine; and the
same might be said of the road, the banks, &c.

Soon after this we reached the Phœnix Park, and
altogether thought our drive a very pretty one; and the
people we saw all looked tidy and comfortable in spite
of broken windows, which, however, were not so general.

LADY MORGAN

March 1841.—I was amused yesterday with hearing
the history of Lady Morgan, from whose pretty little nut-

shell (in Kildare Street) I was just come. Her father and mother were players in a strolling company: the father died, or ran away, I forget which, leaving his wife and two fine girls without a sixpence in the world, and in debt to everybody. Mrs. Evans tells me that she has heard from two different officers, whose regiment happened to be quartered in the town, that they all subscribed to enable Mrs. Owenson and her daughters to get away. Soon after this Miss Owenson went into the family of a very respectable Mrs. Featherstone, as governess (a very young one she must have been) to her only daughter. This pupil, now Lady Chapman, has never ceased to evince great friendship towards her governess. At Mrs. Featherstone's she wrote her 'Wild Irish Girl,' which made quite a sensation. Lady Abercorn, who wanted somebody to *égayer* her tête-à-tête with her old lord, and also to make talk and laugh for her guests, took Miss Owenson as a sort of *dame de compagnie*. When Lord Abercorn chose to pass a season at Baron's Court, Lady Abercorn was venting her regrets upon a friend, asking what she could do to amuse herself. 'Why,' said the friend, ' you take your family physician, whom Lord Abercorn has just got knighted; he and Miss Owenson have a mortal aversion for each other; make up a match between them; that will divert you.' This joking advice was literally followed, and I verily believe the consequence has been a very happy marriage; certainly yesterday she talked only of his unwearied care and affection during her late dangerous illness, of her fears for his health, &c. &c.*

'O'Donnel' was written to commemorate the expedition to Baron's Court; the fine lady, a very exact portrait of Lady Abercorn: the heroine, a highly flattered one of herself, &c. &c. We were lamenting that, aspiring higher, she had left off writing novels, in which she succeeded much better. Mrs. Evans told me that she had made this observation to Lady Morgan herself, who replied that in the days when she wrote novels she had not a place in society and cared not who she offended; now the case was very different, and she should be in continual fear of having names given to her characters, which I believe were more or less portraits in almost every instance.

ANNE OF AUSTRIA.

May 1841.—I have been reading Swinburne's 'Letters from the Courts of Paris, Naples,' &c. &c., very gossiping, therefore entertaining and (I suppose) apocryphal. The most interesting part is at the period of the French Revolution, and afterwards when Swinburne was nego-

---

* This account is substantially confirmed by Lady Morgan's *Memoirs*, in which public attention is invited to every particular of her birth, education, family difficulties, &c. The general conclusion is highly favourable to her.

tiating an exchange of prisoners in 1796. He brings
forward as a discovery the now well known and most
probable conjecture as to the Masque de Fer; that he
was an elder brother of Louis XIV.; that from the
estrangement of Louis XIII. at that period, Anne of
Austria could not give a shadow of apparent legitimacy
to his birth; and that his father was Louis Bourbon, a
bourgeois de Tours—this is the only part of the story
which is new to me. We all know that, the birth of
Louis XIV. being equally questionable as to legitimacy,
the unfortunate elder born was put out of the way.
Swinburne adds, 'Linquet says that a lady at Chartres,
ninety years old, still alive (1786 or 1787), and in her
youth mistress to one of the ministers, was surprised this
should not be known, as it was no secret when she lived
in the world. Madame Campan tells me that her
father-in-law actually occupies the same house at
Choisy that was inhabited by the maitre d'hôtel and
his wife, the favourite *femme de chambre* of Anne of
Austria.' That queen made a *neuvaine* * to St. Leonard,
whose chapel near Choisy was much resorted to for
procuring children to barren ladies. Every day during
her pilgrimage the Queen retired after the ceremonies
to this house at Choisy, and there is a tradition that
some one came to visit her from Rael every evening by
a private road which leads through the meadows to the

---

* A nine days' pilgrimage.

river, where the country people say there was in the memory of man a ford, and the only one for miles on the Seine.*

THE BARON GERAMB AND LA TRAPPE.

July 1841.—I have been reading 'The Journey from La Trappe to Rome,' by the Reverend Father, Baron Geramb, Abbot and Procurator-General of the Trappe. The author is the famous whiskered and tight-laced Baron who, I believe, was under the Alien Act sent out of England in 1812: he was arrested at Hasum, a Danish post near Hamburgh, and cast into the dungeon of Vincennes. He professes himself ignorant of any cause of offence, nor was any ever assigned. As an Austrian subject he had attempted to raise a regiment to resist Bonaparte when he was approaching Vienna in 1807. The entrance of the allied sovereigns into Paris in 1814 gave Geramb liberty, and he not ill describes his utter incredulity when the news first reached him, and his conviction that his informant was a lunatic. The book, very ill translated, contains, with much chaff, a few grains of curious development of human character, and some singular anecdotes, generally founded on extreme bigotry. From Paris he writes in 1837, 'I

---

* A. Dumas, père, has founded a novel on this theory of the *Masque de Fer*, treating Louis XIV. and his supposed brother as twins. But the question is still an open one.

passed to the Temple erected by Chatel, a dirty coach-house with tricolor standards. On the gate is inscribed *Eglise Française.* At the entrance I saw the likeness of the pretended Primate of Gaul. There were books for the service of the new Church, and the following announcement printed in large characters : " On Tuesday next the Primate Chatel will preach on the Dignity of Woman, and after the sermon will present each lady with a bouquet." '

I conclude that Geramb's prediction that the doctrines of Chatel would not spread, has proved true, for in no other work have I read of them. Geramb is constantly eulogising the restored Jesuits, who, I fear, are creeping into their old authority. His personal vanity mixing with all this is very comical. He travels in a common lay dress, resumes his monastic habit at Rome, where he resides in a monastery; goes from thence to the Sacro Speco on Mount Cassino, where St. Benedict, the founder of monastic life in the west, had resided, and which has been since the head seat of the Order. This was in the holy week, and he naturally attaches great ideas of sanctity to the expedition—pilgrimage, I suppose he would call it. In the midst of this two mischances are recorded. ' At Rome I had hired a tolerably decent carriage and three good horses to take me to Subiaco. . . . Scarcely had we been an hour on the road when the rain fell in torrents. I had fallen asleep, and on waking I saw to my inexpressible annoyance that my habit, which was snow white when I got into the voiture, had a pretty deep tinge of green in some parts; the rain had entered through the broken windows, and had run through the green curtains. The vetturino answered my complaints by the observation that a little washing would remedy the evil. . My habit was literally ruined, and I looked more like a dragoon than a Trappist. The superior of Santo Speco sent me the following day a mule, a guide, and a person to carry my trunk. My Trappist habit attracted great attention.

Soon after, on the edge of a precipice, the mule fell down; to get out of my stirrups and fling myself on the other side, was the work of a moment.' The muleteer laments only his mule, whose leg he believes to be broken. The labourers near, who assisted, cried out 'A miracle! miracle! you owe your life to St. Benedict, Father —— ;' and I doubt not 'plenty of Bajochi to us' was added. Afterwards a workman is sent for to execute a column to commemorate this escape. 'I dwelt on my miraculous preservation. "I do not," said the workman, "see any miracle in the matter. The mule was heavy, but *you* were still heavier than the mule; it could not have happened otherwise." I laughed heartily at this drollery, but was, however, not a little annoyed at my *embonpoint*, which had procured for me the advantage of the comparison.'

At Geramb's return to Rome, in 1838, he is made

Abbot, &c. &c. of the Order, and was to exchange the obscurity of the cloister for a residence in the midst of Rome. There I will try to see the face of this strange animal, whom I cannot but believe more knave than fool.

LOUIS PHILIPPE.

Naples: March 1842.—Heard from the Duc de Montebello an interesting story of Louis Philippe. When he was giving to him his last directions upon going as Ambassador to Switzerland, he desired him to enquire at such a town, street, &c. &c., for ' *un nommé Muller, à qui j'ai l'obligation de m'avoir donné son passeport pour sortir du pays quand j'étais proscrit.'* Louis Philippe then told them how with this passport, on foot, he set out for Sweden, and landed at some port there. He was dining at the table d'hôte, and his anxious curiosity was excited by a face bronzed like his own, and very unlike the northern fair-complexioned men who surrounded them. He entered into conversation asked the country of the dark man. ' *Je suis Suisse, Monsieur.'* ' *Et moi aussi; de quel Canton êtes-vous?* ' The King felt it of great importance to his personal safety to ascertain the truth of the assertions of this man, being well aware there were many spies interested in the discovery of his person. By dint of well-applied questions, he discovered this man to be a native of the village where he had been a schoolmaster.

HENRY THE NINTH OF ENGLAND.

Bodrhyddan: August 1844. — From Angharad Lloyd * I have heard a story which is worth recording. Her sister, Helen Lloyd, was (through the interest of Lady Crewe, I believe) governess to the younger daughters of the Duke of Clarence. He, as was his custom, lived with her on terms of familiar intimacy and friendship from the time of her first presentation to the day of his death. He had expressed a strong preference for his second name of Henry, which he liked much better than that of William. The day after the death of George IV., Miss Helen Lloyd met the King at the house of Lady Sophia Sydney; she asked him familiarly whether he was to be proclaimed as King William or as King Henry. 'Helen Lloyd,' he replied, 'that question has been discussed in the Privy Council, and it has been decided in favour of King William.' He added, that the decision had been mainly influenced by the idea of an old prophecy of which he had never heard before, nor had he any evidence that it had ever been made. The drift of the prophecy was, that as Henry VIII. ' had pulled down monks and cells, Henry IX. would pull down bishops and bells.' Helen

---

* Of Rhyl, Flintshire; a Welsh lady celebrated for her knowledge of the Welsh language and antiquities.

exclaimed, 'I have seen that in an old book at home.' The King was astonished and pleased; he desired her to send for the book as soon as possible. Diligent search was made for it, but unhappily it was not discovered till after the King's death. It was found by me.

A. L.

Thus far Angharad; she sent me the book to look at.

A Briefe View of the State of the Church of England as it stood in Queen Elizabeth's and King James his Reigne, to the Yeare 1608. Being a Character and History of the Bishops of those Times, and may serve as an additional Supply to Dr. Goodwin's Catalogue of Bishops. Written for the use of Prince Henry upon occasion of that Proverb—

> *'Henry VIII. pulled down Monks and their Cells,*
> *Henry IX. should pull down Bishops and their Bells.'*

By Sir John Harrington of Kilston near Bath, Knight. London, printed for J. Keston, St. Paul's Churchyard, 1653.

In the life of Dr. Underhill, in this book, I find, ' I should go from Rochester to St. David's in Wales, save I must bait a little out of my way at four new bishoprics erected by King Henry VIII., of famous memory, and therefore I hope not ordained to be dissolved of a Henry IX., of future and fortunate expectation.'

Angharad said that King William wished to be King Henry IX., because, as the Cardinal of York had assumed that title on his medals, he wished to establish the lawful right to bear it, but this she did not write in the paper she sent to me.*

---

* She told me the story, and showed me the book in 1862.

KEAN.*

April 14*th*, 1814.—Saw Kean in Iago, and was less struck than I had been by his performance of Shylock, perhaps because I expected more. The absence of all ranting is in itself a great merit, which in the present state of the stage, degraded as it is, appears even greater. The quiet colloquial tone in which Kean performs the greatest part of this character, gives an effect almost electric to those passages which he strongly (sometimes, I own, too strongly) points. His emphasis seems to me always well laid, proceeding always from a strong and often from a new view of the sense of the passage ; † not like Kemble's, falling sometimes on words where it is so falsely applied that one should almost be tempted to believe that he does not give himself the trouble of understanding the common sense of what he is speaking. I once saw him in Lear, and heard the following passage thus accented :—

> I tax you not, you *elements*, with unkindness,
> I never gave you *kingdom*, call'd you *children*.

Nothing can be more admirable than the strong expression of continual watchfulness which marks Kean's deep eye in Iago, and I think I can never

---

* It does not appear why this entry was postponed.
† 'To see Kean act is like reading Shakspeare by flashes of lightning' (*Coleridge*).

forget the look of deep villany, of dire diabolical revenge, with which in leaving the stage, he directs the eye of the miserable Othello to his murdered Desdemona.

May 27*th.*—I have seen Kean in Othello, and found him in that magnificent part fully equal to my highly raised expectations; the highest dramatic treat I ever experienced. One regret will intrude, the weakness of his voice, and still more the insignificance of his figure, make him a very unfit representation of the rough martial Othello. When he tells what that *little arm* has done; when he tells you that 'every puny whipster gets my sword'—it requires all his wonderful talent to blind one to the ridicule of such expressions applied to that form.* In all the earlier part of the play, Kean saves himself, and you get only transient gleams of his genius. In the first act, the passage which struck me most was the burst of tenderness, displaying the whole character of Othello in these few words, 'And I *loved* her that she did pity them.'

The charm of Kean's Othello seems to me to lie mainly in the intense passion for Desdemona which he seems to be concealing, and which bursts forth as if involuntarily; this seems to form the excuse for Othello, to give nature to the excess of jealousy. In the fine scene in

---

* Before such merits all objections fly,
  Pritchard's genteel, and Garrick's six feet high.
                                        Churchill.

which Othello first conceives suspicion, this was peculiarly evident; and when Iago says, 'I see this hath a little
dashed your spirits,' Kean electrified the house by the
simple words, 'Not a jot.' The bitter look of deep hatred
with which he said, 'I found not Cassio's kisses on her
lips,' seems to prepare one for the catastrophe, and was
finely contrasted with the heartfelt dark dejection with
which the beautiful farewell to '*the glorious circumstance of war*' was spoken. Nothing could be finer
than the speech about the handkerchief, '*and could
almost read the thoughts of people*'—his speaking
eye seemed fully possessed of that power; or more
affecting than the speech, '*Had it pleased Heaven
to try me with affliction*,' excepting the last scene, the
beauty of which is so fully displayed in the tender
heart-broken tones of Kean.

I believe it is quite an original idea, certainly
one which crowns the effect and seems to give the
full view of this magnificent character, when Othello,
just before the last speech, after the innocence of
Desdemona is established, returns to the bed, to give
one last look, one kiss of reconciled love which seems
to cast a gleam over his despair. Then, as if it were
a thing no longer of the slightest importance, he
carelessly says, '*I have done the state some service.*'
When at last he stabs himself, the gradual relaxation
of the limbs, and the last fall, were as fine as anything
could be.

In seeing Othello performed a month ago by
Pope, who stormed and mouthed and ranted the
part, I felt quite enraged with the pit and galleries, who clapped him, while they rarely and coldly
marked any applause of Kean in Iago, which I
consider as the most perfect piece of acting I ever
witnessed. I could believe only that Pope had a powerful
party in the house.   Little did I then imagine that in
these days it was Shakespeare himself, and his Othello,
which had taken possession of the audience, and made
them incapable of applauding his wicked tormentor.
I felt it almost strange that those who could admire
such acting did not hiss that of Kean.   When he
appeared in Othello, the applause was deafening, and
Pope, who was less offensive to me in Iago, was received
in sullen silence ; which convinced me that it was the
characters, and not the actors of them, who moved the
multitude.

LADY HESTER STANHOPE.

Letters from Lady H. L. Stanhope to Sir H. Williams Wynn,
from the Desert in 1813.

The first letter speaks of all the conquests she has
made of great Turks. young Beys, chiefs of Delhi-bachis,
and lastly, of ' the great Emir Mahanna el Tadel, Chief
of the Anasa Arabs: the troops under his command
amount to 40,000 men, who are all ready to draw their

swords for me, and the Millichi is the subject of conversation all over the desert.   You will say, How is it then
you have not yet been to the seat of your empire, to
Palmyra?*   For this reason . . . . I took the determination to set off alone to Homs, or Hamar, and pay at
least my promised visit to Mahanna el Tadel, should he
yet be on the borders of the desert.   I found he had
waited for me twenty-four days.   I sent for him, and
spent a week with *my people* in their tents, and
marched three days with them.   I had previously dis-
armed my servants, saying I put myself into the hands
of God and the great Emir, which succeeded admirably,
for I did not lose the value of a para, and was treated with
the greatest kindness and respect.   I was dressed as a
Bedouin, and ate with my *hands* (not *fingers*), drank
camel's milk, and rode surrounded by 100 lances.
What a sight it is at night to see horses, mares, and
camels repair to the tents! No one can have an idea of
it who has not seen it.   This morning, 12,000 camels
belonging to one tribe were taken to drink at once.

After this experiment I think I can rely on Mahanna's
word, which has once more determined Bruce † and
myself to go to Palmyra under his protection.   The
reason I now find why Masoud Agar would have 1,000

---

* This alludes to the prophecy of Brothers, who had foretold
that she was to restore the empire of Jerusalem.

† The late Michael Bruce, commonly called Lavalette Bruce
from the gallant part he took in assisting Lavalette to escape.

men to accompany me was, that Mahanna's son had vowed that, if he attempted to take me into the desert, the Bedouins would cut off his beard, strip his men all naked, and yet still not hurt one hair of my head; but the honour of escorting their queen should be theirs. I have orderly Arabs at my command, receive despatches every two or three days, giving me an account of what is going forward in the desert, of what battles have been fought, and with what tribe, war has been declared. The Feadars, the powerful enemies, are now driven to the neighbourhood of Bagdad; but parties still come this way, at least about Palmyra; this is the danger of going with the Mahanna, yet please God I must go.

' I have had nine horses given me, three bad and six good ones, and yet I would not take any from the Arabs. The Mahanna offered me his own mare. I respect poverty and independence; I am an example that it succeeds in some parts of the world; for if your very self-important uncle was to come here, and snort to the right and the left, he would do nothing either with Turks or Arabs. To command is to be really great : to have talents is to talk sense without a book in one's hand; and to have manners is to be able to accommodate oneself to the customs and tastes of others, and to make them either fear or love you. —— has done neither at home; a pretty business he has made of his politics, and a pretty scrape he has got you all into.   . It is quite what I

expected; but yet, far from being pleased with my own
penetration, I grieve when I reflect upon the state of
things, for everyone is not made for an exile, like myself.
. . . . If my red shalvers at Constantinople amused
you, what would you say to my present dress? It is
that of the son of a chief, or young chief. A Bedouin
handkerchief bound on with a sort of rope made of
camel's hair; a curly sheepskin pelisse; a white
aba with a little gold on the right shoulder, crimson loop and button, and two crimson strings to
fasten it. This is the *true thing*, with a lance with
black feathers, mounted on a fine mare, but I as yet
ride a horse. I ride quite at my ease, and shall dislike a side-saddle. I am sure the Arabs are delighted
with my horsemanship, which is lucky for me. They,
as well as the Turks, think people who cannot ride
absolute fools. Nobody was ever so popular with
priests and Franks, Greeks and Armenians, as old
North; but the Turks at Damascus considered him as
quite contemptible because he could not ride at all,
and walked fast. . . . . .

Last June a battle was fought between the Anasees
and the Feadars; the former were victorious, and
the new pacha took them into favour. I went over
the field of battle with Mahanna; it is near the ruins
of Salonica. The encampment of the Anasees extended
ten miles at least; of this I am sure, as I saw the remains of their entrenchment. As to what travellers

hear from old priests, dragomans, and Frank doctors, it is all false; they know nothing at all about the Arabs. I never saw any of these people, except Chabeauson a few times out of civility, but went my own way to work. All I know is pure, without the additions and absurdities mixed up with the histories of Arabs by people whom they despise. During my stay at Damascus the pacha received a letter from Mecca recommending him to be upon his guard, for that a strong party of Wahabees had set out upon dromedaries, and it was thought would make for Damascus. You know they have come that way before, and burnt all before them, and put every one to the sword in all the villages they passed through.

A pretty fright everybody was in but me, and for this reason—I have even Wahabee friends, who dare not confess themselves such. Let the worst have come to the worst, I should have gone out to have met them, and put myself under the protection of the chief, and I know I should have been safe; and I had other options, to stay or run away when the pacha did, or to have been escorted by some of the rebel troops to the mountain, where I should have been safe with my friend the Emir Besheer. I don't say without some reason I could have been escorted by (the name illegible), for when they suddenly left Damascus to join the pacha of Aleppo, they sent to me to march with them, and said, if I was waiting at Damascus for the arrival of the caravan with money, there were twenty purses for my use, or I might take what troops I liked to escort me to Palmyra. In short, the Dillas and the Arabs are the only people to be feared in this part ·of the world, and I have them all under my thumb: but there is one thing I must make you aware of; to bungle with the Arabs is to be lost; for though they avoid shedding blood themselves, they have black slaves, who are devils, kept for the purpose when necessary, who are armed with a shocking crooked knife tied round their neck, to rip up people, and a hatchet under their pelisse to cut off heads. These people are much more difficult to manage than the Arabs themselves, as they are so interested and so bloody minded if they take a dislike to a person. . . .

'It was to make an experiment, to try my *influence*. Going like a thief in the dark as *you* did, fearing the Bedouins at the right and left, is abominable. The thing is to look round one, free as the air of the deserts, to observe something like a flight of crows at a distance—to look proudly that way, move your hand, and in one instant see fifty lances spring in your defence; to see them return, exclaiming " Schab—Friends." '

'Latichia, June 30, 1813.

' Without joke I have been crowned Queen of the Desert, under the triumphal arch at Palmyra. Nothing could succeed better than this journey, dangerous as it was, for upon our return we were pursued by 200 of the enemy's horse, but escaped from them. They were determined to have the head of the chief who accompanied us, yet sent me in secret an ambassador to say that I need not fear anything—that everything belonging to me should be respected: such were the orders given by this powerful tribe, by five of their chiefs assembled at Bagdad. . . . They all paid me homage. If I please, I can now go to Mecca *alone*—I have nothing to fear. I shall soon have as many names as Apollo. I am the Pearl, the Lion, the Sun, the Star, the Light from Heaven. . . . I am quite wild about the people, and all Syria is in astonishment at my courage and success.

'To have spent a month with some thousand of Bedouin Arabs, is no common thing. For three days they plagued me sadly, and all the party excepting Bruce almost insisted upon returning. The servants were frightened out of their wits, their eyes always fixed on their arms, or upon me. The dragoman could not speak—he had quite lost his head. All the people immediately about me were *chosen* rascals; and having primed a fellow, who was once with the French army in Egypt, I rode dash into the middle of them; I made my speech—that is to say, I acted—and the man spoke. It so surprised and charmed them, that they all became as harmless as possible, and here ended all unpleasant scenes. . . . Nobody must ever give an opinion of the charms of the Desert, who has not seen above 1,500 camels descend the mountains into an enchanting vale, and a tribe of Arabs pitch their tents upon beds of flowers of ten thousand hues, bringing with them hundreds of living creatures only a few days old—children, lambs, kids, foals, young camels, and puppies.'

Extracts from Mrs. — —'s Letters.

Alexandria, Dec. 3, 1835.

We already begin to hear stories of Lady Hester. The consul here has seen the correspondence between her and Lady Georgina Wolff, each of them laying claim to the being the Messiah's Bride, whose coming they expect shortly, and in the meantime call each other by every bad name under the sun. Lady Hester has had a great fight with the Pacha, having taken it into her head to protect seventy-six rich Arab families, and exempt them from the payment of taxes. After a long debate, the Pacha has given up the point, being unwilling to create a disturbance among his Syrian subjects, who consider Lady Hester as a mad woman, and therefore as holy. She is over head and ears in debt, and kept entirely by the Arabs. . . .

I fear that my chance of seeing Lady Hester is very small: her last fancy is not to see any but French. At present the Duchesse de Plaisance and her daughter are living in her house: the Duchesse was pronounced quite mad in the lunatic asylum in which she was confined some years. They are dressed in white trowsers worn under a gown of the same colour, with enormous sleeves, and wear white calico hats, which end in a high peaked crown. A Frenchman lives with Lady Hester, and he is, somehow or other, soon to be the Messiah. They are always fighting as to which is to be the greatest personage among them. One of these quarrels is said to have ended thus:—'Vous, Madame! vous la prémière! Je vous ferai placer dans ma cuisine.' They are to be married in the New Jerusalem, but the gentleman is impatient and wishes the ceremony to take place now; but Lady Hester will be the Messiah's Bride.

I have written a letter to Lady Hester Stanhope, but I fear have no chance of seeing her. Colonel Campbell has just written to Lord Stanhope to say that, unless her enormous debts are paid, she must leave the country, as he will otherwise apply to our Government to stop the payment of her pension, and apply the amount to the discharge of her debts. . . . A Frenchman whom we met the other day assured us that the following *fact* occurred while he was in Syria:

A French colonel to whom Lady Hester had given a *protection* was robbed and murdered by the Arabs two days after he had left her house. She sent to the nearest government of the Pacha, saying that she *must* have the heads of the murderers in six days. The government promised to obey, but the seventh day came and no heads were produced. Lady Hester sent another messenger, signifying that, if the heads were not before her window in twenty-four hours, she would take her own vengeance on the governor. In twelve hours he came himself to say that he was very sorry he had not been able to discover the actual murderers, and therefore could not produce their heads. He had tracked them to their village, to which he had set fire, and had burnt women and children to the amount of 300 souls! Lady Hester's answer: 'It is a pity that 300 should perish for the crime of four or five, but still this is better than that my vengeance should be unsatisfied.' It is hardly possible to believe in a story of such atrocious cruelty. I can only say that, from another gentleman lately returned from Syria, I heard exactly the same story.

CLAIRVOYANCE.

Sept. 1844.—I begin to think that if one can believe (and I am equally puzzled how to doubt or believe) the facts stated in the following letter, one may believe much that is recorded of witchcraft. That in the means employed, as well as the effects produced, there is much similarity, if not identity, I am firmly persuaded· that many means of which I know nothing, exist, by which an extraordinary power is acquired over some

minds, I believe; that in many instances the imagination increases this tenfold, I am more firmly persuaded.

Extract from a Letter from ——— to Mrs. Rowley, dated
'Paris, September 13, 1844.'

One of my principal friends here is Charles Ledrû,
the celebrated advocate. He is about to plead for one
of the magnetisers, and is acquainted with all of them,
besides being somewhat of a proficient. Two days ago
I went with him to the Palais de Justice, and when his
case was over, he asked me to call *en passant* at the
house of one of his clients, a pretty woman of nineteen,
who wants to get a separation from her husband. We
were shown into a room where she was with her sister,
her father, and a Baron somebody. After hearing her
case, Ledrû proposed to magnetise her, having acciden-
tally discovered that she is a good subject. He threw
her into the desired state in a short time, and we then
proceeded to try whether she was *clairvoyante* or no.
At first there was a succession of failures: I was then
told to take her hand, and think of some one. ' Pensez
à Madame N.' whispered Ledrû, who knows her. I
suspected collusion—assented, but thought of another
person. I give the words of the *clairvoyante* as nearly
as I can remember them.

' Ah! c'est une dame, loin, loin d'ici--vingt-cinq ans,
ou comme ça—grande, c'est-à-dire plus grande que
petite—mince, svelte, figure un peu alongée, bouche

petite, et des yeux—Oh! que ses yeux sont beaux!'
'Pour ses habitudes?' (said I) 'monte-elle à cheval?'
'Oui, beaucoup.' 'Sa santé?' 'Elle est souffrante,
et depuis quelque temps, mais pas tout à fait d'une
maladie fixe.' 'Où est-elle?' 'Dans un château
au milieu d'un parc; il y a une grille, et une
avenue avec des fossés de chaque côté, mais point d'eau.'
'Avec qui?' 'Je vois une femme plus agée, des cheveux
gris, un bonnet avec des rubans, et puis deux enfans—
garçons je crois—l'un, avec des cheveux bouclés—les
jambes nues, beaucoup décolletés, blonds, tout à fait
blonds.' 'Y a-t-il des messieurs?' 'Oui. Je vois un
monsieur blond, et puis encore un—passablement grand,
maigre, et souffrant.' 'Est-ce qu'il porte des mous-
taches?' 'Ah! Je vois une barbe.' If you can guess
the subjects of my thoughts, you will agree with me
that these are strange coincidences.*

I then thought of Lady Charleville, Mrs. M——, my
sisters, &c.; but the power was gone, or at least had
exhausted itself.

Yesterday Ledrû proposed a private trial of Alexis.
Our party consisted of Sir William and Lady de Bathe,
Mrs. M——, and her son, Ker (one of the attachés), and
myself. Marcillet threw him into the trance. We then
bandaged his eyes, covering them with wool and stuffing
all the crevices formed by the nose with wool, so that I

* The description, as regards both persons and locality, was in almost every particular correct; and what is most remarkable, the

am quite sure he could not see ; but he played four games
of écarté with me, and frequently told me my cards before
they were played or even taken up from the table.
I asked him if he would play with cards of my bringing.
' *Volontiers.*'   I went out, enquired of the porter where
I could get cards : he told me of a shop, and *I went to
another*, got my cards, and found no difference whatever
—he played and named them as before.

We then produced our folded papers with writing
within. He failed with mine—I had written Longueville
—but succeeded with Lady de Bathe's and Ker's. He said
I was *malveillant et incrédule*, and had no sympathy
with him, which made him powerless. This I considered, in other words, as saying he could not get on
without some sort of aid. In general, he first told the
number of letters, then enquired if he was right. I
maintained that the experiment was not satisfactory if
any answer was given ; and everybody in the room cried
out that I was too hard upon him, except Marcillet,
who said that Monsieur's *droiture d'esprit* was the very
thing he wished to encounter, and that he would satisfy
me. I walked to the window with young M—— (an

---

same persons (six in number), and no others, were on that same day
at the country house in question. They constituted the family. The
day before, a party of visitors had left, and the day after, a fresh
party arrived. The writer of the letter showed it to three English
friends before putting it into the post, and as there was then no
electric telegraph between London and Paris, collusion was impossible.

Eton lad), made him write the word *Auguste,* folded the paper so that there were five folds between the writing and the light, doubled down the corners, and put it into Lady de Bathe's hands, who gave it to Alexis. I made M——— write and Lady de Bathe deliver it, to obviate the objection as to my want of sympathy. I sate down by him and kept my eye on the paper. He never attempted either to unfold or look through it, and he was in a dark part of the room, the opposite end from the window. Marcillet was not near him. He struggled, and at last named the number of letters. No answer. 'Mais répondez donc, Monsieur,' said Marcillet; 'au moins mentalement, prenez lui la main, *et pensez très distinctement à l'écriture.* I did so. Again a sort of paroxysm, and he exclaimed, 'Un crayon—vite, un crayon,' which was given him, and he wrote 'Auguste,' the paper being still folded. Fortune-tellers have hit on curious revelations, and H. Dobler puts explanation at defiance; but undoubtedly such facts as these are well worth the attention of philosophy.

Extract from a subsequent Letter by the same Writer.

As regards the lady's display of *clairvoyance,* the coincidences (for I believe them to be nothing more) are certainly startling, but I have just met with others equally so. George Smythe [afterwards Lord Strangford] arrived in Paris just before I left, full of a *rencontre,* or adventure, or incipient *bonne-*

fortune in its way, which had befallen him and his travelling companion in Germany. On the Rhine (I think) they made the acquaintance of two ladies, a mother and daughter of remarkable attractions and accomplishments, who turned out to be pianists on a professional tour. They had already visited Petersburg, Moscow, Berlin, Dresden, and Vienna; and afterwards performed at Frankfort,—by the token that Smythe and his friend made their servants attend to take money at the door, hand refreshments, &c.,—a pretty strong proof of the height of their enthusiasm. The mother spoke three languages, French, German, and Italian; the daughter English in addition to the other three. They were respectively about eighteen and thirty-six years of age. Their conduct and character were described as irreproachable.

A few days after hearing Smythe's narrative, I left Paris for London. At Folkestone I found myself forming one of a trio in a railway carriage with two ladies, answering in nearly all respects to his description. They were mother and daughter, about thirty-six and eighteen, both handsome, both lively and attractive; the mother speaking the three languages, the daughter the four. Struck at first sight by the similarity, I led the conversation in such a manner as to discover that they had recently been at the great cities of the North as well as at Berlin, Vienna, and Frankfort, although I did not elicit in what capacity.

After I had interchanged a few sentences in English with the daughter, the mother laughingly interrupted me: '*Choisissez, Monsieur, entre les trois langues, mais je ne parle pas Anglais, et je ne veux pas vous ménager une tête-à-tête avec ma fille.*'

They were going to Brighton, and we parted at Redhill. I immediately wrote to Smythe to tell him where his beauties were to be found. He went to Brighton, tracked *my* ladies, and ascertained that they were not the originals although exact duplicates of his own. Now, the chances are just as great against finding actual duplicates as against the realisation by persons or events of a fancy group or foretold occurrence. The successful mesmerist or conjurer may be simply *le menteur veridique.*'

You remember the fulfilment of Poniatowski's strange fortune: '*Hüten Sie sich vor der Elster,*' 'Beware of the Magpie,' the name of the stream near Leipsic in which he was drowned. When at Leipsic in 1833, I satisfied myself that this warning had been really given him, and was duly recorded at the time.

FAUSTINE.

Extract from Mrs. ——'s Letter to the Writer of the Article on the Countess Hahn Hahn's Novels in the 'Edinburgh Review' for January 1844.

What did this German countess do to bewitch you

into admiring her book? Better the credulity of Miss Martineau (who believes in the mesmeric prophecies of Jane the housemaid, but not in the divinity of the Saviour) than yours who believe in Faustine. In the statistics of insanity there is a case of a lady who went mad from vanity and triumph in her child, whom she imagined to be a cherub singing in heaven. Faustine is simply a woman gone mad from *exceeding selfishness*, and indeed puts me in mind of nothing but the stories I have heard of ——. Also the cart is put before the horse—the cart being Mengen and the horse Andlau—for no woman loves the last man best even if he deserves it (which Mengen does not), because the first had the benefit of all illusion, which is to love as the halo round the saints' heads in pictures.*

Also my English throat cannot swallow Mengen's marrying her, to reward her rapid inconstancy to the

---

* A broad distinction, not generally recognised, is here drawn between man's and woman's love. Is it well founded? Romeo loves Rosaline before Juliet; Waverley, Flora M'Ivor before Rose Bradwardine; and Lord Nevil deserts the brilliant and illusion-creating Corinne for the tame and rather insipid Lucile. But no first-rate writer of fiction that I remember, out of Germany, has represented a woman the victim of more than one grand passion, or (as in Mrs. Haller) has pictured her returning, after a temporary aberration, with affections as good as new, to the first, real and rightful possessor of her heart. In England, we are apt to exclaim with Byron in his suppressed lines:

'Then fare thee well, Fanny, thus doubly undone,
Thou frail to the many, and false to the one.
Thou art past all recalling, e'en would I recall,
For the woman so fallen for ever must fall.'

man she *had* the power to throw off, or her accepting him under the circumstances. Still less can I stand the desertion of little Bonaventura, to go and compose hymns to the organ in a convent. In vain does Hahn Hahn give her heroine the benefit of every excuse, in vain defer her adultery till the husband's house is left, and make the lover a stabbed and slaughtered man. The want of compassion, the want of meek womanly affection, the want of devotion, and, above all, the utter absence of any notion of self-sacrifice, or indeed of any notion except that of sacrificing everybody and everything to self, make Faustine odious and unnatural.

The book has clever dialogues and great cleverness of description in it, and Clement is a well-drawn likeness of Lord —— ——, and did well to shoot himself; but as to Faustine herself being interesting or true to human nature, she is not. . . . Being married to a man you dislike does not incline you to love other men ; and being disappointed in the degree of affection you inspire, rather induces the feeling described in a much more natural story I once read,* where the lady having passionately loved a man called Georges (who forsakes her), and being then passionately beloved by another, privately says to herself while this other is rapturously love-making, '*Ah! comme j'ai du ennuyer ce pauvre Georges.*'

---

* *Marianne,* by Jules Sandeau.

ADDENDUM TO THE FIRST NEWS OF WATERLOO (*ante*, p. 157), AND THE MEETING OF WELLINGTON AND BLÜCHER (*ante*, p. 276).

Communicated by a member of Major Percy's family.

'A few hours after the battle was over, Major Percy started with the Duke's despatches and three captured eagles, travelling day and night. When he arrived in London, he went, *I believe*, first to the Horse Guards, where he found none of the authorities; then to Lord Liverpool, who was, *I believe*, dining at Lord Bathurst's, where Major Percy followed him. "You must come immediately with me to the Regent," said Lord Liverpool, and they got into the carriage of his Lordship. "But what is to be done with the *eagles*?" "Let the footman carry them," said Lord Liverpool. Major Percy always told this with some disgust. They proceeded to Mrs. Boehm's house in St. James's Square, where the Regent and the Duke of York were dining. Lord Liverpool took up Major Percy to the Prince, and said, "I have brought Major Percy, who comes with the news of a great victory for your Royal Highness." "Not Major Percy, but Lieut.-Colonel Percy," said the Prince. Major Percy knelt and kissed his hand. "We have not suffered much loss, I hope," he then said. "The loss has been very great indeed," was of course the reply, upon which the Regent burst into tears.

Major Percy afterwards went to his brother's house in Gloucester Place, and called him up to hear the good news, and then to Portman Square, where he undressed and went to bed for the first time since the battle.

'I well remember the next Monday, when I was taken to see him. I remember the great dark stain on his uniform; the horror I felt, in the midst of all the triumph and joy of the moment, when he told me, in answer to my questions, that it was the blood of an officer killed close to him. Still more when I heard him tell how, in taking off his sash as he undressed, he shook from the folds fragments of the brain which had lodged there.

'I have often heard him describe the interview between the Duke and Blücher, at which he was present; and the ride back to the English quarters over the field of battle covered with the dead and the dying. *It was a bright moonlight night.* The first soldiers they met greeted the Duke with loud cheers, which were taken up and sounded along the whole line of bivouacs; the poor wounded men joined with their feeble voices, and Major Percy said he saw many try to rise as the Duke passed. As the first soldiers who recognised crowded round him, he said, " My poor fellows, you have had a hard day's work." There was a general cry in answer, " We don't mind it : all's right as you are safe." Those words were almost the only expressions uttered by the Duke during that memorable ride. He was deeply affected, and even shed tears.'

Mr. William Bathurst, son of Earl Bathurst, Secretary for the Colonies and War in 1815, states that the despatches were directed to his father, who was not at Lord Harrowby's where Lord Liverpool was dining ; and that Major Percy was with some difficulty persuaded (in Lord Bathurst's absence) to deliver them to Lord Liverpool, the Prime Minister. Mr. Bathurst was dining at Lord Jersey's, and, in company with Earl Grey, had gone to Lord Harrowby's on hearing of the arrival of the news.

Major Percy's account of the ride back by moonlight after the meeting with Blücher, proves that it could not have taken place at *La Belle Alliance*, and confirms, if it needed confirmation, the Duke's statement, that he continued the pursuit till long after dark. Blücher and his staff halted and passed the night at Genappe. 'When Gneisenau,' says M. de Bernardi, 'arrived at daybreak at the *Emperor* public-house, some thousand paces the other side of Frasnes, two miles and a half (German) from the field of battle, he had only with him about fifty Uhlans of the Brandenburgh regiment, who also could go no farther for weariness. There ended the immediate pursuit.' In the ' People's Edition' of Gleig's 'Life of Wellington' (just published), it is stated on the highest possible authority that ' the Duke reached his head-quarters at Waterloo about ten o'clock at night.' It is impossible, therefore, that he could have gone as far as Genappe. Yet as he passed through Genappe when falling back from Quatre Bras, and mentions it in his despatch of the 19th, it is curious that he should have confounded it with Maison Rouge, which he afterwards specified as the real place of meeting to the best and most trusted of his biographers, the Chaplain General.

Extract from Major Percy's Journal.

' Came up from Dover in a chaise and four with three eagles out of the window. They were too long to be shut in it.

' Went first to the Prince Regent (before he came home) at Mrs. Boehm's in St. James's Square. Prince much affected. All London thrown into agitation— people quitting balls and assemblies as the news was conveyed of the wounds or deaths of relatives. Many ladies fainted. There was a rumour, before the news came, of a great battle and retreat, and even defeat. People were much depressed; therefore the reaction was immense.'

ADDENDUM TO THE 'THE TYRONE GHOST' (*ante*, p. 43).

Communicated by a friend.

' I first heard the story of the Beresford ghost from Mr. Cumberland. He told it finely. I was about twelve years old at the time   (this would be sixty years ago). Long afterwards I met with the ghost in print, in a magazine which my father took in regularly. A discussion on tales of mystery produced a letter from one of the Beresford family, containing an account of the real circumstances of the story. The lady of the velvet bracelet, when about to be married for the second time, really had a dream warning her of the unhappiness likely to result from the contemplated union. It was well known to all the family of the intended bride that she had been subject to a disorder which had left a deep scar on her wrist—long before the visitation of the burning spirit ; and she had covered this scar with a velvet bracelet most carefully ever since it had been formed.'

EPITAPHS,
EPIGRAMS, AND INSCRIPTIONS.*

Audaciores sanè sunt interdum Homines quàm aut decet aut per religionem licet, dum Cœli gaudia haud dubia mortuis tribuunt, et pro spe humili, ac solatio, triumphum canunt.

Bishop of Llandaff's Prælectio, xxvii.

———

Ille quidem plenus annis abiit, plenus honoribus, illis etiam quos recusavit. Nobis tamen quærundus ac desiderandus est, ut Exemplar Ævi prioris, mihi vero præcipue, qui illum non solum publice, sed etiam privatum quantum admirabar, tantum diligebam.

Plinius de Virginio Rufo, Epist. lib. 2. ep. 1.

This was transcribed by my brother, C. W. W. W., and intended for an inscription on a bust of Lord Grenville.

———

INSCRIPTION ON THE COMMON PALL USED AT FUNERALS,
AT FRIBOURG.

Cras tibi Mors.

---

* I have selected rather the least known, than the best, of those collected by Miss Wynn.

IN TACHBROOK CHURCH, NORTH WARWICKSHIRE.

Gualterus Landor Roberto generoso pio integerrimo
Patre natus
Duas Uxores duxit, a prima Filiam unicam,
Ab altera Filios iv. Filias iii. suscepit.
Lepidus, doctus, liberalis, probus, amicis jucundissimus.
Anno Ætatis lxxiii. decessit.
Juxta prout vivens moriensque voluit
Composita est Uxor ejus Elizabetha
Filia Caroli Savage
Conjux Mater Fœmina pia optima.
Vixit Annos lxxxv. menses xi.

Walter Savage Landor.

INSCRIPTION ON THE POOR-HOUSE AT BERNE.

Christo in Pauperibus.

INSCRIPTION ON THREE SIDES OF AN OBELISK IN THE
CEMETERY AT ARNHEIM.

Civibus Exteris
Summis infimis
Quocunque Ritû Deum colentibus
Omnibus Vitâ functis
Hanc placidæ Quietis Sedem
Communis Multorum Voluntas
Destinavit.

Tuti quiescant
Læti resurgant
Quotquot Terra tegit.

Terra quos rapuit
Cœlum restituit.

———

IN THE CHURCH OF SANTA MARIA DEGLI ANGELI
AT ROME.

Virtute vixit
Memoriâ vivit
Gloriâ vivet.

Corpus humo tegitur
Fama per ora volat
Spiritus Astra tenet.

FROM AN ANCIENT MONUMENT, ST. SAVIOUR'S CHURCH,
SOUTHWARK.

Like to the Damask rose you see,
Or like the blossom on the Tree,
Or like the dainty Flower of May,
Or like the Morning of the Day,
Or like the Sun, or like the Shade,
Or like the Gourd which Jonah made;
Ev'n so is Man, whose thread is spun,
Drawn out, and cut, and so is done.
The rose withers, the blossom blasteth,
The flowers fade, the morning hasteth,
The Sun sets, the Shadow flies,
The Gourd consumes, and Man he dies.*

ST. MARGARET'S, WESTMINSTER.

Within the walls of this Church
was deposited
The Body of the great
SIR WALTER RALEIGH, KNT.
On the day he was beheaded in Old Palace Yard,
Oct. 18, 1618.

Reader, should you reflect on his error,
Remember his many virtues, and that he was mortal.

---

* The first six lines resemble some in Burns's *Tam O'Shanter* :—
  'But pleasures are like poppies spread,
    You seize the flower, its bloom is shed;
    Or like the snow-fall in the river,
    A moment white—then melts for ever;
    Or like the borealis race,
    Which flits e'er you can point the place;
    Or like the rainbow's lovely form,
    Evanishing amid the storm.'

ÉPIGRAMME APRÈS LA BATAILLE DE RAMILLIES.

C'est bien dommage, sur ma foi,
Que Monseigneur de Villeroy
Soit déjà Maréchal de France ;
Car dans cette grande action
On peut dire sans complaisance
Qu'il a mérité le Bâton.

INSCRIPTION UNDER THE BUST OF ALFRED, AT UNIVERSITY COLLEGE, BY SIR WILLIAM SCOTT.

Quisquis es,
Vel Libertatis amans, vel Literarum,
Illius Viri Imaginem
Piis suspice Oculis,
Qui Patriam
Peregrinis Hostibus afflictam,
Domestica Morum Feritate
Et turpissima simul Ignorantia
Laborantem,
Armis erexit, Legibus emollivit,
Scientiâ exornavit.
Si sis Britannus
Possis etiam gloriari
Militarem Romuli Virtutem
Civilem Numæ Scientiam
Philosophicam Antonini Gravitatem
Unice in se complecti
BRITANNICI ALFREDI Nomen.

W. S.

ON A CALM AND CLEAR SPRING AT BLENHEIM, BY WARTON.

> Here quench your thirst and mark in me,
> An Emblem of true Charity,
> Who, while my bounty I bestow,
> Am neither heard, nor seen to flow.*

———

ARMAGH : ON A DIAL ERECTED OVER THE GRAVE OF
EDWARD BOND, ESQ.,

Who ordered 100*l*. to be given to the Poor, instead of a pompous
funeral, 1744.

> No marble Pomp, no monumental praise,
> My tomb this Dial, my Epitaph these lays.
> Pride and low mould'ring clay but ill agree,
> Death levels me to beggars : Kings to me.
> Alive, Instruction was my work each Day ;
> Dead, I persist Instruction to convey.
> Here, Reader ! mark (perhaps now in thy Prime)
> The stealing steps of never-ending time :
> Thou'lt be what I am ; catch the present Hour,
> Employ that well, for that's within thy power.

The epigram on a bridge at Blenheim, erected by the first
duke, is in an opposite strain :—

> ' This lofty bridge his high ambition shows,
> The stream an emblem of his bounty flows.'

DUNDALK.

Here lies the Body of Robert Moore,
What signifies more Words?
Who kill'd himself by eating of Curds;
But if he had been rul'd by Sarah his Wife,
He might have liv'd all the Days of his Life.

ÉPITAPHE DE ROBESPIERRE.

Passant, ne pleure pas mon sort,
Si je vivais, tu serais mort.

ÉPITAPHE DE LOUIS XVI.

Ci gît Louis, ce pauvre Roi.
On dit qu'il fut bon, mais à quoi?

ST. PAUL'S CATHEDRAL : ON SIR PHILIP SYDNEY, KNT.

Who received his Death in a Battle near Zutphen, in Gelderland,
Sept. 22, 1586.

England, Netherland, the Heav'ns, and the Arts,
The Souldiers and the World have made six parts
Of noble Sydney; for who will suppose,
What a small heap of Stones can Sydney inclose!

England hath his Body, for she it fed;
Netherland his Blood, in her defence shed:
The Heav'ns have his Soul, the Arts have his Fame,
The Souldiers the Grief, the World his good Name.

CHURCH OF THE CAPUCHINS, PIAZZA BARBERINI, ROME.

Inscribed on a flat stone near the high Altar.

Hic jacet Pulvis, Cinis, et nihil.*

———

FIELD OF BLENHEIM : INSCRIPTION ON A COLUMN SENT AND ERECTED BY THE EMPEROR LEOPOLD.

It was afterwards removed.

Agnoscat tandem Ludovicus XIV.
neminem ante obitum
debere aut felicem aut magnum
vocari.

———

* This inscription is or was, in 1722, to be found in the Cathedral of Toledo on a flat stone covering the remains of Cardinal Porto Carrero: 'Suivant qu'il l'ordonna expressément, mais on a mis vis à vis une magnifique Epitaphe en son Honneur.'—*Memoires de St. Simon.*

EPIGRAM.

Lumine Acon dextro, capta est Leonilla sinistro,
  Sed forma esse potest hic Deus, illa Dea.
Blande Puer, lumen quod habes concede *Sorori* (*parenti*),
  Sic tu cæcus Amor, sic erit illa Venus.

Variante.

Lumine Acon dextro, capta est Leonilla sinistro,
  Et poterat forma vincere uterque Deos.
Parve Puer, lumen quod habes concede Sorori,
  Sic tu cæcus Amor, sic erit illa Venus.

This Epigram is said to have been written by Girolamo Amaltheo, who was born in Italy, and lived in the 16th century; he had two brothers, John Baptista and Cornelius. They were all three Latin Poets.

INSCRIPTIONS

ON A STONE WHICH MARKS THE SPOT ON WHICH LORD CAMELFORD FELL IN A DUEL.

Placed by Lord Holland, written by Ugo Foscolo.

Hoc Diis Manibus

voto

deprecatione Iræ.

ON A MEDAL COMMEMORATING THE DESTRUCTION OF THE
INVINCIBLE ARMADA,

And representing a Fleet baffled by Storms.

Afflavit Deus, et dissipati sunt.

ON THE COFFIN OF LÆTITIA BUONAPARTE.

Mater Napoleonis.
Ætat. 87.

FOR A BASSO RELIEVO REPRESENTING A CHILD BLOWING
UPON AN EXTINGUISHED LAMP,

Which decorates the Front of the Receiving House of the Humane
Society, Hyde Park.

Lateat Scintillula forsan.

INSCRIPTION ON A BUST OF BRUTUS IN THE GALLERY AT
FLORENCE,

Which was left unfinished by Michael Angelo.

Dum Bruti effigiem sculptor de marmore ducit,
In mentem sceleris venit, et abstinuit.

ENGLISH VERSION.

Impromptu by D. Sandwich.

Brutum effecisset sculptor, sed mente recursat
Tanta viri virtus, sistit et obstupuit.

CHURCH OF THE SANTI APOSTOLI, ROME : INSCRIPTION ON A MONUMENT TO THE PRÆCORDIA OF CLEMENTINA, QUEEN OF ENGLAND,

Whose body reposes in St. Peter's. A heavy dropsical Cherubim carries her Heart, and with it her Crown.

Hic Clementinæ remanent
Præcordia,
Nam Cor cœleste fecit,
ne superesset Amor.

PANTHEON : INSCRIPTION BY CARDINAL BEMBO ON THE TABLET TO THE MEMORY OF RAFAELLE.

Ille hic est Raphael, timuit quo sospite vinci
Rerum magna Parens, et moriente mori.

PASQUINADE ON THE POPES PIUS VI. AND PIUS VII.,

When the latter went to Paris and crowned Napoleon.

Romani, vi dirò un bel quadro
D' un santo Padre chi fù coronar un Ladro.
Un Pio, per conservar la Fede lascia la Sede,
Un altro, per conservar la Sede lascia la Fede.

A A

INSCRIPTION BY LEO XII. ON THE PAVEMENT UNDER THE
ALTAR OF LEO THE GREAT, IN ST. PETER'S.

Leoni magno Patrono cœlesti
Me supplex commendam,
Hic apud sacros ejus cineres
Locum Sepulturæ elegi
Leo XII. * humilis Cliens
Hæres tanti nominis minimus.

Vixit an. 63 &c. &c.
Ob. 1828 &c. &c.
Hic positus Dec. 1830.

———

FROM THE WALLS OF A WELL-SCRAWLED PORTICO,
TRENTON FALLS.

Les Fenêtres et les Murailles
Sont le Papier des Canailles.

Leo XII. was of the family della Genga, and was reported to
have been very dissipated in his youth. He reigned six years, and
was succeeded by Pius VIII., who reigned only one year, and was
succeeded by Gregory XVI.

CHURCH OF WEDMORE, SOMERSETSHIRE.

Sacred to the Memorie of Captain Thomas Hodges, of the County of Somerset, Esq., who at the Siege of Antwerpe, aboute 1583, with unconquered courage wonne two Ensignes from the Enemy, where receiving his last Wound, he gave three Legacies, his Soule to his Lord Jesus, his Body to be lodged in Flemish Earth, his Heart to be sent to his dear Wife in England.

> Here lies his wounded Heart for whome
> One Kingdom was too small a Roome,
> Two Kingdoms therefore have thought good to part
> So stout a Body and so brave a Heart.

PÈRE LA CHAISE: TO A MOTHER.

Passant, donne une larme à ma Mère en pensant à la tienne.

ON A COLUMN AT NORDLINGEN,

On the spot where fell in battle General de Mercy, erected and inscribed by the young Enghien, afterwards the Grand Condé, who had defeated this veteran.

Sta, Viator, Heroem calcas.*
1645.

---

* 'Pause, for thy tread is on a Nation's dust.'—*Byron.*

A A 2

TIVERTON CHURCH.

To the Memory of
Edward Earl of Devonshire and his Wife.

Ho ! ho ! who lies here ?
'Tis I, the good Earl of Devonshire,
With Kate my Wife to me full dear.
We lived together fifty-five year.
That we *spent* we *had,*
That we *left* we *lost,*
That we *gave* we *have.*

ROUEN.

Inscribed on the tomb of Louis de Brézé by his Widow, Diane
de Poitiers, a specimen of mendacity exceeding any.

Indivulsa tibi quondam, et *fidelissima* conjux,
Ut fuit in Thalamo, sic erit in Tumulo.

PAU.

On a statue erected by subscription, which was intended to
have been that of Henri IV., but Louis XIV. by intrigue
and cabal contrived to have one of himself substituted.

Louis XIV.
Roi de France et de Navarre,
petit fils de notre
grand Henri.

ANCIENT INSCRIPTION REPEATED BY SIR WALTER SCOTT, AND
SAID TO HAVE BEEN FOUND IN THE RUINS OF MELROSE
ABBEY.

The Earth walks on the Earth glistening with Gold,
The Earth goes to the Earth sooner than it was wold,
The Earth builds on the Earth Temples and Towers,
The Earth says to the Earth, All will be ours.

ST. GERMAINS.

On a Monument erected to the Memory of King James II. by
King George IV.

Regio Cineri
Pietas regia.

Ferale quisquis hoc monumentum aspicis
Rerum humanarum Vices meditare.
Magnus in prosperis,
In adversis major,

JACOBUS II.

Anglorum Rex, insignes
Ærumnas—dolendaque
Nimium Fata pio placidoque
Obitû exsolvit
in hac Urbe,
Die 16 Septembris 1701,
et nobiliores quædam
Corporis ejus partes hic
Reconditæ asservantur.

Age like his is full of pleasure instead of care ; not like winter, but like a fine summer evening, or like the light of a fine harvest moon, which sheds o'er all the sleeping scene a soft nocturnal day.—*Montgomery.*

Applied to the Right Hon. T. Grenville, aged 90 years.

F. W. W.

FROM THE CIMETIÈRE DU PÈRE LA CHAISE.

Ci-gît Fournier (Pierre Victor)
Inventeur breveté des Lampes dites sans fin ;
Brûlant une centime d'huile à l'heure.
Il fut bon Père, bon Fils, bon Epoux :
Sa Veuve inconsolable
Continue son Commerce, Rue aux Ours, No. 19.
Elle fait des Envois dans les départemens.
N.B.—Ne pas confondre avec la Boutique en face, S.V.P.
R. I. P.

On entering the shop, a jolly rubicund tradesman accosted us. We intimated a wish to transact business with the widow, 'la Veuve inconsolable.' 'Parbleu, c'est moi ! Je suis, moi, Pierre Fournier, inventeur, &c. La veuve n'est qu'un symbole, un mythe.'

Lightning Source UK Ltd.
Milton Keynes UK
UKOW05f0944090117
291675UK00015B/601/P